Legal Aid in Practice:
The guide to civil and criminal proceedings

OLE HANSEN is a solicitor who has worked as a partner in a London legal aid firm and in a law centre. He is a former Director of the Legal Action Group. The author of several books and many articles, he now works as a senior lecturer at South Bank University, as a writer for newspapers and television, and as a consultant to law centres and legal aid firms.

Legal Aid in Practice:
The guide to civil and criminal proceedings

THIRD EDITION

Ole Hansen SOLICITOR

 Legal Action Group
1993

Third edition published in Great Britain 1993
by LAG Education and Service Trust Limited
242 Pentonville Road, London N1 9UN

First edition as *Legal Aid — How to Use It* 1985
Second edition as *Using Civil Legal Aid* 1989
© Ole Hansen 1985, 1989, 1993

British Library Cataloguing in Publication Data
A CIP catalogue record for this book is available from the British Library

ISBN 0 905099 36 2

Phototypeset by Kerrypress Ltd, Luton
Printed by BPCC-Wheatons Ltd, Exeter

Acknowledgments

Over the years many people have contributed to the thinking represented in this book. They include lecturers and students on LAG courses, and colleagues who have worked on earlier drafts or made other contributions. In general I should mention Cyril Glasser, Louise Watt, Stephen Gerlis, Anthony Burton, Jenny Levin and Walter Merricks. For help on this edition I am especially indebted to Nina Hansen, Simon Hillyard and Ed Cape. They all provided invaluable advice. Responsibility for errors, of course, remains mine.

Special mention must also be made of all the staff of the Legal Aid Board both centrally and in the area offices who have given of their expertise, interest and enthusiasm both in lecturing on LAG courses and in connection with this book.

Final thanks must go to the LAG staff and in particular my editor Paul Crane for his skill and patience.

Advice and assistance and civil legal aid forms are reproduced by permission of the Legal Aid Board. The criminal legal aid forms are Crown copyright and reproduced with the sanction of the Controller of HMSO.

The law is stated for England and Wales at 1 July 1993. References to the *Legal Aid Handbook* and to its Notes for Guidance are to the 1993 edition unless otherwise stated.

Contents

Table of cases

Table of Legal Aid Board Notes for Guidance

References are to the 1993 Handbook unless otherwise stated.

Table of statutes

Table of statutory instruments

CHAPTER 1

Introduction

The legal aid scheme

Legal rights are worthless unless they can be enforced. Legal aid provides payments to lawyers so that individuals are not prevented through lack of means from securing their legal rights. The extent to which this aim has been realised – or not realised – is beyond the scope of this book. Instead it is intended to explain how to make the scheme work to the best advantage of consumers and to the best advantage of lawyers. The objectives are not necessarily incompatible.

All solicitors should know how the legal aid scheme works. It is a solicitor's professional duty to consider whether a client would benefit from legal aid, and, if so, to advise the client of the fact. It makes no difference that the particular solicitor does not do legal aid work. It is a question that the solicitor must address almost as soon as the client comes through the door. Failure to advise a client who is financially eligible about legal aid would probably amount to breach of the solicitor's duty to act with reasonable skill and care, and would therefore be actionable on the part of the client. The Law Society's *Client Care Guide* says: 'You should discuss with the client how legal charges and disbursements are to be met and should consider whether the client may be eligible for legal aid (including legal advice and assistance)'.[1] It also warns that failure to do so could lead to a finding that the solicitor had provided inadequate professional services, and in serious cases a finding of professional misconduct, as well as giving rise to a claim in negligence.

The legal aid scheme is unacceptably complex, and the addition of a new form of legal aid for Children Act proceedings (see below) has only made matters worse. Rationalisation is long over-due. Nonetheless, for the practitioner the basic structure is easily understood if a few guidelines are followed.

---

1   *Client Care – A Guide for Solicitors*, The Law Society, 1991, p20 and the Legal Aid Board's *Legal Aid Handbook*, Sweet & Maxwell, 1992, p447.

First, what is loosely called the legal aid scheme is, leaving aside duty solicitors, three schemes: legal advice and assistance, civil legal aid and criminal legal aid. In addition, assistance by way of representation (ABWOR) exists as a variant of the advice and assistance scheme (see chapter 3).

Secondly, although the workings of the three schemes vary in detail, they have important general features in common. They are almost entirely implemented by solicitors working in private practice. Any solicitor with a practising certificate may take part. The schemes have been modelled on the private solicitor and client model but the solicitor's fees and disbursements and counsel's fees are paid out of public funds. Most of the legislation and regulations flow from this triangular relationship and the consequent need to protect public funds.

Thirdly, all three schemes, in general, are means-tested – the applicant for legal aid must be financially eligible and may be required to pay a contribution. The means tests, the eligibility criteria and the scales of contributions differ between the three schemes and for some exceptional matters legal aid is non-means tested and non-contributory.

Fourthly, although there are anomalies of detail, the lines dividing the schemes are generally clear. Thus the advice and assistance (or 'green form') scheme provides help on almost any matter which requires the application of English law, but will not normally cover representation in any court or tribunal proceedings. Legal aid is necessary to bring or defend court proceedings, and whether it is civil or criminal legal aid depends on the court in which those proceedings take place, *not* on the nature of the case. Thus an application to the Queen's Bench Divisional Court on a case stated to quash a criminal conviction in the magistrates' court will require civil legal aid and not criminal legal aid because the Queen's Bench Divisional Court is a civil court. If the applicant had been given legal aid in the magistrates' court it would have been criminal legal aid.[2] With relatively minor exceptions, legal aid is not available for tribunal proceedings (see chapter 4).

This tidy picture is spoilt to some extent by ABWOR. ABWOR is part of the advice and assistance scheme, but it enables representation to be provided in matrimonial proceedings in the magistrates' courts and before mental health review tribunals and prison boards of visitors.

It is also possible for magistrates' and county courts to authorise representation under the advice and assistance scheme. The confusion that this might engender, however, is limited because such representation is possible only in very restricted circumstances (see chapter 3).

---

2   Magistrates' courts, in particular, and Crown Courts have a dual jurisdiction, of course. In those courts the type of legal aid, whether civil or criminal, will depend on the jurisdiction being exercised.

The administrative structure is similarly divided. The Legal Aid Board has the main responsibility for civil legal aid and advice and assistance, including ABWOR. The courts play the major role in the administration of criminal legal aid.

Legal structure

Each of the schemes is based on statute which defines the area of operation. Detailed rules for the running of each scheme are provided in regulations in the form of statutory instruments and – because the legal aid scheme is administrative as well as legal in nature – general instructions on the application of the regulations are contained in Notes for Guidance from the Legal Aid Board and circulars issued from time to time by other relevant authorities (see below).

The Legal Aid Act 1988 (LAA) sets out the basic law; any section numbers in this book refer to the LAA unless otherwise stated. Part III (ss8 to 13) of the LAA deals with advice and assistance including ABWOR and Pt IV (ss14 to 18) with civil legal aid. Part V is concerned with criminal legal aid and Pt VI with legal aid in special cases, of which only the provisions dealing with contempt proceedings are now relevant. Care proceedings which were also dealt with in Part V are now covered by civil legal aid in Part IV following the Children Act 1989 reforms.

The Legal Advice and Assistance (Scope) Regulations 1989 SI No 550 (hereafter referred to as the Scope Regs) limit the coverage of the advice and assistance scheme (regs 3 and 4) and list the types of proceedings for which ABWOR is available (regs 7 to 9). The detailed operation of the advice and assistance and ABWOR scheme is governed by the Legal Advice and Assistance Regulations 1989 SI No 340 (hereafter referred to as the Advice and Assistance Regs) of which regs 16 to 21 are specifically concerned with ABWOR. Detailed rules governing the means testing of advice and assistance and ABWOR applicants are set out in Schs 2 and 3 to these regulations.

Civil legal aid, in contrast, has one set of regulations governing the general operation of the scheme and another set dealing with means testing. The Civil Legal Aid (General) Regulations 1989 SI No 339 (hereafter referred to as the General Regs) set out the manner in which applications for legal aid should be made, how such applications should be determined, etc. The Civil Legal Aid (Assessment of Resources) Regulations 1989 SI No 338 contain the rules governing means testing, including such matters as aggregation of resources and determination of capital.

The detailed operation of the criminal legal aid scheme is found in the Legal Aid in Criminal and Care Proceedings (General) Regulations 1989 SI No 344 (hereafter referred to as the Criminal Regs), Sch 3 of which sets out the rules for assessment of means. In addition, provisions about advice in police stations and duty solicitor schemes in the magistrates' courts are found in the Legal Aid Board Duty Solicitor Arrangements 1992.

Administration

The Legal Aid Board has the main responsibility for running legal aid. It is set up by Part II of the LAA and its members are appointed by the Lord Chancellor. The LAA requires that at least two members shall be solicitors appointed after consultation with the Law Society[3] and that the Lord Chancellor must consult the General Council of the Bar with a view to appointing at least two barristers.[4] Apart from these provisions, s/he may appoint anybody s/he likes, having in mind the desirability of securing that the Board has sufficient knowledge of the provision of legal services, the work of the courts and social conditions, and management.[5] The constitution of the Board is set out in Sch 1.

Membership of the Board is part time and paid. All of its non-specialist members are from private sector management.[6]

The day to day administration of legal aid is carried out by professional staff in area offices, of which there are 13 organised in five groups. Each group is managed by a group manager who is based in one of the area offices. The other offices are run on a day-to-day basis by an area manager. References to 'area director' in the regulations may be taken as being to group or area managers (Legal Aid Board Area Committee Arrangements para 4). Area committees composed of solicitors and barristers on a voluntary and unpaid basis consider appeals against the decisions of the officials.

Section 3(2) gives to the Board 'the general function of securing that advice, assistance and representation are available in accordance with this Act and of administering this Act'. This provision should be read with s1, which sets out the purpose of the Act as being:

> to establish a framework for the provision . . . of advice, assistance and representation which is publicly funded with a view to helping persons who

3   LAA s3(7).
4   LAA s3(8).
5   LAA s3(9).
6   See June 1988 *Legal Action* 4 and April 1992 *Legal Action* 5.

might otherwise be unable to obtain advice, assistance or representation on account of their means.

The Board is responsible for civil legal aid, advice and assistance (including ABWOR) and paying lawyers for criminal legal aid work in the magistrates' courts. It also runs the duty solicitor schemes in police stations and magistrates' courts. However, the Lord Chancellor may give the Board wider functions, including the assessment of means in civil legal aid cases – at present carried out by the Department of Social Security through the Benefits Agency – and the making of decisions whether to grant criminal legal aid – at present decided by the criminal courts.[7] It is the long-term aim of the Government that the Board should have overall responsibility for all aspects of legal aid.[8]

Under the General Regs reg 6, area directors may decide most of the questions which arise in relation to individual legal aid applications. Directors may delegate their decision-making power to their staff: General Regs reg 3(1) states that 'Area Director . . . includes any person duly authorised to act on his behalf'. Appeals against decisions taken by area directors and their staff are the main function reserved for area committees.[9]

In the main the administration of legal aid has improved immensely since the Board took over. Although the staff are for the most part the same who worked for the Law Society, the change from working for a private organisation seems to have freed them to run the legal aid scheme as the public serivce they always believed it to be.[10] The results have been seen in faster and more efficient processing of applications, better designed forms and a more effective flow of information to practitioners, largely thanks to the quarterly *Legal Aid Focus* which is sent to all legal aid account holders.

The LAA and regulations give a great deal of discretion to area committees and directors. To help applicants and practitioners, therefore, the Legal Aid Committee of the Law Society's Council which was in charge of legal aid until 1 April 1989, from time to time issued Notes for Guidance, indicating, for example, how applicants should decide in which court to bring family proceedings where there is a choice of venue.

These Notes for Guidance were published in the first instance in the *Law Society's Gazette* and reproduced in the *Legal Aid Handbook* (above). Since the Board took over the Notes for Guidance have been

---

7 LAA s3(4).
8 HL Debs, Vol 491 col 607, 15 December 1987.
9 General Regs reg 6(2).
10 *Journal of Law and Society*, Spring 1992, p85.

progressively re-written. The first re-written Notes for Guidance appeared in the 1990 *Handbook* and the process was completed in the 1991 *Handbook*. A few of the new Notes were an improvement (eg Note for Guidance 2-29 on when the green form statutory charge might be waived and 6-10 on persons having the same interest) but on the whole the re-writing made the *Handbook* less useful. A large amount of information found in the 1989 *Handbook*, and which is still relevant, had simply disappeared – from Note for Guidance 5 on ABWOR in Mental Health Review Tribunals, through Note for Guidance 9 on the convolutions of the paying client test to most of the valuable help in applying the statutory charge provided by Note for Guidance 46. Not only is it disappointing to record this in view of the general improvements in legal aid administration, but also it has meant that throughout this book it has been necessary to refer to the 1989 and 1990 *Handbooks* which, therefore, practitioners should continue to keep for reference. However, some of the missing material, for instance Note for Guidance 13-02 on the implications of *Littaur v Steggles Palmer* [1986] 1 All ER 780, was restored in 1992 *Handbook* and one can only hope that this process will continue in future editions.

The 1992 *Handbook* also contained much new material in the form of the 'Standards' which have been issued by the Legal Aid Board to its officials to improve consistency in decision-making. The Standards set out the principles according to which decisions should be made and direct officials to the correct outcome by a series of algorithmic questions. The latter cover the whole process of granting legal aid from a simple and mechanistic ascertainment of fact, as in 'Are the proceedings for which legal aid is sought before: (a) a Coroners' Court' (Answer: 'If YES legal aid is not available') to a complex exercise of judgment, as in 'Are the legal prospects of success: (a) Good? (b) Average? (c) Below Average?'.

The primary intention appears to be managerial, ie, to enable lower paid grades of staff to undertake higher grade work. The openness of the Legal Aid Board in publishing the Standards is, of course, welcome, but nonetheless, most lawyers and applicants for legal aid will find, at least at first sight, that the way in which this additional information is presented obscures rather than clarifies the issues. It is now necessary to consult not merely the primary Act, the secondary Regulations, and the explanatory Notes for Guidance, but also in some instances, the Standards. The latter, although published as part of the Notes for Guidance, follow their own comprehensive scheme and in some instances, although not most, add a further gloss to what has been specifically dealt with elsewhere. Had the intention been to make the Notes for Guidance more 'user-friendly' the

Legal Aid Board had plenty of scope for re-writing and expanding them. But that was obviously not the priority.

As already indicated, the Department of Social Security assesses the means of applicants for civil legal aid. The DSS also issues guidance to its staff about how they should exercise their discretion. This is in the *Legal Aid Instructions*, sometimes known as the *L Code*. Unlike the Law Society's (and the Legal Aid Board's) Notes for Guidance, the *L Code* has never been published. In 1984 a leaked copy of the *L Code* was found to contain instructions to DSS legal aid assessment officers to disclose confidential information from applicants to other members of the DSS who had nothing to do with legal aid but might find the information useful, for instance to detect social security overpayments.[11] Those instructions were contrary to s22 of the Legal Aid Act 1974 (now s38). The Government withdrew the unlawful instructions and undertook a review of the *L Code*, but has nonetheless continued to refuse to publish it. Any references in subsequent chapters refer, accordingly, to the *L Code* as at May 1984.

Accountability

At first sight, the replacement of a private body, the Law Society, with a public one, the Legal Aid Board, should have improved accountability for the running of the scheme. It has not made much difference in practice because for many years it has been the Lord Chancellor's Department, with the greater or lesser involvement of the Treasury, which has taken the important policy decisions about the scheme. That has continued. If there is a difference, it is that the Board, except on one or or two notable occasions, has exercised less independent judgment than did the Law Society. Those, including the present author, who criticised the private profession's control over a public service may yet come to regret that it has now come under the more direct control of a Government which, on the one hand, has shown little enthusiasm for public services and, on the other, has displayed a centralising and authoritarian tendency.

The Lord Chancellor has always been responsible to Parliament for legal aid expenditure. However, because of the delegation of responsibility to the Law Society, this responsibility was somewhat attenuated and little has changed as a result of the Society's replacement by the Board. A Member of Parliament who asks the Lord Chancellor to intervene, as one did in 1985 after civil legal aid had been withdrawn from a child claiming compensation for whooping cough vaccine damage,

11 See May 1984 *Legal Action* 1 and 4.

would still get substantially the same answer. 'The Lord Chancellor is ultimately responsible for legal aid,' said a spokesperson, 'but it is administered by the Law Society and the Department does not normally intervene.'[12]

The main change is likely to come through the appointment of a junior minister to represent the Lord Chancellor, because previously answerability to Parliament for the running of the scheme was further weakened because the Lord Chancellor sits in the House of Lords and was represented in the House of Commons by the Attorney-General and the Solicitor-General, who had no departmental responsibility for legal aid.[13]

Recent changes

New legal aid for Children Act proceedings

As a result of the changes in law and procedure in the Children Act 1989, legal aid has also been recast. Civil legal aid is now used in respect of all Children Act proceedings, and in some circumstances non-means tested and non-contributory legal aid is available to parents and children.

Franchising

See chapter 16.

Multi-party actions

The Civil Legal Aid (General) (Amendment) Regulations 1992 inserted a new reg 152 in the General Regs. Under this the Legal Aid Board has discretionary power to enter into contracts with firms of solicitors to undertake generic work in personal injury cases involving 10 or more claimants. More detailed provisions about the procedure for entering into such contracts and about their contents are found in the Legal Aid Board Multi-Party Action Arrangements 1992; Note for Guidance 16 provides advice about how the new arrangements will work. The new arrangements are confined to claims in respect of death, disease or other physical impairment.

The Board can select the firm or firms to undertake generic work on behalf of all the legally-aided claimants. Contract firms will be obliged to produce detailed six-monthly reports to the Legal Aid Board on the progress of the case and three-monthly reports to the claimants. In return,

12   *Guardian* 5 August 1985.
13   See February 1992 *Legal Action* 3.

contracting firms will be able to claim more money sooner on account of costs. They can claim 75 per cent on account of costs for work done as soon as practicable after doing the work – as opposed to the normal 54 per cent 12 months after the issue of the certificate under General Regs reg 100. Non-contracting firms acting for individual clients will be able to claim money on account under the hardship provisions of General Regs reg 101(1)(b) where proceedings have been in force for more than 12 months under a lead case relating to the multi-party action for which they hold an individual certificate, irrespective of when that certificate was issued.[14]

Restrictions on eligibility

The tightening of means-testing which came into effect on 12 April 1993 in all parts of the legal aid scheme has undoubtedly been the most important change to take place since the inception of the scheme. As a result millions of people have lost their entitlement to legal aid and those who qualify have to pay increased contributions. The details of the changes are set out in the relevant chapters. Most notable has been the withdrawal of green form assistance from all but those at income support level.

It is not the purpose of this book to be polemical but it cannot pass without comment that although Lord Mackay's cuts are not the first occasion on which a Lord Chancellor has deliberately set out to reduce legal aid eligibility – that achievement belongs to his predecessor, Lord Hailsham – the cuts have effectively undermined the original aim of the scheme, as expressed in the Legal Aid Act 1949, to provide help not only to the poor but also to those of 'moderate means'. From being an example of the welfare state Lord Mackay has reduced the legal aid scheme to the level of the Poor Law.

For practitioners, the most important changes are that:

- contributory green form help has been abolished; the only clients who qualify are those entitled to free help;
- civil legal aid dependants' allowances and the lower income limit have been reduced, thus raising contributions;
- civil legal aid and ABWOR contributions are now payable during the lifetime of the case with consequent changes in the rules about reassessment of means.

Child Support Agency

The takeover by the Child Support Agency from the courts of most issues relating to child maintenance means that green form, ABWOR and legal aid in this area are now restricted (see chapter 6).

Criminal legal aid

The main change in criminal legal aid is the introduction of standard fees. New regulations providing for payments on account have effectively restricted their availability (see chapter 15).

Challenging decisions

Where applicants or their legal advisers are dissatisfied with the actions of legal aid officials, the first avenue of redress they should consider is the system of appeals created by the regulations (see pp85 and 215). If that does not provide a successful outcome the next stage is to consider an application for judicial review.

Area committees and area managers, when deciding on an application for legal aid, are acting judicially.[15] An aggrieved party, that is, anyone affected by the decision, may therefore apply to the High Court for an order to quash a decision. The Legal Aid Board will grant legal aid to challenge its decisions by judicial review if the normal criteria are met. Decisions of the DSS when assessing means are also subject to judicial review. Judicial review is, however, a limited remedy. The High Court will interfere with the original decision only where it can be shown that the decision was made on the basis of an error in law, or was a decision that the authority had no lawful power to make, or was a decision which no reasonable authority could have made.

A decision of the Legal Aid Board may also be challenged where it arises as an issue in the course of proceedings which are already before the court. Thus, in *Lacey v W Silk & Son Ltd* [1951] 2 All ER 128, the issue was whether a legal aid certificate protected the unsuccessful party against a full order for costs when the committee issuing the certificate had backdated it. The trial judge held that the committee had no power to backdate and that therefore the certificate was invalid and no protection against a full order for costs.

In addition to these legal remedies, however, applicants and their advisers should consider exploiting the legal aid system's administrative

15   *R v Manchester Legal Aid Committee ex parte RA Brand & Co Ltd* [1952] 1 All ER 480.

hierarchy. In taking a particular decision, officials may be following policy – or they may be taking arbitrary action. If the latter, a complaint to the officials' superiors may be more effective and quicker than a formal appeal under the regulations; if the decision was based on policy, the Board may be persuaded to change that policy.

Pressure may be exerted at various levels: area manager, group manager, area committee, regional director, director legal aid, Legal Aid Board, and the Lord Chancellor.

If the system itself continues to be unresponsive, it should be considered whether external pressure will help: local community leaders, local law societies, the Law Society, Members of Parliament, the press or the Legal Action Group.[16]

Finally, the European Commission and Court of Human Rights may offer a remedy in a case of gross injustice.[17]

Complaints against lawyers and compensation

The fact that the client is receiving legal aid modifies, but does not fundamentally alter, the normal relationship between solicitors, barristers and their clients. The modifications flow from the triangular relationship with the Legal Aid Fund (see above, p2), and have the effect that in some circumstances the lawyer's duty to the client is overriden by his or her duty to the legal aid authorities – for example, the normal duty of confidentiality to the client is overridden by obligations to report to the Legal Aid Board.

Apart from these exceptions, however, solicitors and counsel owe the same duty to legally-aided clients as they do to privately paying clients. Thus, a legally-aided client who suffers loss as a result of his or her solicitor's negligence may sue that solicitor. Similarly, but subject to counsel's more limited liability in negligence generally, the client might sue a barrister. Where a solicitor or barrister has been guilty of professional misconduct, the client may complain to the professions' disciplinary authorities in the normal way.

Solicitors, and less often barristers, may be guilty of negligence specifically in relation to legal aid. One example of this was given in the opening paragraphs of this chapter: failing to advise an eligible client of the advantages of legal aid. Other examples are given in subsequent chapters (see p119, for example). Where a client has suffered through the

---

16   For example, see July 1983 *LAG Bulletin* 1 and 5, August 1983 *LAG Bulletin* 5 and
       September 1983 *LAG Bulletin* 3.
17   See 18 January 1988 *Law Society's Gazette* 25.

legal representatives incurring costs unnecessarily, it may be possible to have those costs reduced or disallowed under General Regs reg 109 or under the Rules of the Supreme Court Ord 62 r11 (see p162). Additionally, solicitors and barristers may be guilty of disciplinary offences arising from the fact that their client was legally-aided. The disciplinary tribunals of the Senate of the Inns of Court and the Bar[18] and the Law Society[19] must hear legal aid complaints. The tribunals may:

a) make the same orders on a complaint as on a charge of professional misconduct;
b) order that any fees or disbursements be reduced or cancelled;
c) order that the solicitor or barrister be excluded from legal aid work permanently or for a specified period.

Special or additional provision

Contempt proceedings

The LAA, in s29, makes special provision for a grant of legal aid where a person is likely to be committed or fined for contempt. In such cases the court may grant representation 'if it appears to the court to be desirable to do so in the interests of justice'.[20]

Legal aid under s29 is available in all courts. It is granted by the court which is considering whether to commit or fine somebody for contempt. The court grants legal representation on a form RCP1 or RCP1A, which also functions as the solicitor's claim for payment. A standard fee, currently of £70.25, is payable but it is possible to apply for a non-standard fee if there were special circumstances, such as the fact that the work was required to be undertaken by the court after one hearing and before another.[21] Claims for payment, except for the Court of Appeal Criminal Division and Crown Court cases where they are made direct to the court, are made to the Legal Aid Accounts Department.

Multi-party actions

See p8 above.

---

18   LAA s33.
19   Solicitors Act 1974 ss47 and 47A.
20   LAA s29(2).
21   See Note for Guidance 18.

Foreign judgments

Civil legal aid is available without a merits test, means test, or contributions to enable some foreign judgments to be registered and/or enforced in England and Wales. General Regs reg 15(1)(b) applies to the registration of judgments under the Civil Jurisdiction and Judgments Act 1982 s4.

Other regulations deal with legal aid to recover abducted children and to register foreign maintenance orders (see chapter 6).

Citizens advice bureaux, advice centres and law centres

Solicitors and barristers in private practice are not the only sources of legal help and advice. Citizens advice bureaux (CABx), independent advice centres and law centres all provide free and non-means-tested legal help. There are nearly 900 CABx in England and Wales. Some, especially in the larger cities, are staffed by full-time paid workers, while others rely on unpaid volunteers. Their capacity therefore varies but they can all offer initial advice and refer the client, if necessary, to a solicitor. Most will write letters on behalf of clients and help with completing forms. Many provide expert advice, especially on welfare benefits, and some offer tribunal representation. A few CABx have resource or 'community' lawyers to provide consultation and training, who may take up a few individual cases.

Independent advice centres deal with much the same problems as CABx, although they may concentrate on housing, welfare benefits and immigration. Like CABx they are able, usually, to refer clients to local solicitors. Some have lawyers working in the centre, usually part time in the evenings.

Consumer advice and housing advice centres offer specialist advice within their areas of concern. Some specialist agencies, such as the Citizens' Rights Office of the Child Poverty Action Group and the Joint Council for the Welfare of Immigrants, offer a centralised national service.

Law centres are staffed by full-time lawyers and legal workers. The centres provide free legal advice to people who live or work within their catchment area, regardless of means, and they provide free representation in certain cases. Law centres usually apply strict criteria in deciding which cases to take on, and concentrate on specific areas of social need, such as housing, welfare benefits, employment and immigration. Where the client is eligible, a law centre may use the legal aid or the green form advice and assistance scheme, but is very unlikely to expect the client to pay any contribution or to exercise the statutory charge.

The Equal Opportunities Commission and the Commission for Racial Equality

Both the Commission for Racial Equality (CRE) and the Equal Opportunities Commission (EOC) may pay for a person to receive legal advice, help and representation on a case that falls within their area of concern. If a person financially assisted in this way is successful, there are provisions similar to those governing the statutory charge (see chapter 10) which enable either Commission to recover the costs of the case.

This form of financial assistance may be particularly helpful in cases of race or sex discrimination in employment, because legal aid is not available to bring proceedings in an industrial tribunal. It should be noted, however, that while it is worth applying, the EOC finances little litigation.

European Commission of Human Rights

The advice and assistance scheme provides help only in relation to English law, and the legal aid schemes provide help only in the English courts. EEC law, being part of domestic law, is covered by the advice and assistance scheme, and references by an English court to the European Court of Justice are covered by civil or criminal legal aid as the case may be. The European Convention on Human Rights, however, is not part of domestic law and therefore no part of proceedings brought to the European Commission of Human Rights (EComHR) or to the European Court of Human Rights in Strasbourg is covered.

The EComHR, however, has its own legal aid scheme. Under the Addendum to the Rules of Procedure of the European Convention on Human Rights r1, the EComHR may 'either at the request of an applicant lodging an application under Article 25 or *proprio motu* [of its own motion], grant free legal aid to that applicant in connection with representation of his case'. This, however, covers only work done after the application has been made. It does not provide for initial help and advice in connection with the making of the application.

Information

Individual solicitors may advertise to the extent of telling the public of the work they do and how much they charge.

The Legal Aid Board publishes a *Solicitors' Regional Directory*. Consisting of 28 volumes, it contains detailed information about solicitors' firms and the areas of work in which individual solicitors claim experience. It states whether a particular firm does legal aid work. The *Directory* is published annually and distributed free to libraries, town halls, social and probation services, the police and courts and other organisations.

The Legal Aid Board has also produced leaflets informing the public about legal aid and the consequences of applying for it. The most important leaflets are 'What happens next?' and 'The Statutory Charge – What it means to you', both of which solicitors should hand to anyone who completes an application for civil legal aid.

Part I

Advice and assistance

CHAPTER 2

Green form scheme

Introduction

Before the 1993 changes, the legal advice and assistance scheme (usually known as the green form scheme) was of great importance to both the public seeking legal help and the practitioner seeking to make a living out of providing it. Now, as a result of the Lord Chancellor's cuts, only the very poorest people are financially eligible (see p32 below).

For those clients, however, who are still eligible, the scheme remains as a valuable resource. Accessible, simple and easy to use, it enables a client to obtain free or subsidised legal help of any kind, short of representation in court, in almost any matter (for the exceptions see p25 below). In some cases even representation is possible.

There are initial prescribed limits on the cost of the work and any expenditure which may be incurred. The initial limits differ for different types of work. They may be extended on application to the Legal Aid Board (see p35 below).

The scheme was introduced by the Legal Advice and Assistance Act 1972. It is now contained in the Legal Aid Act 1988 (LAA) ss2 and 8 to 13. Provisions restricting the scope of the green form scheme are contained in the Legal Advice and Assistance (Scope) Regulations 1989 SI No 550 (hereafter referred to as the Scope Regs). Detailed rules covering the operation of the scheme are set out in the Legal Advice and Assistance Regulations 1989 SI No 340 (hereafter referred to as the Advice and Assistance Regs).

Financial eligibility limits are set out in Advice and Assistance Regs reg 11(1), as amended by specific statutory instruments from time to time. The rules for assessment of resources are set out in Sch 2 to those Regs, most recently by the Legal Advice and Assistance (Amendment) Regulations 1993.

The first item on any solicitor's mental checklist when s/he sees a client on a new matter should be 'can I use the green form?'. As already

19

explained (see p1 above), a solicitor *must* advise a client of the benefits of
legal aid and this includes the green form scheme. Generally, it will be to
the advantage of a client to use the scheme. There are only two exceptions
to that general rule: first, where free, and adequate, help is available from
a law centre, an advice centre or a citizens advice bureau; and secondly,
where the client may need, and has a more than reasonable hope of
obtaining, an order for costs against the Legal Aid Fund under s13 or s18
of the LAA (see chapter 9).

Scope

Work within the scope of the scheme

Advice and practical help may be given by a solicitor, and if necessary
counsel, on any question of English law affecting the client's
circumstances.[1] The advice may be written or oral and the help may
include the solicitor taking action short of formal representation in court
or tribunal proceedings.[2]

Only the solicitor to whom the client has applied for help may claim
payment of fees under the green form scheme and only in respect of work
done within the solicitor's firm or by someone competent who is under
immediate supervision by the solicitor.[3] Barristers' fees can be claimed
under the green form scheme but not the fees of solicitor agents (although
solicitor agents can be paid for in ABWOR cases).[4]

Some work is outside the scheme and that is discussed below (p25).
The main practical limitation is that, in general, a solicitor may not,
under the green form scheme, represent a client or take any formal steps in
proceedings before a court or tribunal.[5] However, advice by way of
representation (ABWOR), which is dealt with in the next chapter,
provides important exceptions to this general rule and a solicitor can
provide help under the ordinary green form scheme in connection with
proceedings in which the client is formally acting in person. Indeed, one of
the main uses of the scheme is to finance legal advice and assistance to
people who, formally speaking, are petitioning in person for divorce (see
chapter 6).

In every case the wide terms of s2(2) and (3) should be considered.
Section 2(2) provides that advice may be given 'on the application of

1   LAA s2(2).
2   LAA s2(3).
3   Advice and Assistance Regs reg 20; *R v Legal Aid Board ex parte Bruce* [1992] 3 All
    ER 321, HL and see p25 below.
4   LAA s10(3)(b); Note for Guidance 2–34 and see p24 below.
5   LAA s8(2) and the Scope Regs.

English law' to the client's circumstances and s2(3) says that 'assistance' means taking 'any steps . . . including steps with respect to proceedings' or helping the client 'in taking them on his own behalf.' Apart from unauthorised representation and a few specific exceptions, as the Law Society pointed out when it ran the scheme,[6] 'There is no restriction upon what a solicitor can do for a client'. (This should, of course, now be read subject to the specific restrictions on the use of the green form scheme for conveyancing and wills introduced on 1 April 1989, see p26 below.)

'Reasonableness'

Solicitors will only be paid for work which it was reasonable to undertake having regard to the matter in which they have been instructed. However, the client – and therefore the solicitor being paid – does not have to show that it is reasonable to seek the help of a solicitor for a particular matter. The non-financial criteria which a client must meet to obtain help within the initial limits are only those set out in s2(2) and (3) – that help is needed 'on the application of English law to any particular circumstances'.

In other words, there is no merits test or test of 'reasonableness', unlike in civil legal aid, before the client can make use of the advice and assistance scheme. That was confirmed implicitly by the Solicitor-General in 1983. After disclosures in the *LAG Bulletin*[7] that the Law Society, which then administered the scheme, had refused to pay solicitors under the green form for advice on welfare benefits entitlement, Sir Patrick Mayhew stated:[8]

> I can confirm that matters affecting entitlement to welfare benefits are matters of law to which the legal aid scheme is applicable and it would not follow, nor is there anything in the legislation to suggest, that because advice, for example, from a lay quarter may be available on a particular matter, legal aid would not be awarded in such a case.

However, Note for Guidance 2–25 states that completion of the Child Support Agency's forms would not be a reasonable use of the green form where no direct legal issues were involved and it would be reasonable for the client to complete the form him or herself – something which obviously depends on the client and the nature of the form.

When the prescribed limit has been reached and the Board is considering whether to grant an extension (see p35), it must decide whether in all the circumstances it is reasonable to do so, a question which effectively requires the application of the civil legal aid merits test.

6   Note for Guidance 2 1989 *Handbook*.
7   July 1983 *LAG Bulletin* 5.
8   HC Debs, Vol 45 col 604, 11 July 1983 and August 1983 *LAG Bulletin* 5.

Examples of what can be done under the green form scheme

Solicitors, therefore, may: conduct correspondence; compromise actions; draft constitutions, agreements, and settlements; and advise on benefits entitlement. In limited circumstances, solicitors can draft wills and undertake conveyancing of property (see further below) – and be paid under a green form. One of the most important uses is to provide help in applying for legal aid. This may involve making investigations and obtaining counsel's opinion in difficult cases. Where legal aid has been refused, the green form scheme may be used to pay for advice on an appeal against the refusal.[9]

The range and variety of work for which a solicitor may be paid under this scheme is so great that, rather than asking in each case whether a task *may* be done under the green form scheme, the question should be 'is there any reason why it should *not* be done on a green form?'. The specific suggestions which follow should, therefore, by no means be taken as an exclusive list.

i) *Personal injury cases.*   Taking instructions; preparing an application for legal aid; making initial investigations (in some cases, for example, pavement tripping, it is often important to make an early inspection and take measurements and photographs); obtaining a medical report; writing letters before action; conducting negotiations (however, unless it is certain that settlement will be reached, legal aid should be applied for as soon as possible in order to prevent delay and to keep up pressure on defendants).

ii) *Crime.*   The use of the green form for crime is considered in detail in chapter 11. At this point it should be noted:

a) that green form help in police stations is not means tested or contributory;

b) that the green form scheme is not confined to police station work but is available generally for advice and assistance in connection with defending and prosecuting criminal cases, for complaints and civil suits against the police;

c) because of the general unavailability of legal aid to undertake prosecutions, the green form scheme can be particularly important to prepare prosecutions for assault or harassment or under the Environmental Protection Act 1990 s82.

iii) *Planning.*   Giving general advice; making representations; negotiating with the local authority; liaising with community groups and

---

9   This was not possible before 1 January 1981 when the Legal Aid (General) Regulations 1980 came into effect. In those regulations, a previous requirement that appeals had to be at the applicant's own expense was omitted – see also p84.

tenants' associations etc. By obtaining extensions on a number of forms, it may possible to raise a considerable sum of money, for instance, to pay for consultants' reports.

iv) *Welfare benefits.* Advising on entitlement and appeals and preparing appeals. Following the controversy referred to above, the Law Society amended its Notes for Guidance to confirm that advice on entitlement to benefits and verifying assessments fell within the green form scheme.[10]

v) *Immigration.* Giving advice; entering appeals; making contact with the Home Office and MPs; preparing applications for permits; advising on nationality and patriality. The scheme has in the past paid for an immigration adviser to travel to the Indian sub-continent to gather evidence. An extension was granted because the adviser was able to deal with a large number of cases at the same time.

Extensions may be granted to pay for blood tests but only if certain conditions are met:[11]

a) if the blood test is required before the Entry Clearance Officer has made a decision, the solicitor must certify that other available evidence is unlikely to satisfy the Entry Clearance Officer that a blood relationship exists on which the decision will hinge;

b) if the blood test is required for an appeal, an extension will be granted if the solicitor certifies that it is necessary for the outcome of the appeal and that there are reasonable prospects that any other grounds for refusing entry can be overcome;

c) if the samples are to be taken abroad it must be in accordance with strict procedure, which, at the moment, on the Indian sub-continent can only be satsified in Islamabad and Dhaka, therefore extensions will be refused unless the relevant person can go to either of those centres;

d) if the samples are to be taken in the United Kingdom it must be by a consultant haematologist, a medical practitioner in a Regional Blood Transfusion Centre or an appointed blood tester.

vi) *McKenzie advisers.* Further, the green form scheme might be used, for example, to pay for the attendance of a solicitor, or member of a solicitor's staff, at a tribunal or court to help a client conducting his or her case in person. In *McKenzie v McKenzie* [1970] 3 All ER 1034, it was established that any person may attend a trial to assist either party by taking notes, quietly making suggestions and giving advice. That was recently reaffirmed in *R v Leicester Justices ex parte Barrow* (1991) *Times*

10   The advice is now contained in the Legal Aid Board's Note for Guidance 2–24.
11   Note for Guidance 2–35.

5 August and applies to both court and tribunal proceedings. Giving help under the *McKenzie* ruling to a client acting in person is within the scheme.[12] However, when solicitors claim costs for acting as McKenzie advisers, the area office will ask to inspect the file to ensure that the claim does not include costs for an element of representation. When solicitors ask for extensions beyond the initial limit in order to act as McKenzie advisers, area directors have been told that it will normally be unreasonable to grant an extension and therefore it should be refused:

– where full legal aid is available and the client will be better served by being fully represented;
– unless the applicant can show that it is necessary to have the services of a solicitor as a McKenzie adviser because of the difficulty of the case, or the importance of the case to the client, or the inability of the client to act on his or her own without legal help.

Disbursements

It is important to remember that the green form provides for payments of disbursements, including reports from experts such as doctors, surveyors, accountants and environmental health officers. Note for Guidance 2-33 was originally issued in 1985 because 'problems have arisen' over what could be recovered. Resolving these problems may be 'technically' difficult, but the Legal Aid Board has provided a list of those disbursements which it will allow and those which it will not. Even the allowable disbursements will only be paid if:

(a) it is reasonable for the solicitor to incur the disbursement for the purpose of giving advice or assistance to the client; and
(b) the amount of the disbursement is reasonable.

The list is:

Recoverable disbursements	*Irrecoverable disbursements*
birth and other certificates	*ad valorem* stamp duties
conciliation referral fees	capital duty
counsel's fees	client's travelling and
enquiry agents' fees	accommodation expenses
experts' fees	discharge of debts owed by the
interpreters' fees	client, eg, rent or mortgage
Land Registry fees	payments
newspaper advertisements	mortgagees' or lessors' solicitors'
fees recoverable on oaths	costs and disbursements

12   Note for Guidance 2–21.

Recoverable disbursements	*Irrecoverable disbursements*
photographers' accounts	naturalisation fees
search fees	passport fees
stamp duties of a nominal	fees payable on voluntary petitions
amount, eg, the 50p paid on a	in bankruptcy
power of attorney	court fees.
travelling expenses of a solicitor.	

Where solicitors want to incur disbursements which appear in neither list, they are urged 'to seek advice and authority from the relevant area office'. To which it might be added that this guidance is issued without specific statutory authority, and the test must be whether a particular disbursement falls within the words of the LAA and the regulations. Neither provides for advance authority of disbursements incurred within the initial limit. While it may be reasonable to suppose that rarely will disbursements listed as 'irrecoverable' fall within the scheme, some might – for example, a client's travelling expenses where they have been incurred as part of the investigation of the case. The Board may, to be helpful, issue guidance, but in this, as in other areas, it must properly exercise its statutory discretion. If the Board fails to do so, its decision may be challenged by judicial review.

Only solicitors or barristers can be paid for giving legal advice under the scheme. In *R v Legal Aid Board ex parte Bruce* [1992] 3 All ER 321, HL, a private welfare rights agency gave advice, which the court held was effectively legal advice, to a solicitor acting under a green form for that solicitor to pass on to his client. The House of Lords held that the fees of the welfare rights agency were not a permissible disbursement. Because the welfare rights agency was not under the immediate supervision of the solicitor, he could not charge a fee for its work, even though he was passing on its advice – see p20 above.

Work outside the scope of the scheme

There are two general categories of work which fall outside the scheme and two specific types of work which were excluded as from 1 April 1989. In addition, there are some categories of client whose access to the scheme is restricted (see below p31). The specifically excluded categories of work are conveyancing and the making of wills. They are dealt with below. The two general categories of excluded work are as follows:

a) The scheme covers only 'the application of *English* law to any particular circumstances'.[13] This means that advice and help with Northern Irish and Scots law is excluded – as is, of course, all foreign law, including the European Convention on Human Rights. EEC law, on the other hand, when it is directly applicable *is* part of English law and therefore within the green form scheme.[14] It should also be noted that help is available under the scheme for the transmission of legal aid applications to the countries which are parties to the European Agreement on the Transmission of Applications for Legal Aid.[15]

b) Unless it is one of the number of special cases where ABWOR is available and has been authorised (see chapter 3, p45 below), the green form scheme does not cover a solicitor taking formal steps or representing the client in proceedings (which includes obtaining a grant of probate) before any court or tribunal.[16] This does not prevent the scheme being used to give help in connection with court proceedings, indeed s2(3) specifically includes 'steps with respect to proceedings' and, as already noted, the scheme can be used to help a litigant formally acting in person (see p23 above). It is 'representation' which is not covered: for instance appearing in court as an advocate, being on the court record, writing letters direct to the court or tribunal as the client's representative (as opposed to drafting them for the client to send), etc.

Conveyancing

This is one of the specific exclusions. Under Scope Regs reg 3, solicitors will be paid under the green form scheme for conveyancing services in *only* two instances:

– where it is necessary to implement a court order or an agreement made in matrimonial proceedings.[17] This is similar to the civil legal aid rule where conveyancing work is necessary to implement an order made in legally-aided proceedings.[18] In any event, most clients benefiting from this provision will end up paying for the work through the mechanism of the statutory charge (see p39 below);

---

13 LAA s2(2) and (3), emphasis supplied.
14 *R v Marlborough Street Stipendiary Magistrate ex parte Bouchereau* [1977] 3 All ER 365, DC.
15 Notes for Guidance 2–07 and 17.
16 LAA s8(2) and Scope Regs reg 5.
17 Scope Regs reg 3(2).
18 *Copeland v Houlton* [1955] 3 All ER 178.

- where the solicitor's help is needed because the client is proposing to enter into a rental purchase agreement or conditional sale agreement.[19]

The green form scheme will not pay for any other conveyancing services. Conveyancing services are defined by Scope Regs reg 2(1) by reference to the Administration of Justice Act 1985 s11(3) as:

> the preparation of transfers, conveyances, contracts, and other documents in connection with, and other services ancillary to, the disposition or acquisition of estates or interests in land; and for the purposes of this sub-section—
> (a) 'disposition'–
>   (i) does not include . . . any disposition in the case of such a lease as is referred to in section 54(2) of the Law of Property Act 1925 (short leases); but
>   (ii) subject to that, includes in the case of leases both their grant and their assignment; and
> (b) 'acquisition' has a corresponding meaning.

This is a very wide definition which catches most work normally thought of as conveyancing, including mortgages. It should be noted, however, that it is specifically concerned with 'acquisition' and 'disposal'. Other solicitor's work in relation to land – for example advice on entitlement to property, or on the construction of a lease or in relation to mortgage arrears – is still covered by the green form scheme.

In addition, of course, as a result of the exclusion in s11(3)(a) and (b) above, the green form scheme continues to cover work in connection with the acquisition and disposal of short leases which are not under seal – and therefore it also covers work done in connection with tenancy agreements.

'Conditional sale agreement' is defined as in s189 of the Consumer Credit Act 1974.

Wills

This is the second of the specific exclusions. In most circumstances, solicitors will not be paid under the green form for work relating to the making of wills.[20] They will, however, be paid where the help is given to a client who is:[21]

- 70 and over; or
- disabled; or

---

19   Scope Regs reg 3(3).
20   Scope Reg regs 4(1).
21   Scope Reg regs 4(2).

- the parent of a disabled person and who wants to provide for that person in the will; or
- a single parent wishing to appoint a testamentary guardian under the Guardianship of Minors Act 1971 s4.

Regulation 4(2)(b) of the Scope Regs details the disabilities from which a client must suffer in order to qualify for help: blindness or partial sight, deafness or hardness of hearing, dumbness, mental disorder, substantial and permanent handicap by illness, injury or congenital deformity. The mental disorder test, in particular, is likely to produce problems in practice. The Scope Regs reg 2(1) imports the definition of mental disorder found in the Mental Health Act 1983 s1(2). This states as follows:

'mental disorder' means mental illness, arrested or incomplete development of mind, psychopathic disorder and any other kind of disorder or disability of mind and 'mentally disordered' shall be construed accordingly.

The section gives a little further help by defining 'psychopathic disorder' as a:

persistent disorder or disability of mind (whether or not including significant impairment of intelligence) which results in abnormally aggressive or seriously irresponsible conduct on the part of the person concerned.

In many instances, no doubt, it will be clear whether or not a client falls within the definition. Some cases, however, will be problematic and solicitors in general practice are, in effect, being asked to diagnose conditions which experts disagree over defining.[22] Deciding that the client is suffering from a mental disorder and is therefore eligible for help will solve one question for the adviser only to raise another: the fundamental problem of whether the client has the mental capacity to instruct a solicitor and to make a will. Again, these are questions the solicitor will have to decide. If decided in the affirmative, the solicitor then has to make sure that the client's testamentary capacity is on record. Otherwise the will is vulnerable to subsequent challenge on the evidence of the client's qualifying for green form help by reason of mental disorder.

When one considers the general effects of the provision, it should be noted that not only the *making* of a will is generally excluded from the green form scheme, but also any advice and assistance *'relating to the making'* of a will. Therefore, preliminary advice about the advisability

22   For a summary of the issues surrounding the definitions see, eg, 1983 *Current Law Statutes* 20–13.

and possible terms of a will is not covered under the scheme. On the other hand, work done in relation to a will which has been made *would* normally be covered. Thus solicitors would be paid under the scheme for advice on the construction or probate of a will and, more obviously, for advice on an intestacy. (Applying for a grant of probate or letters of administration would not be covered, of course, see p26 above.)

Overlap with legal aid

In principle, the green form scheme can be used to undertake much of the work which is also covered by civil and criminal legal aid. For instance, a civil legal aid certificate covers work done before the issue of proceedings, which could also be covered by a green form. A criminal legal aid order may cover work done before it was issued, work which could equally be done under the green form.

It is an absolute rule that the green form scheme cannot be used where the assisted person has a legal aid certificate or order in respect of the same matter.[23] Green form assistance in criminal cases is dealt with below in chapter 11. In civil cases, the rule that green form help is not available where the client has a legal aid certificate does not dispose of all the problems, and options, which may arise in practice.

There is, first, the question of when to apply for legal aid where a case has been begun on the green form. The answer, unless the client has a large contribution and/or it is certain that the case will be compromised, must always be 'as soon as possible'. It is in the interests of the client to make an early application: there will be no delay after the breakdown of negotiations while the legal aid application is being considered, the existence of a certificate normally means there is no immediate limit on the work which can be done and therefore no worry and delay about obtaining green form extensions, and notification to the other side that the client has legal aid will sometimes assist a reasonable compromise (see further chapters 4 and 8 below). It is also in the interests of the solicitor to work under a legal aid certificate as this normally carries remuneration at a higher hourly rate than the green form.

Secondly, after the grant of a legal aid certificate the question may arise whether work should be done under the certificate or whether it could be treated as 'separate' and be done under the green form. The same issues arise as when considering separate green form matters (see p40 below). The implications are likely to be particularly important if the statutory charge arises. Needless to say, the decision should be taken in the

23 LAA s8(5).

interests of the client, rather than on the basis of the solicitor's interest in obtaining the higher hourly rate paid by civil legal aid.

Completing the green form

Any solicitor with a practising certificate in England and Wales (or a member of such a solicitor's staff[24]) may help under the green form scheme. All that is required is that the necessary Form GF1 (see Part V) is completed, the client's means assessed by the solicitor or staff member (see p32 below) and the form signed by the client. The form should always be signed by the client on the first attendance at the solicitor's office, as no payment will be made to the solicitor for work done on an unsigned green form. Equally, a form may not be backdated to cover work done before it was signed.

Completing the form is a relatively simple matter, which should take only a few moments – it requires the client's name and address and an indication of whether s/he has previously had legal aid or legal advice and assistance in connection with the matter in question, together with details of means. At the time the form is completed, however, and before it is signed, the amount of work which it covers and any financial effects, especially the contribution and the workings of the statutory charge (see p40, below), should be carefully explained to the client.

In most cases, the application must be made in person by the client to the solicitor.[25] This may cause problems where, perhaps because of disability or imprisonment, the client cannot go to the solicitor's office and the solicitor is not able to go to the client. Regulation 10 provides that if for 'good reason' the client cannot go to see the solicitor, the client may authorise a representative to attend to complete the green form. The only general requirement is that the representative should be able to provide the necessary information about means.[26] If the application is for help with the making of a will, the representative should also be able to show that the applicant falls within one of the categories entitled to help. There are no requirements concerning the relationship of the representative to the client: the representative could be, for example, a social worker or advice worker. Similarly, there are no rules about the form of the authority or even a requirement that it should be in writing.

Only residents outside England and Wales are generally exempt from the requirement of personal attendance. With prior authority from the

24 Advice and Assistance Regs reg 20.
25 Advice and Assistance Regs reg 9(3).
26 Advice and Assistance Regs reg 10(2).

Legal Aid Board, solicitors may accept postal green form applications from such persons.[27]

General eligibility

In general, the scheme is available to any person whose means are within stipulated limits: nationality, for example, is irrelevant. However, 'person' is defined to exclude a body corporate or incorporate unless it is acting in a representative or fiduciary capacity.[28] Anybody over the compulsory school age (16) may apply under the scheme;[29] in the case of someone under that age application may be made by the parent, guardian or other person in whose care the child is, or by a guardian ad litem or next friend.[30] With the prior authority of the Legal Aid Board, application may also be made by any other person or by the child itself.[31] Where a child needs advice or assistance in a police station, the solicitor may accept an application from the child, without prior authority from the Board, if the solicitor is satisfied that the application cannot 'reasonably be made' by those mentioned above.[32] In Children Act cases a child of any age may, in some circumstances, apply direct to a solicitor for green form help (see chapter 7).

Mental patients may complete a green form and therefore make use of the scheme, if the solicitor is satisfied that the patient is capable of managing his or her own affairs and giving instructions. There has been a misunderstanding in the past about whether a person detained in a mental hospital under the Mental Health Act 1983 was able to give instructions where no guardianship or protection order had been made. The Law Society, when it ran the legal aid scheme, made it clear that if the solicitor considers that the client is capable of giving instructions and managing his or her own affairs, it is not the function of the legal aid office to go behind the solicitor's decision.[33] Applications may also be made by a next friend or guardian ad litem, or, with the consent of the Legal Aid Board, by any other person.[34]

It is possible for groups of individuals to be given help under the green form, although both incorporated and unincorporated bodies are

27 Advice and Assistance Regs reg 15.
28 LAA s2(10).
29 Advice and Assistance Regs regs 3 and 14.
30 Advice and Assistance Regs reg 14(3).
31 Advice and Assistance Regs reg 14(1) and (3)(d).
32 Advice and Assistance Regs reg 14(2).
33 See November 1981 *LAG Bulletin* 247.
34 Advice and Assistance Regs reg 14(3).

excluded (see above). Whether the scheme may be used, and the extent to which others should contribute, depends upon the relative extent of the client's personal interest in the outcome (see below).

A person who has received help and advice under the green form scheme from a solicitor may not be helped under the scheme in respect of the same matter by another solicitor without the prior consent of the Legal Aid Board.[35] 'Another solicitor' in this context means a solicitor in another firm. Note for Guidance 2-12 sets out when authority is likely to be granted for a new solicitor:

- where there is a substantial gap between the first and the second occasion (but one might argue in that event that, in any case, the second occasion is a separate matter – see p40);
- the circumstances have changed materially, for instance a reconciliation has failed (but, again, such circumstances could sometimes constitute a separate matter);
- the client is dissatisfied with the services of the first solicitor, but not merely because the advice from the first solicitor is unpalatable and the client wants a second opinion;
- the client has moved a distance away and communication with the first solicitor is therefore difficult;
- the client wants to follow a particular solicitor who has changed firms.

The Note for Guidance also makes clear that authority will be refused if there is only a short time between consulting the solicitors and there has been no material change in circumstances, if authority has been granted previously, or if there is no reasonable explanation for the change.

If authority is given the new solicitor should start on a new green form – the authority is not to extend the old green form. Therefore, a new means assessment must be carried out (see also 'Change of Solicitor' in chapter 8 below).

Financial eligibility

Generally

Applicants for green form help must satisfy both capital and income tests. Anyone with disposable capital over £1,000 (calculated as below) is disqualified. Anyone with disposable income of more than £61 per week is also disqualified. However, applicants in receipt of income support, family credit or disability working allowance qualify automatically,

---

35   Advice and Assistance Regs reg 16(1).

provided they do not have capital in excess of the £1,000 limit. (Advice and Assistance Regs reg 12).

It is important to note that as a result of the 1993 changes, which apply to all applications made after 12 April 1993, contributory green form assistance no longer exists. Clients either qualify under the scheme for free help, under the rules set out above, or for no help at all.

However, the eligibility rules for the green-form-based ABWOR scheme are very different (see p45) and, of course, so are the civil legal aid rules. Therefore many clients who are ineligible for green form help will be eligible under the other schemes.

Calculating disposable capital

The method of calculating disposable capital is set out in Sch 2 to the Advice and Assistance Regs. Capital is defined as the amount or value of every resource of a capital nature.[36] It therefore includes the capital value of any insurance policy and money in a bank or savings account (and money which has been saved for a specific purpose, such as buying a freehold or paying for a holiday). Where, however, debts are due and payable, these may be deducted. Schedule 2 specifically directs that there should be disregarded the value of the subject matter or claim in respect of which the client is seeking help,[37] the main or only dwelling-house, household furniture, articles of personal clothing and tools and implements of trade.[38]

Deductions must also be made for dependants.[39] Dependants are defined as a spouse whose means are aggregated with the applicant's (see below), or a dependent child or relative wholly or substantially maintained by the applicant. The current deductions are as follows:

	£
for the first dependant:	335
for the second:	200
for all subsequent:	100

(There are no dependants' deductions from capital in respect of civil legal aid because of the higher capital limits which apply.)

The major capital item about which the regulations are unclear is the applicant's car. Is that a household effect? Could it be an implement of trade? 'Any question arising out of this Schedule shall be decided by the

---

36   Sch 2 para 1.
37   Sch 2 para 7(1).
38   Sch 2 para 8.
39   Sch 2 para 8(c).

solicitor to whom the client has applied'.[40] And although the solicitor is instructed to have regard to the guidelines which may be issued by the Legal Aid Board, none have yet been issued. However, normally the car may be safely ignored.

Calculating disposable income

Income is defined as the 'total income from all sources which the person concerned received or became entitled to during or in respect of the seven days up to and including the date of his application'.[41]

Form GF1 is laid out so as to enable the solicitor to carry out the necessary calculation of disposable income in a matter of minutes. One of the first questions is whether or not the applicant is in receipt of income support, family credit or disability working allowance. If the answer is 'yes', there is no need to carry out further assessment of *income*, as the client will automatically be eligible with a nil contribution. (Of course, if the disposable capital exceeds the capital limit, the client will not be eligible at all.) The assessment is concerned with net, not gross, income, and therefore deductions are made on the form in respect of tax, National Insurance payments and maintenance paid over the last seven days to a separated spouse, child or relative who is not a member of the household.[42] Certain welfare benefits are disregarded: disability living allowance, attendance allowance paid as an increase to a disablement pension, and any payments made out of the social fund. (Sch 2 para 9A inserted by Legal Advice and Assistance (Amendment) Regulations 1993 para 10). Deductions in respect of dependants living in the household as from 12 April 1993 are as follows:

	£pw
husband or wife:	25.00
child under 11:	15.05
child 11–15:	22.15
child 16–17:	26.45
child 18 or over in continuing education:	34.80

These allowances change automatically with social security benefits. The allowances for dependent children and other relatives are the same as the income support appropriate to the age of the child or relative. The allowance for a partner is the same as the difference between the income support allowance for a couple and that for a single person. (Sch 2 para 9

---

40   Sch 2 para 3.
41   Sch 2 para 1.
42   Sch 2 para 10.

as amended by Legal Advice and Assistance (Amendment) Regulations 1993 para 9).

Dependants' allowances and aggregation of resources

The resources of a spouse must be taken into account unless the spouse has a contrary interest in the matter, or is living apart from the applicant or it would otherwise be inequitable or impracticable to take the spouse's resources into account.[43] 'Spouse' includes someone of the opposite sex living with the applicant as husband or wife.[44] The applicant is also entitled to allowances in respect of a spouse with whom the applicant is living (see above). Where the applicant is not living with his or her spouse but is making payments to that spouse or a former spouse, child, or relative who has been a member of the applicant's household, the applicant is entitled to an allowance for any payment made or to be made in the seven days up to and including the date of the application.[45]

Where the application for green form help is on behalf of a child, the resources of the child's parents or anyone else who is liable to maintain the child under the Social Security Act 1988 s 26(3) and (4) may be taken into account if it appears just and equitable to do so.[46] In deciding whether it is just and equitable, the solicitor must 'have regard to all the circumstances, including the age and resources of the child and any conflict of interest'. Where a child is making an application on his or her own behalf in respect of a Children Act matter it is unlikely to be appropriate to take the means of anyone else into account.[47]

Extensions of prescribed limit

The initial limit for green form work generally is now set at two times the hourly rate allowed to solicitors under the scheme.[48] In cases involving the preparation of a divorce or judicial separation petition, the initial limit is three times that hourly rate.[49] This is simply a formula, introduced in the 1989 Regulations, for working out the initial limits, which will at least ensure that they keep pace with the hourly payments to solicitors. The formula does not necessarily mean that clients will obtain two or three

43 Advice and Assistance Regs Sch 2 para 7(2).
44 Advice and Assistance Regs Sch 2 para 2.
45 Sch 2 para 10.
46 Sch 2 para 5.
47 Note for Guidance 2–03.
48 Reg 4(1)(d).
49 Reg 4(1)(c).

hours' work in all cases because any disbursements will have to be met within the limits. (It should be noted that the old £90 limit for police station work remains in force.[50]) Unless the Legal Aid Board gives authority to exceed the initial limits, a solicitor may not claim more than that amount under the green form in fees and expenses, including counsel's fees (but excluding VAT). It must be stressed that, when the initial limit has been reached and more work needs to be done, the solicitor should always apply for an extension. A solicitor may not start to charge a green form client privately until a request for an extension has been turned down.[51] Solicitors may possibly not even be able to claim more than the limit as *inter partes* costs where work has been done under the green form because of the indemnity principle as set out in *Gundry v Sainsbury* [1910] 1 KB 645 CA (see discussion in chapter 9). There is evidence to suggest that not enough extensions are applied for – which means either that clients are not having work done for them which needs to be done, or that solicitors are doing the work unpaid, or that solicitors are charging privately for work that should be done under the scheme.

Applications for extensions are made on Form GF3 (see Part V). Solicitors should make sure that the form contains sufficient information to enable the area office to decide first, as reg 21(2) of the Advice and Assistance Regs requires, that it is reasonable for the advice and assistance to be given and, secondly, whether the amount of the estimated solicitor's costs is fair and reasonable. The Legal Aid Board may grant an extension and prescribe such higher limits on fees and disbursements as it thinks fit, and it may limit the advice and assistance to such subject matter as it thinks fit.[52] To avoid delay, solicitors should submit applications for extensions as soon as possible and give as much information as possible to enable the Legal Aid Board to make a decision. In urgent cases, applications for extensions may be made over the telephone. The area office does not want to receive any more papers than necessary but practitioners should remember that the legal aid officials will not know anything about the case in advance. They must be told what the problem is, what work has been done, what needs to be done and why, and the likely cost.

Notes for Guidance 2–17 to 2–20 set out some of the criteria which are applied when considering applications for extensions. The first question is whether legal aid is available for the matter. This prevents the granting of an extension only if the applicant has actually been granted legal aid.[53] If

50   Reg 4(1)(a) and (b).
51   Note for Guidance 2–38.
52   Advice and Assistance Regs reg 21(3).
53   LAA s8(5) and see above.

legal aid has not been granted, the applicant may be given an extension but further questions must be considered:

- has legal aid or ABWOR been refused? If so the area office will probably grant a limited extension only to appeal against the refusal;
- has legal aid or ABWOR been applied for? If so an extension may be granted if a delay in the application is likely and more work is needed;
- should legal aid be applied for? If proceedings are imminent or unavoidable, only a limited extension will be granted to enable an application to be made for legal aid. If the solicitor can show that there is a real prospect of settlement one extension may be granted, but if further work needs to be done the area office will probably require an application to be made for legal aid.

Apart from the question of legal aid, the area office will also consider the following:

- does the applicant have alternative sources of finance?
- is the opponent worth pursuing?
- does the money at stake justify the expenditure?

Extensions will normally be refused to prepare applications to the Criminal Injuries Compensation Board (CICB) on the basis that the CICB carries out the necessary enquiries. After the CICB has made an award or refused to do so, it might be reasonable to grant an extension for advice on the decision and on whether the client should apply for an oral hearing. Such an extension might include obtaining a further medical report or other evidence.[54]

The area office is unlikely to grant an extension to obtain an opinion from counsel in relation to potential litigation and will instead suggest that an application be made for legal aid, unless the opinion is needed on form or type of litigation. An extension may be granted where there is no potential litigation and the matter appears beyond the expertise of a reasonably competent solicitor.

Special criteria apply to matrimonial and family cases which are dealt with in chapter 6.

Unfortunately, practice on giving extensions varies between the legal aid areas. According to practitioners in some areas, extensions are granted almost as and when requested, whereas in other places they are more likely to be refused, in part or in full. Again the practice varies as to when directors consider that a case is more appropriate for an application for civil legal aid rather than an extension to the green form. To some degree, these variations are confirmed by the annual legal aid statistics. It will

---

54   Note for Guidance 2–19(d).

save time to get to know the local practice. However, it is worth pointing out that the Legal Aid Board is trying to standardise the attitude towards extensions, so in a particularly unreasonable case a complaint to the Legal Aid Head Office is probably worthwhile, and publicity in *Legal Action* may help. The principle must be: when in doubt, apply.

Extensions to a green form cannot be sanctioned retrospectively.[55] However, there are special rules covering advice in police stations (see below). There is no appeal against the refusal of an extension to the green form. However, it is possible to submit fuller information and ask the area office to reconsider, and it is always possible to challenge by means of judicial review.[56]

Payments to solicitors

Prompt payment for completed work is the essential basis for any successful legal aid practice. Payments under the green form are so simple to obtain that there is no excuse for delay. The solicitor must complete the reverse of the green form (see Part I), stating briefly the work done: interview with client, drawing instructions to counsel to advise, etc. The solicitor should show on the form how the application of English law was relevant to the work done. The amount of time spent, letters written and telephone calls made must also be inserted. At various times the Legal Aid Board will issue guidelines for the assessment of green form fees. Practitioners are notified of the guidelines by circular letter and they are also published in the legal press. The rate for work done on or after 1 April 1992 (not uprated in 1993) is £43.25 per hour; long letters and telephone calls are paid on a time basis and the allowance for short letters and telephone calls is £3.35 per item. The rates are higher for solicitors in Greater London – Legal Aid Area 1. They can charge £45.75 per hour and £3.50 per item.

Claim forms should be submitted when the matter has been completed; or when the Legal Aid Board has refused to extend the limit and the limit has been reached; or when the client has obtained a legal aid order or certificate covering the same matter.

The green form is sent to the area office of the Legal Aid Board for assessment of the amount payable together with Form GF2 which has space for 14 claims to be listed and made at the same time. The frequency with which such claims are sent must depend on the nature of the practice. A firm which does a large amount of green form work will no doubt send

---

55   *Drummond v Lamb and others* [1992] 1 WLR 163 (HL).
56   See *R v Legal Aid Area No 15 ex parte Cromer* April 1990 *Legal Action* 21.

in the form as and when there are 14 claims to be made, whereas other firms may make a practice of submitting claims on a fortnightly or monthly basis.

The Legal Aid Board pays the solicitor the 'assessed deficiency' – that is the amount of costs and disbursements which has been assessed as due *less* any amounts due to the solicitor from the client in respect of the statutory charge (see below). The Legal Aid Board includes green form payments in the general legal aid cheque which it sends to firms or credits to their accounts through BACS fortnightly. The accompanying payment advice does not, however, list the name of each green form client for which payment is being made; it gives only the first name on Form GF2; and the total paid on that form.

In the interests of efficiency, it is probably worthwhile, in a firm which has several fee-earners doing green form work, to send the forms to one person for submission to the Legal Aid Board. In most practices it may be a good idea to open a special green form account to which payments may be credited, and a system should be set up to ensure that the fee-earner is informed when a green form is paid so that he or she can, if appropriate, close the file.

Statutory charge

Under the green form scheme, the solicitor has first claim on anything which has been recovered or preserved by the client in the matter, up to the amount of the costs payable out of the Legal Aid Fund to the solicitor.[57] This is known as the statutory charge. The Legal Aid Board deducts whatever is due under the statutory charge before paying the assessed costs to the solicitor.

The statutory charge attaches to any property, money or rights obtained by the client under any compromise or settlement which has been arrived at 'in connection with that matter' or to bring to an end any proceedings. The test is whether whatever the client has obtained – property, money or rights – has been obtained 'in connection with that matter', ie, the matter which has received green form assistance.[58] It is not a question of whether it is as a result of the green form help that the client has obtained the benefit, it is merely whether the client has been receiving green form help in connection with that matter. Clearly, the scope of the charge is wide and, but for a number of specific exemptions, the charge may attach to anything which the client has obtained after receiving help

57   LAA s11(2).
58   LAA s11(2)(b).

under a green form. As a result of the redrafting in the 1988 Act, however, the statutory charge does not attach if the money or property is recovered or preserved when the assisted person is no longer receiving advice and assistance under the scheme on the particular matter. There are also some specific exemptions for the statutory charge (see chapter 10).

Nonetheless, it applies in most cases and it may come as an unpleasant surprise to the client to find, at the conclusion of a long and hard-fought case, that the whole or a substantial part of what has been won is taken by the solicitor to pay for the work done. Many clients assume, understandably unless told to the contrary at the beginning, that legal advice and assistance is either free or that only the contribution is payable. It is therefore important to explain to the client at the beginning the possible effects of the statutory charge. It is essential to take the charge into account when deciding on terms of settlement and to explain it again to the client at that point, before s/he makes a final decision.

The statutory charge applies also to legal aid, although with some differences. The operation of the charge, including the exemptions, is discussed in detail in chapter 10.

Separate matters

Separate matters must be dealt with on separate green forms.[59] However, the regulations give no definition of what constitutes a 'separate matter'. The question arises, for example, when a client goes to a solicitor with financial problems. Do all the debts constitute one matter, or may each debt be regarded as a separate matter? Equally, are problems relating to statutory sick pay to be treated as separate from a claim for personal injuries in negligence? The answer may have important consequences for the client:

a) *Entitlement to help.*   Where a client already has legal aid in respect of the same matter, green form help is not available. Further, if the client has previously had help from another solicitor in respect of the same matter, it will be necessary to obtain authority from the Legal Aid Board before further green form help may be given.

b) *The size of the statutory charge.*   Where property is recovered or preserved in respect of some of the work done for a client, the cost of other work will not be recoverable from the client under the statutory charge but will instead be borne by the Legal Aid Fund if it is in respect of a separate matter.

c) *The amount of work that may be done without an extension.*   Where costs have been incurred up to the initial limit and more work is necessary, that work could be done on a different green form, if it is a separate matter, and thus it would not be necessary to apply for an extension. An application for an extension should be avoided if possible; it might be refused and will certainly cause a delay and involve the solicitor in more formalities.

In each of the circumstances detailed in (a) to (c) above the question of whether work is done in respect of a separate matter will be made on the basis of reg 17 of the Advice and Assistance Regs, which provides:

> Where more than one separate matter is involved each matter shall be the subject of a separate application for advice and assistance provided that matters connected with or arising from proceedings for divorce or judicial separation, whether actual or prospective between the client and his spouse, shall not be treated as separate matters for the purpose of advice and assistance.

Thus except in matrimonial proceedings, reg 17 gives the solicitor a wide discretion in determining what is and is not a separate matter. The first decision is the solicitor's, but the final decision, subject to appeal and challenge by judicial review, is the area office's. If the solicitor decides wrongly he or she may not be paid for all the work done. In order to help, the Legal Aid Board has issued Notes for Guidance 2-13 to 2-16.

Note for Guidance 2-16 sets out general criteria:

- First, any application for green form help more than six months after an earlier green form was *presented for payment* will always be a separate matter.[60]
- Secondly, rather obviously if too cautiously, 'genuinely different problems' are 'probably separate matters justifying separate green forms'. It is submitted if they are genuinely different matters then they definitely, not 'probably', justify different green forms.
- Thirdly, where two matters arise from the same set of circumstances the chances of their being genuinely separate matters diminish. It is submitted however they do not disappear: a client's need for advice and assistance with an industrial injury benefit claim and an action against his or her employers following an accident at work would quite clearly in most circumstances be two separate matters.
- Finally, the Legal Aid Board advises that if two matters lead to a single action, cause or matter, it is unlikely that they can be treated as

---

60   See also Note for Guidance 2-12.

separate matters. Conversely, of course, if they lead to separate actions etc., it is highly likely that they can be treated as separate matters.

Specific examples are set out in Note for Guidance 2-15:

-   As a general rule each of a client's debts cannot be treated as separate matters. However, the Legal Aid Board agrees that where separate proceedings are issued in respect of each debt, separate green forms are justified for each set of proceedings.
-   Separate green forms are normally not justified for advice about separate welfare benefits. It is submitted, this cannot be an inflexible rule. For instance, where an appeal is made or legal proceedings begun in respect of a particular benefit, it would be justifiable to treat that as a separate matter.
-   Problems or remedies arising out of housing difficulties would not normally be separate matters. The Legal Aid Board gives the example of 'possession/repairs etc.' It is submitted this guidance can only be correct insofar as it relates to housing difficulties arising out of the same legal relationship of, for instance, landlord and tenant or mortagee/mortgagor. Rent arrears arising out of one tenancy must be a separate matter from a dispute over repairs in another tenancy, and advice and assistance with homelessness or housing benefit would equally be separate matters from advice about a tenancy.

In each instance the decision to treat matters as separate or not must be reasonable, but there will be many cases where to reach either conclusion would be equally reasonable. In such cases the determining factor must be to obtain the result which will be most beneficial to the client. Usually this will mean keeping matters separate.

Legal academics undertaking research for the Lord Chancellor's Department have suggested that such practices are a misuse of the green form.[61] Provided that the solicitor is acting on the client's instructions and giving a professional and disinterested service, it cannot be misuse of the scheme to maximise its benefits for the client and diminish, as far as possible, its disadvantages.

The question of separate matters in matrimonial cases is dealt with in chapter 6.

Conclusion

The eligibility cuts have diminished the importance of the green form scheme, but nonetheless the range of work which solicitors may undertake

---

61   See 2 September 1988 NLJ 631.

under the scheme is immense. Used boldly, the scheme can be of enormous advantage to clients and solicitors alike. When it was introduced, it was widely hoped that the scheme would result in solicitors entering new fields, particularly in relation to welfare benefits and tribunals.[62] Those hopes have not been realised – as is shown year after year in the breakdown of types of work done under the scheme published as part of the *Legal Aid Annual Reports* (HMSO). By and large the work done under the scheme falls into the traditional categories: matrimonial, criminal etc.

It is noticeable that law centres use the green form for a very different mix of work than do private practitioners. The low maximum limit on the work which may be done without authority is certainly a problem, and the low hourly rate paid to solicitors is another, but, without a doubt, one of the major reasons that the scheme has not been used to the full has been a lack of appreciation of its potential within the practising private profession as a whole.

62   See, for example, May 1973 *LAG Bulletin* 83.

CHAPTER 3

Assistance by way of representation

Introduction

The green form scheme may be used to advise and help an eligible person who is involved in court or tribunal proceedings – even to the extent of the solicitor sitting next to him or her during the hearing and giving assistance under the principle in *McKenzie v McKenzie* [1970] 3 All ER 1034 (see p23). Nevertheless, as a general rule, help under the green form may not extend to taking formal steps or providing representation.

There are five exceptions to the general rule, and in cases that fall within those exceptions solicitors may use the green form scheme to represent clients and to take formal steps on their behalf, almost as if the clients had been granted full legal aid certificates. Representation under the green form scheme is known as assistance by way of representation (ABWOR). The five exceptions where it is available are:

a) domestic proceedings in the magistrates' courts, or family proceedings courts as they are now also known,[1] except for Children Act proceedings (which are covered by civil legal aid, see chapter 7);

b) appeals against prohibition notices under s10A of the Fire Precautions Act 1971 in the magistrates' courts;[2]

c) applications to mental health review tribunals (MHRTs);[3]

d) disciplinary proceedings before prison governors;[4]

e) parole hearings before a discretionary lifer panel.[5]

It is necessary to apply to the Legal Aid Board for a grant of ABWOR in civil cases.

In addition to the cases listed above, forms of ABWOR are used to pay duty solicitors in the magistrates' courts in criminal cases and for

---

1 Scope Regs reg 7(1) and Sch.
2 Scope Regs reg 7(1) and Sch para 1(h).
3 Scope Regs reg 9(1)(a).
4 Scope Regs reg 9(1)(b).
5 Scope Regs reg 9(1)(c).

representation on applications for warrants of further detention. That is dealt with in chapter 11.

Further, a limited form of ABWOR may be authorised by a magistrates' court or county court in specified circumstances under Scope Regs regs 7(1)(b) and 8. These will be further dealt with below at p51.

Financial eligibility

Anyone who qualifies for free green form help also qualifies for free ABWOR. But the reverse is not necessarily true.

The eligibility rules for ABWOR are the same as for green form, except that in ABWOR:

- the income limit is higher, £147 per week, and applicants with a disposable income of more than £61 per week pay contributions (see below) (Advice and Assistance Regs reg 11(2) as amended by Legal Advice and Assistance (Amendment) Regulations 1993 reg 5(b));
- the capital limit is higher, £3,000 (but with the same dependants' allowance) (Advice and Assistance Regs reg 11(2));
- capital is disregarded completely where the solicitor is satisfied that the applicant, or any of the persons whose resources should be aggregated with the applicant under Sch 2, is in receipt of income support (Advice and Assistance Regs reg 13(3)).

Contributions

Clients with a disposable income of over £61 per week must pay one third of the excess as a weekly contribution from the date when ABWOR is approved either until it is withdrawn or during the lifetime of the proceedings. Clients granted the limited form of ABWOR by magistrates' or county courts (see p51) pay one week's contribution (Advice and Assistance Regs reg 12 as substituted by Legal Advice and Assistance (Amendment) Regulations 1993 reg 6.)

The contributions must be collected by the client's solicitor and they may be paid weekly or in such other instalments as may be agreed (Advice and Assistance Regs reg 28(1) as substituted by Legal Advice and Assistance (Amendment) Regulations 1993 reg 8(a)).

When the solicitor claims costs, the full contribution history must be set out on Form ABWOR 3.

Method for obtaining ABWOR approval

As already noted, it is necessary to obtain approval from the Legal Aid Board before ABWOR can be given. If the client is financially eligible for ordinary green form help the solicitor will normally have provided initial advice and assistance on the basis of that form with, if necessary, extensions beyond the initial cost limit.

To apply for ABWOR the solicitor should complete the form ABWOR 1A. It requires personal details about the client, specifies the nature of the proceedings for which representation is sought and, on the reverse side, provides for details about any opponent, any children, previous proceedings and a short statement of the case, including, if appropriate and known, details of any opponent's financial resources and of any corroborative evidence. The completed form is sent together with supporting documents to the Legal Aid Board.

The test applied by the Board depends on the nature of the proceedings for which ABWOR is required (see below). If the application is approved, the Legal Aid Board sends the solicitor Form ABWOR 2. Refusal is by letter. Decisions about the grant, extension or withdrawal of ABWOR are taken by the area director and can be challenged by appeal to the area committee within 14 days.[6] The committee considers the matter afresh. Its decision is final and it must give reasons.[7]

Effects of ABWOR approval

The effect of approval is normally to remove the financial limit on the work which may be done. The regulations allow the Legal Aid Board to attach conditions and limitations to its approval.[8] The Board may also impose a financial limit.[9] Approval does not give authority to instruct counsel, and reg 22(4) states that 'it shall be a condition of every approval' that the Legal Aid Board must be asked for prior permission:

a) to obtain an expert's report;
b) to tender expert evidence; or
c) to perform an act which is 'either unusual in its nature or involves an unusually large expenditure'.

Permission to do any of these things may, however, specifically be included in the general grant of approval. If it is not, then an application

---

6   Advice and Assistance Regs reg 26.
7   Advice and Assistance Regs reg 27.
8   Advice and Assistance Regs reg 22(4).
9   Advice and Assistance Regs reg 22(5).

for authority after ABWOR has been granted should be made on Form ABWOR 6.

The Legal Aid Board has made clear that the obtaining of blood tests is something which requires prior permission unless that has been given in the approval of ABWOR itself. It makes no difference that a court has adjourned for the taking of blood tests or even ordered them.[10] Therefore, if necessary, practitioners should make it clear that they require permission for blood tests when applying for ABWOR.

It should also be noted that approved ABWOR includes negotiations for the settlement of the proceedings which are covered and 'reasonably relate to the scope of the particular ABWOR approval'.[11] The scope of ABWOR approval, however, does not include the implementation of a settlement other than the obtaining of a final order.

Scope

Domestic proceedings in family proceedings courts (magistrates' courts)

ABWOR may be given for domestic proceedings in the magistrates' court under Scope Regs reg 7(1). The proceedings for which ABWOR is available are specifically listed in the Schedule to the Scope Regs and, since the introduction of civil legal aid for Children Act proceedings (see chapter 7), consist principally of proceedings under the Domestic Proceedings and Magistrates' Courts Act 1978. Where an application is being made under both the Domestic Proceedings and Magistrates' Courts Act and the Children Act it is necessary to apply both for ABWOR, and civil legal aid, for the children.

The Board *must* refuse an application for ABWOR for domestic proceedings unless the client can show reasonable grounds for taking, defending or being a party to proceedings.[12]

The Board *may* refuse an application if it appears unreasonable to give authority in the particular circumstances of the case.[13] The test is therefore the same as the civil legal aid 'merits test'.

ABWOR will normally be granted to take proceedings for financial

---

10   Note for Guidance 3–22.
11   Note for Guidance 3–22.
12   Advice and Assistance Regs reg 22(5).
13   Advice and Assistance Regs reg 22(6).

provision in the family proceedings court (magistrates' court). In most instances it will only be refused if:[14]

- divorce proceedings are pending or imminent, ie, if the marriage has broken down, in which case the Board will consider that all matters should be dealt with in the divorce proceedings; or
- there will be no personal benefit to the applicant.

That an applicant is receiving income support is likely to be relevant. It does not prejudice his or her right to take proceedings or his or her right to ABWOR, but s/he will have to show that if the proceedings are successful s/he will receive some personal benefit. That does not necessarily mean that s/he has to show that there is a reasonable prospect of obtaining more from the court than s/he is receiving in income support. S/he may intend to take a job and come off benefit, for example. Or s/he may have other reasons for bringing proceedings: for example, to settle issues about custody, welfare or paternity or to obtain a personal protection order.

To obtain ABWOR approval for child maintenance applications it will be necessary to show that the court rather than the Child Support Agency has jurisdiction and ABWOR approvals granted after 5 April 1993 for financial provision applications will not cover child maintenance (other than for step-children of the absent parent) unless expressly stated. ABWOR will be granted to defend domestic proceedings but, in the absence of special circumstances, only where there is a dispute on the issues.

It should be noted that civil legal aid is also available for the domestic proceedings in a family proceedings court covered by ABWOR. However, a statutory ground for refusal of legal aid is that in the particular circumstances of the case it appears more appropriate that the applicant should receive ABWOR.[15] Section 15(3)(b) is used to ensure that only those who fall outside the green form limits are granted legal aid for this type of proceedings. The proportion of legal aid certificates granted in this area is extremely small (see below p107).

There is also another kind of overlap – between the jurisdiction of the magistrates' court in family matters and that of the High Court and the county court. In a non-Children Act case in a family proceedings court (magistrates' court) the client will apply for ABWOR, in the High Court and the county court for civil legal aid. The criteria applied by the Legal Aid Board when considering which venue an applicant should use are discussed on p96 below.

Where ABWOR has been approved for domestic proceedings in the

14   Note for Guidance 3–12.
15   LAA s15(3)(b).

family proceedings court, the solicitor must notify the other parties to the proceedings and the court in which the proceedings are pending as soon as practicable.[16] This should be done by letter (there is no prescribed form).

Appeals under Fire Precautions Act 1971 s10A

The rules are the same as for domestic proceedings in the magistrates' courts.

Mental health review tribunals

ABWOR is available for proceedings before MHRTs under Scope Regs reg 9(a). It is available to the patient and, where the application is being made by a 'nearest relative',[17] to that person as well. Applicants need only satisfy the second limb of the merits test – that is ABWOR may be refused if it appears unreasonable in the particular circumstances of the case that it should be granted.[18] The burden would be on the Board to show that it was unreasonable and it is difficult to envisage circumstances in which that would be the case.

Solicitors are expected to prepare the case within the initial green form limit before applying for ABWOR. This preparation should include obtaining the hospital's statement and interviewing the patient, where necessary obtaining an extension. The application for ABWOR should usually include the hospital statement. If the client is not eligible for a green form, an application should be made immediately for ABWOR on form ABWOR 1.

The MHRT should be notified when ABWOR has been authorised, but the regulations do not so require.

Solicitors should remember that unless specific permission is given, approval of ABWOR does not authorise the obtaining of an expert's report – in this context a psychiatric report. They should therefore specify any reports required when they apply for ABWOR.[19] The Legal Aid Board expects solicitors to exercise their professional judgment to decide whether a report is needed. The same applies to second opinions.

The Legal Aid Board will normally refuse authority to instruct counsel because solicitors are considered sufficiently experienced.

For those applicants who have difficulty in finding a solicitor with the requisite experience, the Law Society has set up a panel of solicitors with

16   Advice and Assistance Regs reg 24.
17   Mental Health Act 1983 s26.
18   Advice and Assistance Regs reg 22(5) and (6).
19   Or apply later on Form ABWOR 6.

some expertise in this work to whom it refers potential clients. However, clients are free to instruct any solicitor of their choice. Clients or solicitors who want information about the panel should contact the Panel Administration (see Part V, p327).

Disciplinary proceedings before prison governors

ABWOR is available to anyone who is appearing before a prison governor on a disciplinary charge provided that the governor has previously ordered that the person should be legally represented.[20]

The normal financial eligibility criteria apply, but, of course, most of the applicants, since they are in prison, are likely to qualify on means. If the prisoner must make a contribution, the Prison Department will arrange for it to be paid.

ABWOR will be granted only if the governor has first decided that legal representation for the prisoner is desirable. Evidence that the governor has so decided must be sent with the application for ABWOR, usually in the form of a letter. The first question, therefore, apart from financial eligibility, is whether the governor has decided that representation is desirable. In *R v Secretary of State for the Home Department ex parte Tarrant; R v Board of Visitors of Albany Prison ex parte Leyland; R v Board of Visitors of Wormwood Scrubs Prison ex parte Tangney, Clark, Anderson* [1984] 1 All ER 799, the Divisional Court held, on an application for judicial review, that prisoners facing disciplinary charges before a board of visitors (who had jurisdiction at the time) might be allowed legal representation at the discretion of the board, but they were not entitled to that representation as of right.

The Divisional Court went on to set out the factors which a board (and therefore a governor) should take into account in deciding whether representation was desirable:

a) the seriousness of the charge and the potential penalty;
b) whether any points of law were likely to arise – which would be rare except in mutiny charges;
c) the capacity of the prisoner to put his or her own case;
d) procedural difficulties, bearing in mind that prisoners awaiting adjudication would normally be kept apart from other prisoners which would hinder them in preparing their cases;
e) the need for reasonable speed in making an adjudication; and
f) the need for fairness between prisoners and between prisoners and prison officers.

20   Scope Regs reg 9(b).

If the governor has permitted representation the Legal Aid Board may only refuse ABWOR if it appears unreasonable to grant it in the particular circumstances of the case. In other words, it is not necessary for the applicant to show reasonable grounds for defending the proceedings.

Since a system of representation was first introduced in November 1983, boards of visitors have not been generous in deciding that representation was necessary in particular cases. By 1 October 1984, representation had only been ordered in 95 cases, according to Mr JH Appleton, the Chair of the Board of Visitors at HM Prison Gartree, speaking at the Board of Visitors' annual conference.[21] Since then the numbers have declined even further. In 1990/91 the Board paid for representation in only 62 cases.

Discretionary lifer panels

Unders s34 of the Criminal Justice Act 1991 some prisoners who have been given discretionary life sentences have the right to apply to a panel of the Parole Board for a release on licence. ABWOR is available for prisoners to be represented and may only be refused if it appears unreasonable to grant it in the particular circumstances of the case.[21A] As in the case of representation before Mental Health Review Tribunals, specific authority from the Legal Aid Board is required before practitioners obtain reports from experts such as psychiatrists, and authorisation must therefore be sought in the initial application or later on Form ABWOR 6.

Approval by magistrates' and county courts

A magistrates' court or a county court may authorise a solicitor to provide ABWOR to a party to proceedings before the court.[22] However, the solicitor will only be paid up to the prescribed limit.

Although this provision may be helpful, the preconditions governing its use should be noted. These conditions were made more stringent in 1989 under the Scope Regs than they had been previously, with the perverse primary intention of making it more difficult for county court duty solicitor schemes to be funded through the use of Scope Regs reg 8. However, the rules are the same for magistrates' courts and county courts,

---

21   Reported at November 1984 *Legal Action* 4.
21A Scope Regs reg 9(c).
22   Advice and Assistance Regs reg 22(2).

although set out separately under Scope Regs regs 7(1)(b) and 8 respectively. The court can authorise representation only:

a) where the client is not receiving and has not been refused legal aid in the proceedings;
b) where the court is satisfied that the hearing should proceed that day;
c) where the court is satisfied that the client would not otherwise receive representation;
d) where the representation is by a solicitor who is already within the precincts of the court for a purpose other than giving ABWOR under this provision.

The solicitor will not be paid more than the current prescribed initial limit for the assistance given. However, the ABWOR, rather than the normal green form, means tests apply. Therefore in all cases an ABWOR 1 form must be completed to confirm the client's financial eligibility before the application is made to the court.

Scope Regs reg 8 might be used in the county court in urgent cases, for example to represent the respondent in injunction proceedings; or where legal aid is not normally granted, for example to represent squatters, certain tenants in rent arrears or debtors generally.

In the magistrates' courts, Scope Regs reg 7(1)(b) is not confined to criminal cases and might be used, for example, to provide representation on maintenance arrears summonses. The use of the regulation in criminal cases is covered in chapter 11.

The Legal Aid Board issued guidance on the use of Scope Regs regs 7(1)(b) and 8 in the *Law Society's Gazette*.[23] It has not been reproduced in the *Legal Aid Handbook*. Helpfully, it states that advice and assistance given under Scope Regs reg 7(1)(b) and 8 will be treated as a separate matter under Advice and Assistance Regs reg 17. This can be very useful in practice. For instance, a solicitor is already giving green form advice on a particular matter, such as maintenance arrears. The client needs help in the magistrates' court on the hearing of an arrears summons, which happens to take place when the solicitor is in court on other business. The solicitor can ask the court to authorise representation under Scope Regs reg 7(1)(b), complete a form ABWOR 1, and then undertake representation and be paid for it up to the prescribed limit without diminishing the amount of work which can be done under the original green form.

That court-approved ABWOR is a separate matter also means that where a client has received help from a solicitor on a green form under Scope Regs reg 7(1)(b) and 8, perhaps on a possession summons, that

23   (1989) 86/46 LS Gaz 11.

client can go to another solicitor and obtain help with the same proceedings under another green form without first obtaining approval from the area office (see p41 above).

The guidance from the Legal Aid Board also advises about the mechanics of claiming costs and providing evidence about the court's authorisation of representation. It suggests that the latter could take one of three forms:

- an endorsement of the completed ABWOR 1 in terms such as: 'I hereby confirm that this court requested/approved a proposal that ABWOR be provided pursuant to reg 7(1)(b)/8 of the Legal Advice and Assistance (Scope) Regulations 1989 in respect of a hearing on (insert date). Signed ....(Clerk to the justices of the ..... court) dated.......';
- a county court order confirming that ABWOR was approved;
- a letter from the court in the appropriate terms and signed by an appropriate officer.

The written confirmation that ABWOR was authorised must be sent to the area office together with the normal ABWOR claim form, ABWOR 3 (see p54).

Some courts have never heard of Scope Regs regs 7(1)(b) and 8, and so it is advisable to check with the court staff before making an application so that, if necessary, the judge, district judge or magistrates can be provided with copies of the Act and Regulations and guidance in the *Law Society's Gazette*.

Withdrawal of ABWOR

The area office may withdraw ABWOR at any time under Advice and Assistance Regs reg 25 if, 'as a result of information which has come to its knowledge', it decides:

a) in the case of domestic proceedings and Fire Prevention Act 1971 s10A appeals only, that the client no longer has reasonable grounds for taking, defending or being a party to proceedings; or

b) in all cases, that the client requires the proceedings to be conducted unreasonably so as to incur unjustifiable expense; or

c) that it is unreasonable in the particular circumstances of the case that the client should continue to receive ABWOR.

Neither the client nor the solicitor has a right to be heard before a decision to withdraw ABWOR is taken. However, an appeal can be made against the decision to the area committee under Advice and Assistance Regs reg 26.

Where ABWOR is withdrawn, the solicitor must immediately inform the client, and in domestic proceedings the court and any other party.[24]

Costs

At the end of the case the solicitor claims payment on a report on case form, ABWOR 3 which sets out details of the time spent and the work done. The costs claim includes those costs which were incurred on the green form prior to approval, and therefore such costs are not claimed on the original green form (as described in chapter 2). The original green form should, however, be sent with Form ABWOR 3 and any other necessary supporting documents to the area office.

The rates of payment are normally varied annually. MHRT ABWOR is paid at a considerably higher rate. The rates (from 1 April 1992 and not uprated in 1993) are:

All ABWOR except MHRT   *£ per hour*
Preparation	£43.25 (£45.75)
Advocacy	£54.50
Attendance at court when counsel assigned	£29.50
Travelling and waiting	£24.25
Routine letters and telephone calls £3.35 (£3.50) per item	

ABWOR in MHRTs
Preparation	£52.00 (£55.50)
Advocacy	£63.00
Attendance when counsel assigned	£29.50
Travelling and waiting	£24.25
Routine letters and telephone calls £3.70 per item	

The figures in brackets apply where the fee-earner has an office in the Greater London legal aid area (Area 1).

The structure of ABWOR fees is similar to criminal legal aid fees, and practitioners should refer to the comments on p244 in chapter 15 about maximising fees. It is especially important to turn travelling and waiting time into preparation or advocacy time whenever possible.

The Legal Aid Board pays the amount of the 'assessed deficiency' in the same way as in a normal green form case. Counsel is paid direct.[25] Where counsel has been instructed without being authorised in advance and the

---

24   Advice and Assistance Regs reg 25(2).
25   Advice and Assistance Regs reg 29(5).

area committee does not think that the proper conduct of the proceedings required that counsel should be instructed, the area office will assess the fees due on the basis of a solicitor alone having done all the work. It will then assess in each case how much counsel should be paid. Payment is made to counsel direct and the solicitor is paid the balance.[26] Where counsel's fees are assessed at more than what a solicitor would be paid, the solicitor is responsible for paying the balance, but may recover this from the client's contribution or under the statutory charge. Solicitors and counsel have 21 days within which to appeal by written representations to the Legal Aid Board, which will then review the decision of the area committee.[27]

Provision is made in Advice and Assistance Regs reg 31 that in summary matrimonial cases where another party has been ordered to pay costs, payment to the solicitor is not delayed while they are collected. These costs, of course, form part of the solicitor's statutory charge, and therefore, in a green form case, would normally be deducted by the Legal Aid Board before the assessed deficiency is paid. However, solicitors who want to be paid immediately on the conclusion of a case may assign the charge over the costs due from the other side to the Legal Aid Board, and in those circumstances the Board may make full payment to the solicitor, without waiting for the *inter partes* costs to be collected.[28] It should be noted that this does not apply to the statutory charge on property recovered or preserved under s11(2)(b) (see above p39) – the solicitor must still take the charge into account when submitting the claim for payment.

If a person who has received ABWOR is unsuccessful in the proceedings, no order for costs may be made against him or her until the court has determined what it is reasonable for him or her to pay, having regard to all the circumstances, including the means of all the parties and their conduct in connection with the dispute.[29] This is similar to the protection for legally-aided parties. An unassisted party who is successful in proceedings where the other party has ABWOR may obtain an order for costs against the Legal Aid Fund under LAA s13. On both these points, see further chapter 9.

Payments on account of disbursements

Since 1 April 1992, it has been possible to claim payments on account of

---

26   Advice and Assistance Regs reg 29(6).
27   Advice and Assistance Regs reg 29(7).
28   Advice and Assistance Regs reg 32(3).
29   LAA s12(1); Advice and Assistance Regs reg 34 and Sch 5.

disbursements where the Legal Aid Board has granted ABWOR.[30]
Payments on account of solicitors' and barristers' fees are not available.
Applications must be for more than £30. A form – ABWOR 5 – was being
devised but had not been issued as this book went to print, and the Legal
Aid Board suggested that practitioners use a standard form letter.

Even where there is no assessed deficiency, solicitors must submit a
statement of costs, the amount of any contribution payable and the value
of any statutory charge. This can be done by letter if no claim for payment
is being made. If the solicitor has been paid more on account than the
amount assessed to be payable from the Legal Aid Fund, the balance will
be recouped.

30   Legal Advice and Assistance (Amendment) Regulations 1992 reg 30A.

Part II

Civil legal aid

CHAPTER 4

Applying for a civil legal aid certificate

Introduction

Legal aid is available for virtually all types of civil proceedings, whether in progress or contemplated. About 50 per cent of the population is financially eligible with or without having to pay a contribution out of income or capital. In the vast majority of cases it is in the client's interest to apply for legal aid if s/he is financially eligible. A solicitor is under a professional duty to advise a client about the availability and advantages of legal aid (see chapter 1). Failure to do so, even if the solicitor does not him or herself undertake legal aid work, may amount to professional negligence, may result in the solicitor being unable to demand that the work be paid for privately and may, if repeated, amount to professional misconduct. It is a duty which continues throughout the professional relationship.[1]

A legal aid certificate does not cover work done before its date of issue and it may not be backdated. However, once a certificate has been issued to take proceedings it covers work done before those proceedings are instigated even if the matter is settled without proceedings ever being issued. Therefore, in order to avoid delay and to avoid a client having to pay privately for work which should have been covered by legal aid, it is important to make an application as soon as it is appropriate.

The questions to be decided before an application is made are:

- is legal aid available for this type of proceeding?
- is the client eligible?
- is it in the interests of the client to apply for legal aid?

Each question is considered in detail in this chapter, but it should be stressed that in the majority of cases the answers will be immediately apparent.

The main provisions regulating civil legal aid are Pt IV (ss14–18) of

---

1 Professional Standard 1.1, *Guide to the Professional Conduct of Solicitors*, Law Society, 1990, para 10.02; 1992 *Handbook*, p446.

and Sch 2 to the Legal Aid Act 1988 (LAA) and the Civil Legal Aid (General) Regulations 1989 SI No 339 (hereafter referred to as the General Regs). The detailed provisions for calculation of eligibility and contributions are contained in the Civil Legal Aid (Assessment of Resources) Regulations 1989 SI No 338 (hereafter referred to as the Resources Regs). In addition, Notes for Guidance 4 to 14 are concerned with civil legal aid.

There are special rules about legal aid for family proceedings and proceedings under the Children Act 1989. They are considered in chapters 6 and 7.

Throughout this chapter, and the rest of the book, reference is made to the Legal Aid Board, its area directors and area committees, as the administrators of the legal aid scheme (see chapter 1 for an explanation of the administrative structure). References will be made to the various sections of the LAA and the different regulations but it is important to remember that individual officers are given a wide discretion and that, accordingly, detailed practice may vary. Area directors can take the final decisions on the granting and refusal of certificates and exercise all the functions of an area committee except the determination of appeals.[2] Area directors can also authorise others, normally their staff, to act on their behalf.[3] In the interests of their clients, solicitors should therefore try to establish a friendly and smooth-running relationship with the staff in their area office.

Scope

The availability of civil legal aid depends on two factors: first whether it is available for the court or tribunal in which the proceedings are or will be taken; and, secondly, whether or not the proceedings are excepted – that is proceedings for which legal aid is specifically excluded. The proceedings covered by civil legal aid are set out in Sch 2 Pt I to the LAA, as follows:

a) proceedings in the House of Lords, Court of Appeal, the High Court (including the Divisional Court) and the county court;
b) proceedings before a person to whom any of the above have referred a case;
c) domestic proceedings in the magistrates' (family proceedings) court and proceedings in which a parent or guardian opposes the making of an adoption order where the court is asked to dispense with

consent (although in non-Children Act cases legal aid is usually replaced by ABWOR, see chapter 3);

d) proceedings under the Children Act 1989;

e) proceedings before the Lands Tribunal, the Employment Appeal Tribunal, the Commons Commissioners and the defence of proceedings brought under the Fair Trading Act 1973 Pt III in the Restrictive Practices Court.

In general, legal aid is not available for proceedings outside England and Wales, with one exception – the Court of Justice of the EEC on a reference made by a court in this country for a preliminary ruling under Article 177 of the Treaty of Rome, provided that the reference is made in respect of proceedings for which civil legal aid is available.[4]

The 'excepted proceedings' for which legal aid is not available are set out in LAA Sch 2 Pt II. The most important single category of excepted proceedings are undefended divorce proceedings (for which help is available under the green form scheme, see chapter 6 below). Other proceedings for which legal aid is not available are:

a) defamation (but see below);

b) relator actions;

c) election petitions;

d) judgment summonses.

Three points arise in relation to defamation proceedings. First, legal aid is not available where the proceedings are 'wholly or partly' in respect of defamation, so that even where it is only one of several causes of action in the same proceedings legal aid will not be granted. Secondly, legal aid *is* available to defend against a counter-claim for defamation and, thirdly, legal aid *is* available to bring or defend the similar action of injurious or malicious falsehood.[4A]

Legal aid for appeals

Legal aid is available for interlocutory appeals and for appeals to the Court of Appeal and to the House of Lords.

When the prospective appellant or respondent does not already have legal aid, an application should be made in the usual way on Form CLA 1 (see Part V). Where appropriate it should be accompanied by an emergency application Form CLA3 (see Part V) but the area director is unlikely

---

4   *R v Marlborough Street Stipendiary Magistrate ex parte Bouchereau* [1977] 1 All ER 365, a decision on criminal legal aid which is equally applicable to civil legal aid.

4A Now confirmed by the Court of Appeal in *Joyce v Sengupta* [1993] 1 All ER 897.

to consider compliance with the time limits to be, in itself, a sufficient justification for an emergency certificate (see further below).

If the applicant already has legal aid for the proceedings, a new application for a fresh legal aid certificate *may* be necessary. Alternatively, it may be that an application should be made to amend the existing certificate. Which course should be taken depends on the nature of the appeal.

The following rules apply:

a) if the appeal is *to* the House of Lords or *from* a magistrates' court a fresh application for a new certificate is required;[5]

b) in all other circumstances, except (c) below, the existing certificate should be amended to bring or defend an appeal or bring an interlocutory appeal;[6]

c) the *defence* of an interlocutory appeal is within the scope of the original certificate and no application to the Legal Aid Board is necessary.

For a discussion of the distinction between final and interlocutory appeals see Notes 25 to 27 to RSC Ord 59 r1 in the Supreme Court Practice (the *White Book*).

Applications for legal aid to appeal should be made as soon as possible. The solicitor should tell the shorthand writer that a transcript is likely to be needed and warn the opposing side that an appeal is probable and that an application for legal aid or an amendment to the certificate is being made. The opposing party should also be asked to consent to an extension of the normal four-week time limit for giving notice of appeal. If the opposing party does not agree, emergency legal aid should be applied for, limited to applying for an extension of time. The Court of Appeal will take the delays caused by legal aid into account on such an application even though they might cause injustice to an unassisted party. The reason is that the injustice would be even greater if an appeal was dismissed just because legal aid could not be obtained in time.[7] If the opposing party has unreasonably refused to agree to an extension of time and made application to the court necessary, an application should be made for costs.

Where the applicant had ABWOR in the magistrates' court, that covers preparing and serving a notice of appeal and applying for a case to be stated.[8]

5   General Regs reg 46(2).
6   General Regs reg 46(1).
7   *Norwich and Peterborough Building Society v Steed* [1991] 135 SJ 414.
8   Scope Regs 1989 Schedule para 1 and *Mawdsley v Mawdsley* (1983) *Times* 10 January.

Although legal aid is available for appeals to the High Court from the Pensions Appeal Tribunal it is not worth applying. This is because the Pensions Appeal Tribunal (England and Wales) Rules 1980 provide that the Tribunal must meet the costs properly incurred by the applicant in bringing an appeal. At best, therefore, legal aid will not be of any benefit, and if the applicant has to pay a contribution s/he will be worse off.

The time limit for appealing to the Employment Appeal Tribunal is 42 days from the date the industrial tribunal decision is sent to the appellant. If the notice of appeal is not delivered within the required time, it must be accompanied by an application for an extension of time setting out the reasons for the delay. The need to apply for legal aid is not necessarily a good reason for delay. The appellant should therefore inform the registrar and the other party of the intention to appeal and ask the latter for an extension of time.

General eligibility

Legal aid is available to anyone who falls within the means limits, irrespective of nationality, domicile, or country of residence. Thus foreign nationals involved in litigation in England or Wales may apply for legal aid (although there are special provisions regarding assessment of means for foreign residents, see p82). The only 'persons' to whom legal aid is not available are 'bodies corporate or unincorporate' unless they are acting in a representative, fiduciary or official capacity.[9] Thus limited companies, industrial and provident societies, partnerships and trade unions will not be eligible. The courts will not allow an assignment of a cause of action from a corporate body to an individual if it is a sham to enable legal aid to be obtained to pursue the action (*Advanced Technology Structures Ltd v Cray Valley Products and another* (1992) *Times* 29 December). The trustees of an unincorporated club, or the partner in a firm or shareholder in a company may apply for legal aid in an individual capacity, subject to the provisions on taking other resources or facilities into account in General Regs regs 30, 32 and 33.

If a bankrupt is a party to proceedings in a personal capacity, as opposed to those in which the trustee in bankruptcy is concerned, the bankrupt may apply for legal aid. However, the application will not be granted if a successful outcome would only be of benefit to the creditors. If a receiving order is made while a person is legally aided, this should be reported to the Legal Aid Board, since it is a ground for the discharge of the certificate.[10]

Children and mental patients are entitled to legal aid as much as anyone else, although applicants for legal aid must normally be of full mental capacity and full age, that is 18 years old (in contrast to the green form scheme which is available to anyone of full mental capacity over the compulsory school leaving age of 16). This means that applications must normally be made on behalf of children or mental patients by someone of full age and capacity.[11] Until 1 April 1992, those making the application were required to sign an undertaking but that is no longer the case.

Finally it should be noted that in some circumstances children involved in proceedings under the Children Act 1989 or the inherent jurisdiction may apply for legal aid on their own behalf (see chapter 7).

Financial eligibility

It is important that a solicitor assesses the financial eligibility of a person wishing to apply for legal aid before the application is made, because:

a) if the client is clearly ineligible the application will be a waste of both the client's and the solicitor's time and may result in an unnecessary delay; and

b) the amount of any contribution may be a decisive factor in determining whether or not it is in the client's interest to apply for legal aid.

The rules for assessing financial eligibility for civil legal aid are set out in the Resources Regs. Eligibility and contributions both depend on calculations of disposable income and capital. For those purposes the resources of spouses are aggregated unless they have opposing interests. 'Spouse' is defined as someone of the opposite sex with whom the applicant is living in the same household as husband or wife.[12] When children apply for legal aid only their own resources and not those of their parents are taken into account.[13]

Any transactions made by the applicant deliberately to deprive him or herself of financial resources may be disregarded by the assessment officer.[14] This applies mainly to capital items and is intended to catch those who incur unreasonable or unnatural expenditure to reduce their

10 General Regs reg 80.
11 General Regs reg 16.
12 Resources Regs para 7.
13 Civil Legal Aid (Assessment of Resources) (Amendment) Regulations 1990.
14 Resources Regs para 9.

assets. It can be particularly important in practice when an applicant for legal aid who would otherwise qualify financially has received a lump sum of money such as a redundancy payment. In such circumstances it would be in order for the applicant to use the money to pay off consumer debts, including hire purchase debts, to buy needed household items, or to take a holiday. In some circumstances, it would even be allowable to make payments to children or relatives, for instance to buy a car for a child in full-time education. However, payments made to reduce debts secured on a person's dwelling-house would not be allowed, and the applicant would be assessed as though he or she still had the cash.

Disposable income

The method for calculating disposable income is set out in Sch 2 to the Resources Regs. It is done by first calculating the income received by the applicant and then deducting from that certain set allowances. The method of calculation is set out on pp86 to 88.

The income which is taken into account is that which it is estimated the applicant may reasonably expect to receive during the period of computation.[15] The period of computation is normally the period of 12 months following the application for legal aid, although the assessment officer may take a more 'appropriate' period.[16] Although disposable income is therefore future income, in the absence of other means of calculating it, the assessment officer will carry out the calculation on the basis of the preceding year's income.[17] It is sometimes important, however, to remember that taking the past year's income as the basis for the calculation is a matter of convenience, and in any instances where that would not be appropriate, perhaps when making an application for someone who is self-employed, the circumstances should be made clear on the financial questionnaire form, CLA4A (see below).

An applicant on income support, or with a spouse on income support, qualifies for legal aid and pays no contributions out of either income[18] or capital.[19] However, recipients of family credit and disability working allowance may have to pay a contribution out of either income or capital.

All income, from whatever source, is taken into account unless it is one of the welfare benefits specifically excluded. They are: attendance

15   Resources Regs Sch 2 para 1.
16   Resources Regs reg 3(1).
17   Resources Regs Sch 2 para 1.
18   Resources Regs Sch 2 para 5.
19   Resources Regs Sch 3 para 7.

allowance, constant attendance allowance, disability living allowance and payments from the social fund.[20]

Deductions are made in respect of:

- housing expenses, including, for example, not only rent and mortgage payments but also repairs and insurance;
- necessary cost of employment, or business, including child minders, fares and union subscriptions;
- payments to an occupational or a personal pension scheme, income tax, national insurance, council tax;
- maintenance or periodical payments made to a spouse, former spouse, child or relative not living with the applicant.

Allowances are made in respect of dependants living with the applicant. In respect of children and other dependent relatives they are the same as income support allowances for persons of the appropriate age (Resources Regs Sch 2 para 11(b)(ii) as amended by the Civil Legal Aid (Assessment of Resources) (Amendment) Regulations 1993 reg 13(b)). Spouses are given an allowance equal to the difference between the income support allowance for a couple and that for a single person (Resources Regs Sch 2 para 11(b)(i) as amended by the Civil Legal Aid (Assessment of Resources) (Amendment) Regulations 1993 reg 13(a)). The legal aid allowances are therefore uprated automatically at the same time as the income support allowances. From 12 April 1993 they are:

	£ pa
Spouse	£1304.00
under 11 years	£785.00
11-15 years	£1155.00
16-17 years	£1379.00
18 and over	£1815.00

Disposable capital

The rules for calculating disposable capital are set out in Resources Regs Sch 3. All resources of a capital nature, except those which are specifically excepted, are taken into account. That means that jewellery and life insurance policies, for example, must be taken into account. Where the capital does not consist of money a valuation will be carried out. That will normally be done on the basis of an open market value unless there is only a restricted market for the capital resource in question, in which case

20   Resources Regs Sch 2 para 6.

the restricted market value will be taken into account.[21] It may be important to point out on the application form if only a restricted market is available.

Life insurance or endowment policies are valued at the amount which the applicant can readily borrow on them.[22]

Where applications are made by company directors, business people or the self-employed owners of businesses, it will be necessary to assess the value of the applicant's business assets.[23] This may be done on the basis of the liquidation value.[24] To assess this the value of the business will be reduced by percentages. The fixed assets are brought in at their full value but stock is reduced by 50 per cent and debts and prepayments are reduced by 20 per cent. The liabilities of the business are deducted and the remaining value further reduced by 33 per cent to arrive at an assessment value.[25]

Certain items of capital are disregarded:
- the subject matter of the dispute for which legal aid is being sought;
- the applicant's only or main dwelling-house;
- household furniture and effects;
- articles of personal clothing;
- tools and equipment of trade, unless the applicant is an owner of a business (in which case the rules described in the previous paragraph apply).

In addition, any capital payment which the applicant has received, from whatever source, in relation to the incident which has given rise to the dispute is disregarded.[26] In *R v Legal Aid Board ex parte Clark* (The Times 14 October 1992 CO/958/92), the assisted person had received legal aid to pursue an action for medical negligence. As a result of the injury she had received due to the alleged negligence she had retired early and received a lump sum payment from her employers paid specifically in respect of her early retirement due to injury. The Legal Aid Board wanted to take this sum into account on a reassessment of means on the basis that it was one step removed from the incident and therefore should not be disregarded. The Divisional Court, however, held that the expression 'in relation to' should normally be given a wide meaning and that the payment to the assisted person fell within the regulation and should be disregarded.

This disregard, therefore, could cover, for instance, a payment under

21   Resources Regs Sch 3 para 2.
22   Resources Regs Sch 3 para 12.
23   Resources Regs Sch 3 para 5.
24   Ibid para 5(b).
25   1987 84/43 LS Gaz 3391.
26   Resources Regs Sch 3 para 14B.

an insurance policy to someone who has been disabled in an accident and who is applying for legal aid to take proceedings over the accident. It would also cover a payment in lieu of notice to an employee who is applying for legal aid to take proceedings for wrongful dismissal.

Applicants of pensionable age are given a special capital allowance if their annual disposable income, net of any income derived from capital, is less than the lower income limit. The amount of the allowance depends on the amount of their disposable income, excluding income derived from capital.[27] The allowances as at 12 April 1993 are:

Annual disposable income £	amount of capital disregarded £
up to 370	£35,000
371–670	£30,000
671–970	£25,000
971–1270	£20,000
1271–1570	£15,000
1571–1870	£10,000
1871–2294	£5,000

'Pensionable age' is defined as 65 for men and 60 for women.[28] The applicant will be given the benefit of the allowance if his or her spouse, whose means are aggregated, is of pensionable age.

There are no dependants' allowances against capital as there are for income (and under the green form scheme).

Discretionary disregards

Finally, it should be noted that the assessment officer has a general discretion in respect of both income and capital to disregard any amounts 'having regard to the circumstances of the case'.[29] This is frequently used to make deductions in respect of expenditure which is not provided for under the Resources Regs, such as hire purchase debts or school fees, or debts due for payment within 12 months.[30] Practitioners could also argue that it should be used in respect of capital generating income on which, for instance, a disabled non-pensioner is dependent.

Limits and calculation of contributions

In order to qualify for free legal aid, an applicant's disposable income and

---

27   Resources Regs Sch 3 para 14A(1) as amended by Civil Legal Aid (Assessment of Resources) (Amendment) Regulations 1993 reg 14.
28   Resources Regs Sch 3 para 14A(2).
29   Resources Regs Sch 2 para 14 and Sch 3 para 15.
30   Resources Regs Sch 3 para 14.

capital must be below the 'lower' capital and income limits which are changed from time to time. The limits (as at 12 April 1993) are:

Income £2,294 per year;

Capital £3,000.

There are also 'upper' limits beyond which an applicant is disqualified from obtaining legal aid. In order to qualify an applicant must have disposable income and capital which is no more than:

Income £6,800 (£7,500 in personal injury cases);

Capital £6,750 (£8,560 in personal injury cases and see below).

The limits are usually changed annually in April and announcements appear in *Legal Aid Focus*, *Legal Action* and the *Law Society's Gazette*.

Applicants whose disposable income and/or capital falls between the lower and upper limits will have to pay a contribution, possibly out of both income and capital. In respect of applications for legal aid received by the Legal Aid Board on or after 12 April 1993, contributions out of income are paid monthly for the life of the certificate at the rate of 1/36th of the sum by which the applcant's disposable income exceeds the lower income limit. In respect of applications made before 12 April 1993 the contribution out of income remains one quarter of the amount by which applicant's disposable income exceeds the lower income limit, and it is paid in twelve equal instalments over the first year of the certificate.

The capital contribution is the whole amount by which the applicant's disposable capital exceeds the lower capital limit, irrespective of when the application was made.

The upper income limit is absolute – legal aid is simply not available to someone with a higher disposable income. Where an applicant exceeds the upper capital limit, however, refusal is not automatic. Resources Regs reg 4 provides that an applicant whose disposable capital is above the upper limit may only be refused legal aid where it appears, in addition, that he or she could afford to proceed without legal aid. In practice that means that legal aid will be refused unless it seems as though the likely costs of the action will exceed the applicant's contribution (see also Guidance Regs reg 27). If an applicant is seeking legal aid on that basis, that should be made clear when the application is submitted.

The Board's discretion under Resources Regs reg 4 with regard to the upper capital limit is quite separate and different from the assessment officer's discretion under Resources Regs Sch 2 para 14 and Sch 3 para 15. First, if capital (or income) is disregarded by the assessment officer it is left out of account not only for qualification purposes but also in the calculation of the contribution. An applicant who is given legal aid by the Board under Resources Regs reg 4 despite having capital over the upper limit will have to pay the whole of his or her capital over the lower limit by way of contribution in the normal way. Secondly, the assessment officer's discretion extends to income whereas the Board's does not. Thirdly, the Board's decision can be challenged by appeal whereas the assessment officer's cannot (see below).

How the assessment of means is carried out

The assessment of the applicant's means is carried out by the Benefits Agency of the DSS. The applicant completes the means questionnaire (see p82), which the solicitor submits with Form L17 from an employer (if applicable) and the main legal aid application form. Although the applicant does not have to provide documentary evidence of capital with the forms, the DSS may ask for evidence of resources or expenses, such as payslips, bank books, receipts for child minding, rent books or mortgage statements. If the DSS requires further information, it will send Form L22 to an applicant who is not married and Form L23 to a married applicant.

In some cases of particular difficulty, usually where the applicant is self-employed, the DSS may ask for an interview. Obviously there may be problems if the DSS asks for an interview at an office which it is difficult to reach, or if the applicant is disabled. The L Code is regularly reviewed (see p6) but in 1984 it provided in para 836 that:

> a legal aid applicant can usually be expected to attend for interview in normal working hours, but officers should be prepared to arrange time and place to suit an applicant's convenience as far as is reasonable, eg an applicant may wish to attend an A[ssessment] O[ffice] near his place of work during his lunchtime. A home visit should be arranged when it is known that an applicant has difficulty in moving around because of age or incapacity, and special arrangements, including a domiciliary visit, may be necessary for the lone woman with children.

There is no right of appeal against a financial determination by the DSS. The L Code para 842 provides:

> as there is no right of appeal against the [DSS's] decision, it is of special importance that the calculation of disposable income and disposable capital should be based on complete and accurate facts. It is the responsibility of the interviewing officer to see that all the requisite information is included in the applicant's statement. . . .

However, the DSS will supply a copy of its calculations to an applicant or his or her adviser who is dissatisfied with the assessment, and the calculations will be reviewed by a more senior officer on request.

Payment of the contribution

If a contribution is payable, the applicant will be informed in the offer of legal aid. Contributions payable out of capital are usually payable in a single lump sum before the certificate is issued. However, if the capital assessed includes items which will take time to realise, the Legal Aid Board should be asked to issue the certificate and wait for payment for a reasonable period.

Contributions out of income are usually payable in monthly instalments. If the application for the certificate was made before 12 April 1993, contributions out of income will only be payable for 12 months after the date of issue of the certificate. However, where the application was made on or after 12 April 1993, contributions out of income continue to be payable during the lifetime of the certificate.

If the Legal Aid Board decides at any time that the contributions paid by an assisted person are sufficient to meet the likely costs of the case, it has power to waive further payment – and should the position change, to revive the obligation to pay. In each case the certificate will be amended.[31]

If an assisted person falls into arrears, he or she will be reminded to pay the contribution by a letter from the Legal Aid Board, and the solicitor will be notified at the same time and told to do no further work under the certificate. If the contribution is left unpaid the certificate will be discharged after 31 days unless the assisted person asks for a reassessment. Therefore, solicitors should explain to their clients the importance of telling them if they have difficulty paying the contributions (see further under 'Reassessments' in chapter 8).

A comparison of civil legal aid and green form eligibility and contributions

A client eligible for green form assistance will be eligible also for legal aid, although the reverse is not true. It is not unusual for a person to be financially *ineligible* for help under the green form scheme but to be *eligible* for civil legal aid, sometimes even without a contribution. The reasons are that:

a) anybody with a disposable capital of more than £1,000 cannot receive

---

31   General Regs reg 52(2) and (3) as substituted by Civil Legal Aid (General) (Amendment) Regulations 1993 reg 9.

ordinary green form help, whereas a person with disposable capital up to £3,000 may obtain legal aid without paying a contribution out of capital, and even above the legal aid upper capital limit of £6,750 there is a discretion to grant legal aid if the costs of the action are likely to exceed the person's maximum contribution; and

b) anyone with a disposable weekly income of over £61 is ineligible for green form help but may still qualify for civil legal aid, usually with a contribution (but sometimes even without a contribution, mainly because the green form test makes a fixed allowance for housing expenses whereas the civil legal aid test takes the actual expenditure into account).

Merits test

The aim of the merits test is to ensure that legal aid is given only for cases which warrant the spending of public money. It applies to all applications for civil legal aid, except some under the Children Act 1989 (see chapter 7).

Section 15(2) and (3) set out the criteria which an applicant must fulfil. These are further elaborated in General Regs regs 29, 30, 32, 33, and Note for Guidance 6 which contains, at 6.11 'Standards on Consistency of Decision Making in Connection with Consideration of Civil Legal Aid Applications'. As mentioned in Chapter 1, the Standards are issued to legal aid officials and, as well as setting out the principles according to which they should make their decisions, also seek to direct them to the correct outcome by a series of algorithmic questions. In some respects they add a further gloss to the advice in specific Notes for Guidance and therefore it is necessary at times to refer to them.

Section 15(2) and (3) imposes two general tests. The first is that a person must not be given legal aid for any proceedings 'unless he shows that he has reasonable grounds for taking, defending or being a party thereto'.[32] Matthews and Oulton in their classic text[33] (one author became Chief Taxing Master and the other the permanent head of the Lord Chancellor's Department) stated what is still the position. The applicant must show that 'there is an issue of fact or law which it is reasonable to submit to the court for decision'. The burden is on the applicant.

The second test is under s15(3)(a), which provides that the Legal Aid Board may refuse legal aid, even where the applicant has satisfied the first

32   LAA s15(2).
33   Matthews and Oulton, *Legal Aid and Advice*, Butterworths, 1971, p123.

test, where it appears to the Board that 'in the particular circumstances' of the case it is 'unreasonable' that the applicant should receive legal aid. If legal aid is refused under this head it is for the Board to show that it would have been unreasonable to grant legal aid. This second test is designed, in part, to weed out the case which, although good in law and on the evidence, is not worth bringing because the cost of so doing would be disproportionate to any advantage which might be gained by the applicant. It is sometimes called the 'paying client' test, the question being 'would the cost of the proceedings be considered justified by a person with the means to pay?'. Examples are given in Note for Guidance 6-08 of cases where it is likely that legal aid would be refused under this reasonableness test:

- the claim is small;
- the estimated costs of the proceedings are likely to outweigh the benefit to the client;
- the applicant wants to enter a substantive defence to allegations in a divorce petition and the only issue is whether they are true but it is accepted that the marriage has broken down;
- in a possession action arrears are not in dispute, it is unlikely an immediate order for possession will be made and the only issue is the terms of a suspended order;
- the defendant has no means to satisfy a judgment;
- the applicant would get no personal benefit from the proceedings.

Legal aid is also likely to be refused if the case is one where a solicitor would, in the view of the Legal Aid Board, normally not be involved,[34] for example: arithmetical calculations in variation proceedings, mortgage arrears or applications to suspend a warrant of possession or execution; applications for extra time to meet a High Court judgment; application to register a county court or High Court maintenance order in the magistrates' court. It should be noted, however, that as in all cases where the reasonableness test is involved, this does not mean that legal aid will not be granted in these cases – merely that solicitors must explain why, in the circumstances of a particular case, legal aid should be granted. For instance, legal aid is frequently granted to apply for the suspension of county court warrants of possession.

The Standards in Note for Guidance 6-11 provide more detailed advice. Officers' decisions should meet the Standard that 'Legal aid should only be granted to pursue a case in which costs are likely to exceed the value of any benefit gained thereby where: (a) there is a high prospect of success and the opponent is likely to indemnify the applicant for legal

34 Note for Guidance 6–08(e).

costs; or (b) what is at stake is of such overwhelming importance to the applicant that it overrides the question of costs.'

The algorithmic questions which follow are designed to ensure that legal aid will generally be refused for all claims worth less than £1,000, or if for personal injuries claims, less than £500. Legal aid will also be refused where the claim exceeds the likely costs by less than £1,000 unless there is a high prospect of success and the opponent is likely to pay the costs. Where the benefit to the applicant cannot be quantified in monetary terms, legal aid will be refused unless that benefit can be shown to be of such importance that it would justify the costs of the proceedings.

The Standards do not provide any examples of cases with sufficient benefit to the applicant but Note for Guidance 6-08 specifically points out that cost-effectiveness may be outweighed by other matters and gives three examples. The first is the importance of the case to the applicant, of which more below. The other two examples are, strictly speaking, not exceptions to the cost-effectiveness or paying client test at all. Rather they are instances where the matters at stake are greater than they appear at first sight and where a privately paying client of adequate means would be well advised to take action. Another example is possession actions. The amount of rent arrears and the fact that they are not in dispute may suggest that legal aid would not be cost-effective but if the landlord is claiming possession and there may be grounds on which a court could be persuaded not to make an order then it could be reasonable to grant legal aid. The third example is where allegations in a divorce petition could affect questions of residence or finance if left uncontested, in other words, where it is necessary to contest allegations which may have serious financial or other practical implications. This is further considered in Chapter 6.

Until the Notes for Guidance began to be re-written in 1990, they contained specific examples of cases where the cost-effectiveness or paying client test was outweighed by other factors. Thus, the 1989 *Handbook* (and previous editions) stated in Note for Guidance 9(e):

Proceedings brought under the Race Relations Act 1976 or the Sex Discrimination Act 1975 may carry little potential benefit to the applicant in purely financial terms but considerable benefit from the point of view of the applicant's personal status. The proceedings brought under these Acts are directed towards the elimination of discrimination as well as towards financial compensation, and in the light of the distress caused to the applicant by the discrimination complained of it may be considered that the applicant has shown reasonable grounds for taking proceedings, notwithstanding that the potential financial benefit is insignificant.

The relevant law and regulations have not changed since that Note for Guidance was last published in 1989 and discrimination cases are still one of the possible exceptions to the paying client test, although, of course, they are also cases for which the applicant might receive help from the Commission for Racial Equality or the Equal Opportunities Commission (see below). It should be noted that an error in Note for Guidance 6-08(b)(iii) in the 1991 *Handbook*, which suggested that discrimintation cases should normally be refused legal aid under the paying client test, is corrected in the 1992 edition.

Other cases mentioned before the revision of the *Handbook* in 1990 as exceptions to the paying client include claims for welfare benefits or maintenance from a spouse:

> Nevertheless there are circumstances in which [the 'paying client'] test is not appropriate and would not comply with the statutory criteria. Such cases are those in which the reason for applying for legal aid is the financial plight of the applicant and his [more likely to be 'her'] need to benefit from the provision of the law designed to mitigate that plight, for example, the obtaining of a financial benefit under welfare legislation or of maintenance from a spouse. In such cases it is unrealistic to consider what decision a properly advised client of adequate means would make, and attention has to be directed to the value of the benefit sought for that particular applicant, bearing in mind the chances of success and the cost of achieving it.[35]

To repeat, despite the omissions in subsequent editions of the *Handbook*, and the attitude of some area offices, none of the statutory criteria has changed since that Note for Guidance was last published. Practitioners should refer legal aid officials to the earlier guidance and, where appropriate, challenge refusals of legal aid by appeal and by judicial review.

Legal aid might also be granted according to the 1989 *Handbook* where an applicant's 'status, reputation or dignity' is at stake 'although the financial benefit is small'.[36] However, this would appear to be contradicted, in the spirit if not the letter of the 1992 Note for Guidance 6-08(b)(iii) which gives as an example of non-cost-effective proceedings where 'the only matter at stake is the loss of stature [sic], dignity or reputation.'

The reasonableness test is further designed to justify refusal of legal aid where the applicant has another remedy or service available. Under

35   1989 *Handbook*, Note for Guidance 9(c).
36   1989 *Handbook*, Note for Guidance 9(d).

General Regs reg 30, an application for legal aid may be refused where it appears that the applicant has either:

- other rights or facilities available which make legal aid unnecessary; or
- a reasonable expectation of obtaining financial or other help from a body of which he or she is a member; and
- has failed to take reasonable steps to obtain those rights, facilities or other help.

Note for Guidance 6-08(c) explains that this refers to help which is available from, for instance: legal expenses insurance; the Commission for Racial Equality, the Equal Opportunities Commission, motoring organisations, trade unions, an estate in a probate action (see further General Regs reg 33 below), a firm where the applicant is a member of a firm. What it means is that an applicant who has other services available must explain why he or she does not want to use them. It does not mean that legal aid will be refused whenever there is another service available. For many years legal aid was refused to members of trade unions which provided legal services. The Legal Aid Board now accepts that, if a trade union member does not want to be represented by the union solicitor, despite the availability of this service, legal aid should not be refused on that ground alone. In each case the terms and conditions and the effectiveness of the other representation on offer could be a crucial factor. The Standards provide that legal aid should be granted if the other facilities available to the applicant are less advantageous than legal aid.

Note for Guidance 6-08(j) purports to explain why legal aid is rarely granted for bail applications to a High Court judge in chambers. The stated reason is that 'it would seem to be more appropriate to rely on the Official Solicitor procedure under RSC Ord 70.' This could be confusing because the Official Solicitor procedure was replaced by appeals to the crown court under the Criminal Justice Act 1982 s60. RSC Ord 70 now deals with matters entirely unrelated to bail applications.

Civil legal aid is available to make bail applications to a High Court judge in chambers. However, applicants will need to show special reasons why such an application should be made, in view of the cheaper crown court procedure which is available and covered by magistrates' court criminal legal aid orders (see p247). Note for Guidance 6-08(j) sets out the information which should be included with any application for civil legal aid to apply to a High Court judge in chambers. Most of it is obvious – such as the history of previous applications and the length of time the applicant would otherwise have to spend in custody pending trial. The most important points to explain are why bail was refused, why the refusal was unreasonable or how the grounds have altered, and any special social or other reasons why bail should be granted.

In a probate action or other action where the applicant is acting in a fiduciary or representative capacity, the Legal Aid Board is entitled to take into account the value of any fund out of which the applicant may be indemnified.[37] The application may be granted on the basis that payment is made from such a fund, or refused unless that would cause hardship.

Where the applicant is one of a number of people with the 'same' interest, all of whom may benefit from the successful outcome of proceedings, special provision is made in reg 32 of the General Regs. The first point to note is that this provision only comes into play when there are other persons than the applicant with the same interest who are not parties to the action. If they are parties at the time that the application for legal aid is submitted, the Legal Aid Board will rely on the normal rules of taxation to apportion costs between legally-aided and non-legally aided parties. Secondly, 'same' interest in this context means seeking an identical outcome to the proceedings, such as an order, injunction or declaration which would benefit them all equally without the issuing of separate proceedings.[38] Different persons with individual claims for damages arising out of the same event do not come within this provision, because separate claims for damages will always need separate actions (see also chapter 1 regarding group actions). This, of course also means that there will be cases where applicants have both 'same' and different interests as other parties – for instance, a tenant in a block of flats claiming both an injunction for a leaking roof to be repaired ('same' interest as other tenants affected by the leak) and damages for water penetration (different interest). Whether or not Regulation 32 would be applied would then depend on which was the main purpose of the proceedings.

Where reg 32 applies the Legal Aid Board must consider whether the applicant would 'be substantially prejudiced' by a refusal of legal aid. This means that legal aid will be granted if the applicant would be substantially prejudiced by not being able to take proceedings but will be refused if other persons would take proceedings without the applicant and, as a result of those proceedings, the applicant would get what he or she wanted.[39]

If legal aid is granted, the Board will ask the the other interested parties to make a contribution bearing in mind their respective interests. Those contributions may be added to the applicant's contribution (although

37 General Regs reg 33.
38 Note for Guidance 6-10.
39 Note for Guidance 6-10.

payment of this additional amount may be waived if the Board is subsequently satisfied that the applicant has unsuccessfully taken all reasonable steps to obtain payment from the others).

Lastly, s15(3)(b) provides an additional specific ground for refusal where it appears 'more appropriate that [the applicant] should be given assistance by way of representation'. It is only in summary matrimonial cases that civil legal aid and ABWOR overlap. This aspect of s15(3) is dealt with in chapter 6.

Advantages and disadvantages

In the vast majority of cases a client will benefit from legal aid, but there are exceptions and an application should not be made automatically whenever a client is eligible.

In all cases solicitors should advise the legal aid applicant to consider carefully the implications of litigation – is it worth the money to be paid by the client and/or put at risk through an order for costs. This means calculating the contribution, considering the possible effects of the statutory charge and the terms of any costs orders, and weighing those financial considerations against the value of the subject matter to the client and the likelihood of success. (Advice to the client is further considered in the next section; costs orders and the statutory charge are considered in chapters 9 and 10.)

In relatively small claims it may not be worth the client's while to be represented by a solicitor in private practice, because even if legal aid is granted the client may have to pay most or all of the costs. It might be more advantageous for the client to bring proceedings in person, perhaps with help from the solicitor on a green form, or from an advice centre or citizens advice bureau. The client may live or work within the catchment area of a law centre which can help. In cases of race or sex discrimination the Commission for Racial Equality or the Equal Opportunities Commission may be asked for financial assistance (see further chapter 1).

In general, however, the consequences of having legal aid are overwhelmingly beneficial. Assisted persons have state finance to litigate, even though they may have to pay a contribution or, eventually, the whole cost under the statutory charge. They also have a guarantee that, subject to reassessment and the statutory charge, whether they win or lose, they will not have to pay more than a fixed monthly amount at any time. Further, if unsuccessful, assisted persons have to pay only so much of the successful party's costs as is reasonable after a further assessment of means under s17(1) (see p154 below).

These advantages in many cases create a third, tactical advantage over non-legally-aided opponents. It is not unusual, for instance, for insurance companies to maintain a firm and hostile front to a claim until they receive notice of issue of a legal aid certificate. Lord Denning MR recognised this advantage in *Manley v The Law Society* [1981] 1 All ER 401, CA, where he observed that legal advisers:

> must remember that they are funded at the expense of the State and that they are putting the defendant (who is not legally-aided) to a great deal of worry and expense in contesting the case – defendants who would not recover any of their costs even if they win. This puts the legal advisers for the plaintiff in an extremely strong bargaining position. There is inequality of bargaining power. They should *not* abuse it at the expense of the defendant.

Another advantage to the legally-aided client is that the amount of the lawyer's fees, because of the basis upon which they are calculated, is likely to be less than if the client were paying privately.

However, there may be disadvantages in applying for legal aid. First, there is the time and trouble involved in making an application. It takes about four weeks to process a legal aid application where no contribution is payable and longer where a contribution is required, although in an emergency legal aid can be obtained in a matter of minutes (see chapter 5). In complicated cases, the assessment of means by the DSS may involve attending an interview, often in a place many miles away from where the client is living. The provision of detailed financial information may require a statement signed by the applicant's employer.

The delay may not necessarily be confined to the initial stages. The solicitor's duty to report to the Legal Aid Board (see chapter 8), the necessity sometimes to ask for authority, and the complexity and formality which often accompanies the payment of the lawyer's fees and accounting to the client at the end of the case (see chapters 9 and 10), may result in the case proceeding at a slower pace than if it were not legally-aided.

Then there are the contributions. As a result of the calculations outlined here, the solicitor should be able to advise the client more or less how much the contribution will be. In some cases, the contribution may be as much as, if not more than, the eventual costs of the case. In personal injuries cases it is possible for contributions out of income and capital to reach £7,295, and in other cases £5,252, in the first year alone. If the client is successful, all or most of the contribution may be returned, but the Legal Aid Fund does not pay interest on the money it holds and it is not unusual for a High Court action to last three or more years, by which time the value of the money may have declined considerably.

Finally, if the client is successful in defending an action against a party who is legally-aided and unable to pay the full amount of any standard basis costs after assessment under s17(1), the client may be out of pocket: only a successful unassisted defendant may apply for costs against the Legal Aid Fund under s18.[40]

In summary, all these issues must be considered before applying for legal aid or before accepting an offer of legal aid – although it must be stressed again that in the vast majority of cases, if it is in the client's interest to become involved in proceedings, it will be clear that an application for legal aid will be to the benefit of the client and should be made. Indications that the decision to apply requires careful thought are: a high contribution; that the other party is legally-aided; or that there is a relatively small amount at stake.

Timing the application

An application for legal aid should be made promptly (though not prematurely, see below). If an application is put off until litigation is inevitable, after perhaps months of negotiation on the green form, several months' further delay will be caused for the client. An application must be made as soon as litigation seems likely. In most personal injuries cases, for example, it is sensible to send off the signed and completed legal aid form at the same time as the letter before action to the prospective defendants – in such cases it is usually necessary for the client to receive legal aid, and/ or to issue proceedings before the defendants make an adequate offer. Similarly, in many types of matrimonial case it is clear from the outset that a court order will eventually be required to compel a husband to disclose his means, and in such cases a legal aid application should be made as early as possible (see also p104). It is also in the solicitor's interest to get legal aid as soon as possible. Some work, such as preparation and investigation of a claim, can be done either under a legal aid certificate or a green form, but work done under a certificate is usually paid at a higher rate – although it also takes longer to get the money.

Nonetheless, the solicitor should ensure that all readily available alternatives to proceedings have been exhausted before an application is made, for example that a letter before action has been sent, and also that any evidence showing a *prima facie* case which can be obtained fairly

40   See, for example, *Almond v Miles* (1992) *Times* 4 February and *Awad v Pillai and Nathanielse* [1982] RTR 266, CA, p150.

easily, such as a relevant police report, is submitted with the application. (Where such evidence is not available, for instance, in the case of the police report, because a prosecution is pending, that should be made clear in the application.) An application to defend proceedings will be refused if the proceedings have not actually been issued, even though it is virtually certain that they will be.

Obviously there is no point in making an application which will be refused. Before submitting the application, solicitors should consider whether they need further evidence in order to advise whether proceedings should be taken or defended. If this is not done and the application is made prematurely, it may be refused, or the applicant may find that, rather than a full legal aid certificate to take proceedings, the Legal Aid Board issues a certificate subject to a limitation, such as obtaining counsel's opinion or a police report. Apart from causing unnecessary delay, submitting an application prematurely in this way may increase the cost to the client. For example, it may be necessary to obtain counsel's opinion or to make further investigations solely to satisfy the Legal Aid Board. If such steps were not necessary to prosecute the action, their cost may possibly not be recovered if the applicant should win the case: their cost will then be recouped from the client's contribution and/or whatever has been recovered or preserved on behalf of the client in the litigation. Therefore, an application must be as full as possible.

If more work is required in order to show that the applicant has a case, this may be done under the green form. If necessary, the Legal Aid Board may grant an extension.

In some circumstances, of course, it is not possible to submit an application which would justify full legal aid being given – and the application form may even specify that only limited legal aid is required. For example, an area office may suggest that an application for legal aid should be made where a green form extension to obtain counsel's opinion has been refused (practice varies in different legal aid areas).

Making the application

Applications should normally be submitted to the Legal Aid Board office for the area where the solicitor is practising. But there are exceptions. Applications from people resident outside the United Kingdom should be sent to the London (No 1) Area Office. Applications for legal aid submitted throught the Lord Chancellor's Department under the Hague Convention on the Civil Aspects of International Child Abduction or the European Convention on Recognition and Enforcement of Decisions concerning Custody of Children (see p106) should also go to the London Office. Other applications under those conventions may go to any area office. (Legal Aid Board Area Committee Arrangements para 3).

Where a solicitor is party to the proceedings in respect of which legal aid is being sought, the application should be sent to an area other than that in which the solicitor practises. Applications for legal aid to bring judicial review proceedings in respect of an area office's decision should be made to another area office.

In addition, particular offices may be designated to deal with all applications in respect of multi-party actions: for instance Manchester has dealt with all Benzodiazepan claims and Nottingham with all home income plan cases.

Legal aid applications, other than in family cases (see chapters 6 and 7) are made on the orange and white Form CLA1 (see Part V). All applications for legal aid, except for non-means tested Children Act cases, must also be accompanied by an appropriate statement of means questionnaire. The statement of means questionnaires are:

- Form CLA4A to be used in all cases unless another form has been specified;
- Form CLA4B for applicants on income support;
- Form CLA4C for applicants who live abroad;
- Form CLA4F for children.

CLA4C has detailed requirements to which solicitors should draw applicants' attention to avoid delay. 'Abroad' in this context means outside the United Kingdom.[41]

In addition, applicants who are in employment should send a Form L17 signed by their employers to verify their earnings. If it proves impossible, or slow, to obtain this the DSS should accept recent pay slips; as many as possible should be sent. Solicitors should be able to fill in the Form CLA4B if the applicant has brought details of the income support benefit. Otherwise, the most practical course is to give the applicant the form CLA4A or CLA4B and L17, if appropriate, ask the client to complete the form or forms and to return them to the solicitor as soon as possible so that the necessary forms can be sent off together to the area office.

However in most cases Form CLA1 should be completed by the solicitor on behalf of the client. The form can be completed quickly by an experienced person but may be a little daunting to the inexperienced, and some technical knowledge is required in stating the case and deciding what accompanying documents are necessary. In any event, an individual

41   General Regs reg 13.

solicitor, not a firm, must be nominated on the form and must sign it, and the solicitor can be paid under the green form for completing it. The solicitor must first decide whether an application is necessary in the particular circumstances.

If the client already has legal aid, the first question is whether the new legal work may be done under the existing certificate. Even if an authority or an amendment to the certificate would be required, these could be obtained more quickly than a new certificate and no new maximum contribution would arise. Generally, a certificate may not relate to more than 'one action, cause or matter'.[42] The test is whether the proceedings or causes of action may be included in the one action under the same cause number or in the same originating process. If not, then separate legal aid applications must be made for each action or originating process. Where there is doubt, the solicitor should check with the area office. Regulation 46(3) provides some limited instances where a certificate may cover more than one cause or matter:

- family proceedings (although nonetheless it has been the practice to specify narrowly which proceedings are authorised by a particular certificate, see p103 below);
- where a grant of probate or letters of administration is necessary to bring the legally-aided action; and
- proceedings to enforce or give effect to an order or agreement made in the legally-aided proceedings. This includes bankruptcy or winding-up proceedings. (See also the provisions covering legal aid for appeals, p61.)

Another rule, less likely to cause problems, is that one person should have one certificate. Even when acting for co-plaintiffs or co-defendants, wife and husband, parents and children, the solicitor must ensure that each person makes a separate application. If the facts are identical each application need not, of course, contain a full statement but may refer to another. When submitting applications from spouses or co-habitees, the procedure can be further shortened by the use of photocopies but with original signatures.[43]

The following points should be borne in mind when completing the form:

- it should be legible. Legal aid officials maintain that it takes much longer to process a badly written application; and all parts of the form should be completed, including details of any previous applications.

---

42   General Regs reg 46(3).
43   See 'Multiple Applications – Children and Spouses/Cohabitees', 1992 *Handbook*, p443.

- The file of a previous application may be at the area office and may contain information relevant to the granting or refusal of legal aid, saving time in processing;
- properly completed means assessment Form CLA4A, CLA4B, CLA4C or CLA4F and, if appropriate, L17 will save time in processing;
- properly completed declarations on page 8. This permits the immediate issue of the certificate if the assessment, when it is received, shows that no contribution is payable;
- the name of the individual applicant's solicitor, which is always required, as well as the full name and address of the solicitor's firm;
- the nature of the proceedings which it is proposed to take. It is not for the legal aid authorities to advise the applicant or his/her solicitor which proceedings are most appropriate;
- signed confirmation that the solicitor holds a practising certificate and has given the required information to the applicant.

In making an application the solicitor must consider what information may be required by the Legal Aid Board in order for it to decide whether or not the applicant has a *prima facie* case: applications must always contain, or be accompanied by, sufficient information to enable the area director to decide whether or not the applicant should be given legal aid according to the merits criteria.

Explaining the effects of legal aid

The certificate that the solicitor, or the solicitor's representative signs on each legal aid form, and the Law Society's Written Professional Standard entitled 'Client Care – A Guide for Solicitors', together require that:
- the statutory charge is explained to applicants and they are handed a copy of the Legal Aid Board leaflet 'The Legal Aid Statutory Charge – What it means to you';
- applicants are given the leaflet 'What happens next';
- applicants are advised about their obligations including paying contributions, and informing the Legal Aid Board about changes of address and changes of means;
- applicants are advised that if they lose the case they may be ordered to pay a contribution towards their opponents' costs;
- applicants are advised that if they win their opponents may not be ordered to pay the full costs or may not be able to do so.

Those are the official requirements but solicitors should provide some additional information. They must explain that the DSS will investigate the client's means and that the client must co-operate in the investigation.

This may otherwise come as an unpleasant shock. They should also explain how contributions are paid and how long it may take for the application to be processed. They should warn the client that an offer of legal aid (see below) may be made before the certificate is issued and tell the client to consult them about an offer if s/he is in doubt whether to accept. They should stress to clients that re-assessments of means take place not only when their income or capital goes up but also when it goes down and that if their means are reduced they should immediately inform their solicitor and the Legal Aid Board in order to avoid the certificate being discharged for non-payment.

The most difficult part to explain is the statutory charge. The Law Society's Client Care leaflet contains a precedent letter (on p45) explaining the statutory charge and related matters. An alternative version is set out in Part V of this book.

Refusals and appeals

If an application is refused, the area director must notify the applicant, stating in general terms the reason: whether it is on the ground of means or merits. If refusal is on the ground of merits, the decision must state whether it considers that the applicant has no reasonable grounds for being involved in the proceedings or whether the director considers that the grant of legal aid in the particular case is unreasonable.[44]

The applicant has a right of appeal only against a refusal on merits. The appeal must be made to the area committee within 14 days.[45] No form has been specified and appeals are simply done by sending a letter setting out the reasons. The area committee has power to extend the time for appealing and will usually do so since, in any event, the applicant may always submit a fresh application. However, given the short time for appealing and the fact that an appeal can be easily withdrawn, practitioners should consider whether they should appeal first and obtain their clients' instructions afterwards.

The appeal is a reconsideration of the application and therefore the area committee will take into account any new information.[46] Applications are frequently turned down only because the solicitor has failed to provide sufficient information. Therefore, solicitors should ask themselves why the application was refused and what further factual information and/or legal argument would enable the application to

---

44   General Regs reg 34.
45   General Regs reg 35.
46   General Regs reg 37.

succeed. An appeal without new information or argument is unlikely to succeed.

Most appeals are dealt with in writing but a hearing is arranged if the applicant asks for one. The applicant may conduct the appeal him or herself or may be represented by a solicitor, legal executive, counsel or any other person.[47]

A solicitor may be paid under the green form scheme to advise on an appeal against refusal of legal aid and to prepare the notice of appeal and supporting documents, but not to represent on the appeal. The legal aid authorities have in the past considered that the area committee hearing an appeal is sitting as a tribunal. The green form scheme does not extend to representation before tribunals apart from specified exceptions; see p20 above. There is nothing in the regulations, however, to prevent solicitors from receiving payment under the green form if they go to appeals to advise clients on the spot. They might even address the area committee, provided of course that any time so spent was not charged for; see p23 above.

Even where an appeal has been refused, the applicant is free to make a fresh application, or even successive applications. This might arise, for example, where an appeal against a refusal of legal aid to apply to the Divisional Court for judicial review had been unsuccessful. If the client has sufficient funds to apply to the Court for leave to apply for judicial review, it may be worth doing so. The other side is not normally represented and thus will incur no costs, so the client will become liable only for his or her own costs. Leave is discretionary, and therefore if leave is granted it would be extremely difficult for the area director or the committee to justify a refusal of a fresh application for legal aid on the merits.[48]

The Legal Aid Board has the power to make a 'prohibitory direction' to prevent a person who has been repeatedly refused legal aid from continuing to submit applications: General Regs regs 40 and 41.

Offers and grants

When an application is approved and no contribution is payable, the Legal Aid Board will issue a legal aid certificate. The Board sends one copy to the applicant and two copies to the applicant's solicitor.[49] If a contribution is payable, the Board will send the applicant an offer of legal

---

47   General Regs reg 38.
48   *R v Legal Aid Board ex parte Hughes* (1992) 24 HLR 698.
49   General Regs reg 42.

aid, which sets out the contribution payable and the terms on which legal aid will be granted.[50] The applicant has 28 days in which to decide whether to accept.

Calculating eligibility

The following outlines how to calculate at April 1993 rates whether a client is eligible for civil legal aid and the approximate contributions. If the client is eligible under the green form scheme, payment can be claimed for doing the calculation. Detailed rules of assessment are in the Civil Legal Aid (Assessment of Resources) Regs 1989.

Capital

1 Take into account:
a) cash savings, bank accounts, national savings certificates, shares etc
b) sums that could be borrowed on security of insurance policies
c) fair realisable value of items of value, eg, boat, caravan, jewellery, antiques etc
d) sums which could be withdrawn from a business or borrowed on the assets of a business without impairing its profitability or commercial credit.
2 Disregard
a) household furniture, articles of personal clothing and tools and equipment of trade
b) value of owner-occupied house
c) subject matter of the dispute
d) social fund payments
e) if client is a pensioner, an amount based on disposable income (see table p68).
3 Sum obtained is disposable capital.
4 If disposable capital is over £6,750 (£8,560 for personal injury cases), client is not eligible for civil legal aid (unless s/he is on income support).
5 If disposable capital is under £3,000, client is eligible and pays no contribution from capital.
6 If disposable capital is between £3,000 and £6,750, client's contribution is whole amount over £3,000 (unless s/he is on income support).

50 General Regs reg 43.

Income

Client on income support is automatically eligible for free civil legal aid. In other cases, if client's capital is not over upper limit:

1   Take weekly household income net of tax and national insurance contributions.

2   Add child benefit, but disregard attandance allowance, disability living allowance and social fund payments.

3   Deduct weekly equivalent sums for:

a) expenses connected with employment, eg, travelling expenses, trade union dues, child-minding payments

b) rent (net of housing benefit) or mortgage repayments

c) council tax (net of benefit)

d) maintenance payments for children not living in household.

4   Multiply by 52 to find yearly income, excluding expenses.

5   Deduct yearly allowances for partner and other dependants, as shown in table.

6   Resulting sum is net yearly disposable income.

7   If yearly disposable income is over £6,800 (£7,500 in personal injury case) client is not eligible for civil legal aid.

8   If yearly disposable income is under £2,294, client is eligible for civil legal aid and pays no contribution.

9   If yearly disposable income is between £2,294 and £6,800, deduct £2,294 from yearly disposable income and divide by 36.

10   Resulting figure is monthly contribution out of income, payable throughout the case.

Example

A married man has take-home pay of £250 per week. His wife has no earnings and they have no capital. They have two children, aged 4 and 12. His fares to work are £10 per week. They pay £60 rent and £10 council tax per week.

Weekly income:

earnings	£250.00
child benefit	£18.10
	£268.10
less:	
fares, rent and council tax	£80.00
	£188.10
	× 52

Yearly income	£9,781.20
less allowances:	
partner and two children	£3,244.00
Yearly disposable income	£6,537.20
less lower income limit	£2,294.00
	£4,243.20
	÷ 36
Monthly contribution	£117.87

CHAPTER 5

Emergency applications

Introduction

The average time from a legal aid application to the issue of a certificate is about 30 days for a non-contributory certificate and about two weeks more for a contributory certificate. The process may be short-circuited where, in the words of reg 19(2)(b) of the Civil Legal Aid (General) Regulations 1989 (hereafter referred to as the General Regs): 'it is in the interests of justice that the applicant should, as a matter of urgency, be granted legal aid'. The application is made on a Form CLA3, which requires the applicant to state why legal aid is required urgently. The Form CLA3 should be accompanied by an application for a full certificate on Form CLA1, CLA2 or CLA5, together with the necessary means forms CLA4A/B/C/E, L17 (unless already submitted) and any necessary accompanying documents. If, because of the urgency, it is not possible to send Form L17, pay slips should be sent instead.

In addition to urgency, the applicant must show that s/he satisfies the usual merits test and is likely to meet the means test.[1]

A postal application may be dealt with in as little as 48 hours, and in extremely urgent cases the area office may grant emergency legal aid over the telephone, but only on the basis that the solicitor undertakes to send to it immediately the emergency application and other documents. The telephone procedure 'should be used only in cases of extreme urgency' and applications will not be considered late in the day when solicitors have had time to send them earlier. A solicitor who abuses the telephone application procedure will soon become known to his or her area office.

In addition, solicitors may in some circumstances be paid for emergency work done before the grant of a certificate provided it was undertaken outside normal office hours.[2]

---

1 General Regs reg 19(2)(a) and see chapter 4.
2 General Regs reg 103(6).

Relevant circumstances

An emergency certificate may be granted where delay would cause a risk of miscarriage of justice, an unreasonable degree of hardship to the applicant, or exceptional problems which ought to be avoided in the handling of a case. However, an emergency certificate will not be granted to avoid inconvenience or to enable steps to be taken in proceedings which could wait until the grant of a full certificate. Before applying for an emergency certificate a solicitor should consider whether the necessary work could be done under the green form scheme, or under an existing certificate with an amendment (which could be granted at least as quickly as an emergency certificate). The solicitor should also consider whether an alternative to immediate steps in a court action might offer temporary protection, for example: rehousing, requesting an adjournment or sending a letter before action and asking for an extension of time.

Regulation 20 of the General Regs sets out the grounds on which an emergency certificate can be refused. These are:

a) one of the grounds on which a substantive certificate can be refused (see above p72);

b) that the applicant is unlikely to fulfil the conditions under which legal aid is granted;

c) that legal aid is not required as a matter of urgency.

Note for Guidance 5-01 sets out some of the general criteria which will be applied to an application for emergency legal aid:

- if the reason for urgency is an imminent hearing date, emergency legal aid will be refused if an adjournment could be arranged without undue difficulty for the applicant, the opponent and the court;

- an emergency certificate is also likely to be refused if the urgency has been created by delay on the part of the solicitor or client;

- an emergency certificate is likely to be granted if the applicant's liberty is threatened;

- an emergency certificate is also likely to be granted if delay causes risk of miscarriage of justice, unreasonable hardship to the applicant or exceptional problems in handling the case.

Specific examples are given in Note for Guidance 5-02:

a) Non-molestation injunctions in matrimonial cases.
   Taking – certificate will be granted if there has been recent physical violence which is likely to be repeated but refused if the respondent is already under some other restraint (eg, a bail condition) or the behaviour was 'merely anti-social';
   Defending – certificate will be granted if there are serious allegations

wholly or substantially denied, or if the respondent is unable to defend the proceedings because of, eg, illiteracy or mental handicap, or if there is a real risk that the respondent might go to prison. But a certificate would be refused if the matter could be resolved by undertakings.

b) Assault and trespass injunctions between unmarried couples will be treated in the same way.

c) Ouster injunctions in matrimonial cases.

Taking – certificate will be granted if non-molestation conditions exist and if the applicant is in a refuge or temporary accommodation having recently been excluded from the home, if the applicant is the owner of the home, if the interests of the children require that the applicant has sole occupation of the home. But it will be refused where the applicant has been out of the home for some time (such as 10 days) or if the respondent has left voluntarily and is unlikely to return;

Defending – certificate will be granted if the non-molestation conditions exist and there has been an *ex parte* ouster order made with no opportunity for the respondent to discuss the issues. But it will refused if the respondent has left voluntarily and has no intention of returning.

d) Emergency legal aid will be granted to take ancillary proceedings to prevent disposal of assets where the applicant has no money or other resources to meet immediate financial needs, but refused where the applicant can apply for income support or has other resources available. Emergency legal aid to defend ancillary proceedings will only be given where existing proceedings require immediate action and the applicant would be prejudiced if no action was taken.

These examples are, of course, not exclusive, and emergency legal aid is available in all types of cases and is particularly common in relation to illegal eviction and homelessness.

The financial means of the applicant are relevant in two respects. First, if it appears that the applicant is probably not financially eligible the application for the emergency certificate is likely to be refused. Secondly, if the applicant has enough capital above the lower limit (see p69) to pay privately for the initial action which needs to be taken urgently, the area office will normally expect him or her to do so. This should not affect the applicant adversely, because in any event the whole of the excess over the lower capital limit may be required as a contribution. However, in such a case the applicant and/or the solicitor should ensure that the DSS is informed of the liability for costs so that it may be taken into account in assessing the applicant's disposable capital.

Applications for emergency legal aid are granted or refused by the area director. There *is* a right of appeal to the area committee against a refusal of, or the terms of, an emergency certificate,[3] although some officials seem unaware of it. However, pressure of time in most cases means that appeals are rare – especially since the area office will usually be willing to expedite the consideration of the full certificate where it has refused an emergency certificate. Sometimes it may be worthwhile discussing with the area office the reasons for refusal and whether, with more information, the emergency certificate would be granted. In any event, where an application for an emergency certificate is refused, the application for the full certificate proceeds (and the applicant may make further applications for emergency certificates). Finally, where the applicant is unable reasonably to supply information which the area director requires, the director has discretionary power to issue the emergency certificate 'subject to such conditions as to the furnishing of additional information as he thinks fit'.[4]

Issue of certificate

When the area office issues an emergency certificate, it sends one copy to the applicant and one to his or her solicitor. The General Regs apply to emergency certificates as they do to full certificates, and so a copy must be filed with the court and notice sent to other parties (see below p126).

It is not necessary to wait for the arrival of the certificate before taking action. A court will allow the certificate to be filed when it is received, and it is always possible at least to inform the other side that emergency legal aid has been granted even if all the details cannot be given.

When telephone applications are granted the area office will fax a notice confirming that fact, giving details of the proceedings for which legal aid has been granted and the certificate number. A formal certificate is sent later.

It should be noted that solicitors may ask for payments on account of disbursements in the same way as when a full certificate has been issued.[5] In theory, solicitors and counsel could also apply for payments on account of fees under reg 100 of the General Regs, but they are unlikely to be able to do so in practice because of the limited duration of emergency certificates.

An emergency certificate is to take urgent action only and is therefore frequently limited in scope; for example, to apply for an injunction or to issue a writ. For the same reason its duration is usually limited in time, for

3   General Regs reg 35.
4   General Regs reg 19(3).
5   General Regs regs 101 and see below p128.

example to 14 weeks or until a full certificate is issued. The duration of an emergency certificate may be extended by amendment, in which case a copy of the amendment must be sent to the court and notice of it to the other parties.

If a full certificate is issued while the emergency certificate is in force, the certificates merge and the effect is as though the assisted person had full legal aid from the date of issue of the emergency certificate.[6] If a full certificate is not granted, the Legal Aid Board must decide whether to revoke or discharge the emergency certificate. For a discussion on this, see p140 below.

Work prior to issue

It is a general principle that legal aid takes effect only from the date of issue of a certificate.[7] However, reg 103(6) contains a limited exception to that rule. Work done by a solicitor immediately before an emergency certificate is issued is 'deemed to be work done' while a certificate is in force, provided three conditions are satisfied:

a) the work is done when the appropriate area office is closed and therefore an application for an emergency certificate cannot be made;
b) the solicitor applies for an emergency certificate at the first available opportunity;
c) the application for the emergency certificate is granted.

Two points in particular should be noted here. First, the regulation does not cover work done by barristers. Secondly, solicitors will be paid only if an emergency certificate is granted. This requirement reduces the effectiveness of this provision. Solicitors should ensure that as much work as possible is covered by a green form and, to the extent that it is not, they will need to consider whether to ask the client for funds on account to cover the eventuality that an emergency certificate will not be issued (such funds should, of course, be returned as soon as an emergency certificate is issued).

Solicitors' responsibilities

It is important that solicitors should explain to their clients the commitments that they undertake when they apply for emergency legal aid or when work is begun in reliance on reg 103(6) of the General Regs. It

6   General Regs reg 23.
7   General Regs reg 103(1).

should be stressed to clients who look likely to pay a contribution when assessed that, although they are not paying anything at the outset, they will eventually have to do so, whether or not they decide to go ahead with the action after they have obtained their emergency remedy. They should be specifically warned about the consequences of revocation. In effect, by signing the legal aid forms, obtaining the emergency certificate and instructing the solicitor to go ahead, some applicants are taking a decision which could have the same financial effects as paying privately for the emergency action. The only difference could be that if their contribution is payable out of income they will be given time to pay by instalments. That is easy to overlook at the time the application is made.

It is also particularly important that clients who apply for emergency legal aid should be informed about co-operating with the DSS in its assessment of means, supplying information about the merits of the case and accepting an offer of legal aid promptly. The Law Society's Professional Standards apply here as much as anywhere else. The specimen letter in Part V below also contains advice to a client who has applied for emergency legal aid.

CHAPTER 6

Family proceedings

Introduction

Family proceedings have peculiar features which call for treatment in a separate chapter: a choice of courts with overlapping jurisdictions; no legal aid generally for decree proceedings; special provision for the use of the green form; and, in the magistrates' courts, an overlap between civil legal aid and assistance by way of representation (ABWOR).

Family proceedings, of course, frequently involve applications under the Children Act 1989. This chapter deals with legal aid in respect of Children Act applications where they are brought with other proceedings, such as a petition for divorce. The next chapter deals with legal aid for 'free-standing' Children Act applications and for adoption and wardship.

Costs and the statutory charge, which cause special problems in family proceedings, are mentioned in this chapter but are dealt with in detail in chapters 9 and 10.

Choice of venue

Many types of matrimonial relief may be obtained in both the magistrates' court and the divorce court, including injunctions, maintenance and lump-sum orders.

Proceedings which are not under the Children Act in the magistrates' (or family proceedings) court are covered mainly by ABWOR (see chapter 3, p44), whereas proceedings in the divorce court, now known as the family hearing centre, are covered by civil legal aid. Magistrates' court proceedings are on average considerably less expensive than proceedings in the divorce court, and ABWOR is cheaper to administer than civil legal aid. Naturally, the custodians of legal aid finances prefer applicants to use the magistrates' court rather than the divorce court.

The Act makes specific provision for legal aid representation to be refused to an applicant 'where it is more appropriate that he should be given assistance by way of representation'.[1]

Note for Guidance 6-08(f) states that an application for legal aid will be refused where the needs of the applicant would be fulfilled in a court with lower costs than that specified in the application. Similarly, Note for Guidance 6-08(g) says that legal aid will be refused and the applicant told to apply for ABWOR where the magistrates' court would be as effective as the High Court or the county court in providing a remedy. It refers specifically to exclusion and protection orders in the magistrates' courts and states that 'If the magistrates' court proceedings give the applicant the protection he/she needs then it may be unreasonable to grant legal aid for High Court or county court proceedings, but reasonable to direct the applicant towards ABWOR.' The operative word is 'if'. Note for Guidance 6-08(g) does not say that if the wider powers of the divorce court to grant injunctions are needed then the application should be for legal aid to take proceedings in that court. But, nonetheless, that follows.

Notes for Guidance 6-08(d) and (g) should be read together with Note for Guidance 7-22, which, while it purports to be dealing only with Children Act legal aid applications, gives advice which is equally valid in relation to all family cases where there is a choice of venue and, in fact, repeats largely the old Note for Guidance 11 (in the 1990 *Handbook* but Note for Guidance 25 in the 1989 *Handbook*) which set out in much more helpful detail than Notes for Guidance 6-8(f) and (g) how area office discretion is exercised in this area. (See chapter 1 for a discussion of the re-writing of the Notes for Guidance.)

Note for Guidance 7-22 gives examples where it would be 'appropriate' to take proceedings in the family hearing centre (divorce court) rather than the family proceedings (magistrates') court. The examples include where:

a) other family proceedings are already pending in another court;
b) an order made by another court is to be varied, extended or discharged by that court;
c) the remedy sought is not available in the magistrates' court – such as an application for a lump sum of more than £1,000 or a transfer of property order;
d) the proceedings are exceptionally grave or complex;
e) some novel and difficult point of law is involved.

As far as d) above is concerned, many practitioners would argue that,

---

1   LAA s15(3)(b).

for example, the family hearing centre is the more suitable forum for most cases because it has a professional judge on the bench who will provide a better quality of adjudication than lay magistrates. Such an argument would clearly not suffice in *every* case, but should be used in a case involving particularly complicated circumstances.

The family hearing centre procedure when making financial orders is more thorough than that of the family proceedings court, even as recently improved. The disadvantages of the old magistrates' court procedure were recognised in *Belt v Belt* (1984) 14 Fam Law 154, where, in allowing an appeal against a magistrates' court order, Wood J said that he:

> had every sympathy for the justices who dealt with an extremely difficult matter in a careful way. It was clear that the matter was more suitable for the divorce jurisdiction where discovery could be ordered and the assistance of accountants could be obtained.

Nowhere in the new Notes for Guidance is it explicitly stated, as it was in the old Note for Guidance 11 (1990 version; Note for Guidance 25 1989 version), that 'multiplicity of proceedings should be avoided', so that ABWOR or legal aid to apply for periodical payments or a protection order in the magistrates' court should be refused, and consequently legal aid granted to apply in the divorce court, to a client whose marriage had broken down and who wanted a divorce. However, the principle still stands. The legal aid authorities have been concerned for many years about the duplication of work when divorce proceedings followed magistrates' court proceedings, and still want to avoid that happening.

Nor do the re-written Notes for Guidance say, as they did before, that in the first instance it is for clients and their legal advisers to decide which court is the most suitable for the client's needs. However, that must still be the case. It is the solicitor's professional duty to advise the client on the most suitable remedy and that is not affected in any way by the fact that the client is receiving, or applying for, legal aid. In practice, the effect of the regulations and the Notes for Guidance is that solicitors must be able to justify their advice as to choice of court to the Legal Aid Board in the same way as they would to privately paying clients; and solicitors should also make the reasons for their advice clear when the application for legal aid or ABWOR is submitted or it may be refused. Any certificates which are not in connection with divorce or judicial separation will be automatically limited to the family proceedings court unless the application spells out that legal aid is required for the family hearing centre and why.

Green form in uncontested proceedings

The Civil Legal Aid (Matrimonial Proceedings) Regulations 1989 added a new para 5A to the 'excepted proceedings' in Sch 2 Pt II to the 1988 Act for which civil legal aid is not available. Since 1977, in fact, uncontested proceedings for a decree of divorce or judicial separation are the major excepted proceedings (for the few instances where it remains available, see p103 below). Help is available, however, under the green form scheme, and the initial prescribed limit on work done under that scheme is three times the hourly rate where the work includes the preparation of a petition for divorce or judicial separation. It should be noted, however, that when a solicitor is advising a respondent, or the work does not include the preparation of a petition, the normal lower limit of two times the hourly rate applies. In each case, of course, any disbursements must also be contained within the prescribed limit (see p24 above).

Solicitors may apply for extensions beyond the limits. Note for Guidance 2-22 says that where the higher initial limit applies they are expected to perform most tasks within it:

a) preliminary advice on the grounds for divorce or judicial separation, the effects of a decree on status, the future arrangements for the children, the income and assets of the family and matters relating to housing and the matrimonial home;

b) drafting the petition and the statement of the arrangements for the children and, where necessary, typing or writing the entries on the form;

c) advising on filing the documents at court and the consequential procedure, including service if no acknowledgement of service is filed;

d) advising the client, when the acknowledgement of service is received, of how to apply for directions for trial, and typing or writing the entries on the form of affidavit or evidence;

e) advising as to attendances before the judge to explain the arrangements for the children and as to what, if any, evidence will be required by the judge other than that of the petitioner; and

f) advising on obtaining the decree absolute.

Further, as pointed out in chapter 2, the Legal Advice and Assistance Regulations 1989 (hereafter referred to as the Advice and Assistance Regs) reg 17 provides that:

> matters connected with or arising from proceedings for divorce or judicial separation, whether actual or prospective between the client and his spouse, shall not be treated as separate matters for the purpose of advice and assistance.

This means that matters such as maintenance (including advice on a Child Support Agency assessment) and custody cannot be treated as separate from obtaining the decree. However, it does not mean that every legal problem following a marriage breakdown has to be dealt with on the same green form. The operative words are 'proceedings' and 'client and his spouse'. So, for instance, homelessness or children being taken into care, which could be said not to arise or be connected with the matrimonial proceedings, could be dealt with under separate green forms. (For a general discussion of 'separate matters' see p40 above and for specific examples, Note for Guidance 2–16.)

As a result of reg 17 of the Advice and Assistance Regs, the green form remains effective until the proceedings have come to an end, and when the solicitor submits a claim for payment s/he should, unless it is clear that everything has been dealt with, retain a copy of the claim for payment for future reference.

The initial limit is unrealistically low if the solicitor undertakes complicated negotiations under the green form. Some area offices, at least, recognise this fact since the introduction of more complex statements of arrangements for children (Forms 4) and are, almost as a matter of course, prepared to grant extensions of two hours. Certainly the only safe course is to ensure that enough of the allowance is retained for the decree proceedings. Solicitors should therefore be extremely careful about undertaking negotiations for financial provision under the green form where any property or capital is involved. If it seems likely that substantial negotiations will be necessary to arrange financial provision, the solicitor should apply for legal aid (see below, *but* note the different criteria in relation to applications in relation to children, where the applicant for legal aid must show that the proceedings will be contested). This will not only help to ensure that the work will be paid for, but also that the solicitor will be paid at the higher legal aid rather than green form rates.

Extensions will be given to the green form to pay for reports by conciliation services. In order to qualify for payment, a conciliation service must satisfy certain criteria:[2]

a) the advisers should be qualified social workers or probation officers, although suitably trained marriage guidance counsellors might also be acceptable;

b) the service must have provision for initial and continuing training of the advisers;

c) the service must have the resources to prepare reports for solicitors clarifying the issues between the parties;

2   (1987) 84/35 LS Gaz 2735.

d) the service must confirm that both parties will be seen by their solicitor and receive legal advice on the report;
e) the management committee of the service must contain representatives of the local legal profession and the local judiciary must confirm its support if it does not have a representative on the committee.

Further information can be obtained from area directors. The extension will normally be £32.50: £9.50 solicitors' fees and £23.00 for the report.[3] These figures are increased from time to time.

A client receiving help under the green form in decree proceedings is *not* receiving ABWOR; the client is *not* represented by the solicitor – s/he is acting in person with the solicitor's help and advice. However, the client is exempt from the usual court fees. Under the Matrimonial Causes Fees Order 1980 art 4, petitioners who are not receiving legal aid do not pay court fees if they are in receipt of income support, or family credit, or advice and assistance under the green form scheme.

Another special provision for the green form client is found in the Family Proceedings Rules 1991 (SI No 1247). Although acting in person, the green form client may provide the solicitor's name and address as the place at which documents should be served.

If the question of an order for costs against an opponent should arise, the green form petitioner is acting in person and therefore may not obtain the solicitor's costs from the respondent. The petitioner in these circumstances is entitled only to the costs allowed under the Litigants in Person Act 1975, which would include disbursements and time spent by the litigant in person working on the case at up to two-thirds of the amount which would have been allowed if the work had been done by a solicitor. A green form contribution is not a disbursement, however. In most cases, to include a claim for costs in the petition would be more trouble than it is worth. If the petition is one of the very few which is ordered to be heard in open court, and the petitioner as a result is given legal aid (see below p104), the petition may, if necessary, be amended.

Scope of legal aid

Legal aid *is* available for substantial ancillary proceedings[4] – indeed expenditure on matrimonial ancillary proceedings is the largest item in the annual civil legal aid accounts. Legal aid may also be obtained to apply for an injunction, for orders concerning children, or making or opposing any

3 (1992) 89/12 LS Gaz 13.
4 LAA Sch 2 Pt II para 5A(b).

other substantial application in matrimonial proceedings[5] and to take or defend proceedings under the following legislation: the Domestic Violence and Matrimonial Proceedings Act 1976; the Married Women's Property Act 1882; and the Matrimonial Homes Act 1967.[6] In all these instances application is made on the blue Form CLA2A (formerly CLA2), which is similar to Form CLA1 but requires additional information about the marriage and any children.

Since 1 February 1984, legal aid for ancillary proceedings has been limited to securing only one substantive order. If the assisted person requires legal aid for another application s/he must apply for a new certificate or, if there is an existing certificate, ask for that to be amended. Although the regulations allow either course to be followed, where costs have been incurred under an existing certificate and there is a possibility that the statutory charge will apply, generally speaking, that certificate should be discharged rather than amended and an application made for a new certificate.

In *Watkinson v Legal Aid Board* [1991] 1 WLR 419 (CA) the Court of Appeal held that a legal aid certificate in its amended and unamended form constituted a single certificate, and therefore that costs incurred before an amendment could be recovered through the means of the statutory charge on property obtained by the assisted person after the amendment. Lord Donaldson of Lymington MR said (p425):

> The moral of this forensic tale is twofold. First, that solicitors should never apply for a certificate to be amended, if they could equally well apply for a fresh certificate . . . Second, that in matrimonial proceedings where there is likely to be what might almost be described as an 'annual pay round' in the form of successive applications for a revision of the amount of periodical maintenance payments, solicitors should use every endeavour to procure the discharge of a legal aid certificate once its purpose has been fulfilled (see regulation 80(c)(iii) of the Civil Legal Aid (General) Regulations 1989) and before any new step is taken in the proceedings for which legal aid is required.

Lord Donaldson's statement may have been a little too sweeping. If the assisted person's contribution under a new certificate seems likely to exceed the costs of the new application, then it may be in his or her interest to apply for an amendment rather than a new certificate. However, in most cases it would be to the advantage of the client to apply for a new certificate. *Watkinson v Legal Aid Board* is considered further in the general context of the statutory charge in chapter 10.

5   LAA Sch 2 Pt II para 5A(a), (c), (d) and (e).
6   LAA s14 and Sch 2 Pt I.

Whether the application is for a new certificate or an amendment, the area office must be satisfied that the further application is necessary and may ask for details of the costs incurred to date and, in the case of a request for an amendment, also ask for an assurance from the solicitor that the effects of the statutory charge have been explained to the assisted person.

Applications to bring child maintenance proceedings will be refused where the Child Support Agency has jurisdiction. Certificates issued on or after 5 April 1993 for contested matrimonial proceedings, maintenance or ancillary relief do not cover representation in respect of child maintenance (except in respect of step-children of the absent parent) unless expressly stated. However, where child maintenance is negotiated as part of a comprehensive settlement, the work done in that connection, and any advice on the implications of Agency assessments, may be paid under the certificate (*Legal Aid Focus* 8).

If legal aid is required to bring child maintenance proceedings, it must be clear from the application why the courts, rather than the Child Support Agency, have jurisdiction (*Legal Aid Focus* 8).

Legal aid is available to bring appeals and applications in respect of parentage under the Child Support Act 1991 ss 20 and 27. Applications should be made on the Children Act Form CLA5. (*Legal Aid Focus* 8).

On an application for legal aid to apply for a residence or contact order, or for an order declaring that the court is satisfied with the arrangements for the children, legal aid will be granted *only* if there is reason to believe that the application will be opposed.[7] Legal aid to apply for a contact order is usually limited to obtaining one substantive order for defined contact. If further legal aid is required, the applicant must apply for a new certificate or ask for an amendment of the certificate, and the same considerations will apply as to ancillary proceedings: the area office may ask why the further hearing is necessary, for an estimate of the costs to date and, if the request is for an amendment, ask for an assurance from the solicitor that the effects of the statutory charge have been explained to the assisted person (see *Watkinson v Legal Aid Board*, above). Certificates for applications for residence orders 'will not necessarily be subject to the same limitations'.

The nature of the desired order should be accurately specified in the application for legal aid. Legal aid to apply for a residence order does not, for example, include authority to make an application for a contact order. And, again as in the case of separate applications for financial relief, if there is any chance of the statutory charge applying it is better to apply for a new certificate rather than an amendment (see p102 above).

7   LAA, Sch 2 Pt II para 5A(c) and (d).

With such restrictions it may be difficult at times for the solicitor to avoid excessive delay and fragmentation of the client's affairs. This can be minimised, however. The golden rule is to apply for legal aid promptly whenever proceedings seem likely, and before the green form and any extensions have been exhausted. At the first interview with a divorce client the solicitor should complete all the necessary forms and have them signed or sworn then, or where appropriate shortly afterwards, ie, the petition, the statement of arrangements for the children, the reconciliation certificate, an affidavit of means, the green form (of course), *and* legal aid forms for any proceedings that may be necessary and for which the applicant meets the informal criteria set out above. The last is particularly important in relation to maintenance pending suit when, at the same time that the legal aid application is sent to the area office, the solicitor should file notice of intention to proceed and the affidavit of means and apply to the court for a hearing date. The area office will refuse to give emergency legal aid for maintenance pending suit applications but will expedite the application. By the time the hearing date comes round the applicant is likely to have received legal aid.

It is important to note that if it becomes necessary to enforce a maintenance order, the usual kind of legal aid certificate will not cover the registration of a divorce court order in the magistrates' court; nor will the area director authorise enforcement proceedings where the applicant is on income support and the arrears are effectively owed to the DSS.

Legal aid to defend a petition

In only the following very limited circumstances may an applicant obtain legal aid for decree proceedings:

a) the petition is defended or the application is to defend the petition;
b) the court directs that the petition should be heard in open court; or
c) the petitioner needs legal aid because of physical or mental incapacity.[8]

The Legal Aid Board wants to restrict, as far as possible, the use of legal aid money in defended divorce proceedings. Note for Guidance 6-08(b)(iv) affirms that legal aid will normally be refused to defend a petition, where the marriage has broken down and the only issue is whether the allegations in the petition are true. The reason an application would be refused in those circumstances, the Note explains, is that it would not be a cost-effective use of legal aid. However, the Note also acknowledges that the position could be different, and legal aid could be

8   LAA Sch 2 Pt II para 5A.

granted, where the allegations in the petition, if left uncontested, could affect matters of residence or finance.

Yet someone may want to defend a petition because of the allegations made against them. This was recognised by the Court of Appeal in *McCarney v McCarney* [1986] 1 FLR 312, which suggests that the Legal Aid Board's policy could be successfully challenged by judicial review. Lord Donaldson, the Master of the Rolls, with the agreement of the rest of the Court, stated *obiter* that:

> For my part I would only say that it is certainly for consideration whether legal aid committees ought to refuse legal aid solely on the basis that none of the allegations would prejudice the applicant in ancillary proceedings; because, where a sufficiently serious allegation is made against somebody, he is really entitled to contest it even if it would have no direct effect upon the result of the proceedings. It would obviously be wrong for me to criticise the legal aid authorities in their absence or, indeed, at all, since we have no jurisdiction. They are an independent body, which has a very difficult task. But I do draw attention to this matter since it seems to me that this may be a mistaken view of of the way in which legal aid should be administered.[9]

If a certificate is issued to defend a petition it is usually limited to work done up to the time when the petition is set down for hearing in the defended list. At that point it is, therefore, necessary to ask for an amendment. Solicitors who apply for an amendment to cover defending a divorce petition should expect that they will be asked to certify that a defended suit cannot be avoided and explain why, to describe any efforts made to achieve a settlement and to describe counsel's views, if any. If necessary the area office may ask for the papers.

Abduction and foreign maintenance orders

Legal aid is available – without the requirement of the means or merits tests or a contribution – to applicants from certain foreign countries as a result of international treaties to which the United Kingdom is party. Regulation 14 of the Civil Legal Aid (General) Regulations 1989 (hereafter referred to as the General Regs) covers applicants for legal aid who have first submitted applications to the Lord Chancellor's Department for help in obtaining the return of their abducted children under the Child Abduction and Custody Act 1985. That Act covers children habitually

---

9   The issue was considered most recently in *R v Legal Aid Board ex parte Woolcock* (unreported) CO 410/01 where a refusal of legal aid was upheld because the area committee had considered the implications of *McCarney*.

resident in countries which have ratified the Hague Convention on the Civil Aspects of International Child Abduction or the European Convention on Recognition and Enforcement of Decisions concerning Custody of Children.

The following countries have ratified the Hague Convention: Australia, Canada, France, Hungary, Luxembourg, Portugal, Spain, Switzerland, and all states of the USA. Some countries have signed but not yet ratified: Belgium, Germany, Greece, Italy and The Netherlands. The European Convention has been ratified by Austria, Belgium, Cyprus, France, Luxembourg, Portugal, Spain and Switzerland. Signatories who have yet to ratify are: Germany, Greece, Ireland, Italy, Liechtenstein and The Netherlands. (See also p81.)

Legal aid covers the travelling and accommodation costs of the collecting parent and child.

Regulation 15(1)(a) of the General Regs deals with appeals to a magistrates' court against the registration of, or refusal to register, a maintenance order, under the Maintenance Orders (Reciprocal Enforcement) Act 1972. That Act covers orders made in the states designated in the Reciprocal Enforcement of Maintenance Orders (Hague Convention Countries) Order 1979 as amended from time to time.

Legal aid is made available on the same terms under reg 15(1)(b) of the General Regs for the registration of the judgments of other EEC countries under the Civil Jurisdiction and Judgments Act 1982.

Adoption

An adoption order may be made in the magistrates' court, the county court or the High Court. Magistrates' court proceedings are cheaper than proceedings in the other two courts and, therefore, on an application for legal aid, the area office will have to be persuaded that proceedings in the more expensive courts are justified. Note for Guidance 30 (1989 *Handbook*) provided that one justification might be where a difficult point of law was involved. The arguments (not mentioned in the Note) about the composition and procedures of the courts described on p98 above, might also be put forward.

If the proceedings are brought in the magistrates' court, ABWOR is available but *only if* the proceedings are contested.[10] In uncontested cases, therefore, green form advice and assistance only may be given.

Adoption applications by a parent and step-parent involve an additional hurdle. The Adoption Act 1976 s14(3) provides that where

10 Scope Regs Sch para 2(e).

such couples apply to adopt, 'the court shall dismiss the application if it considers the matter would be better dealt with under section 42 (orders for custody etc) of the Matrimonial Causes Act 1973'. When an application is made for legal aid, therefore, the area office must be satisfied that an adoption order, rather than an order under s42, is appropriate.[11]

Civil legal aid in magistrates' courts

The magistrates' court proceedings covered by ABWOR are covered also by civil legal aid, by virtue of s14(1)(a) and Sch 2.

Availability of legal aid will be relevant only where the applicant falls outside green form financial limits but is eligible for legal aid (see chapter 4 above). The effect may be severe – the legal aid contribution may be up to eight times as much as that payable under the green form scheme. The area director may refuse an application for legal aid if the applicant is eligible for ABWOR, using the power under s15(3)(b).

This form of legal aid is now rarely used (in 1990/91 only 94 certificates were issued), and is likely to disappear altogether.

Until 14 October 1991, application was on a Form SJ1, which was a distinguishing yellow. Now the normal Form CLA2A is used.

Appeals

An assisted person needs a new certificate only if the appeal is *to* the House of Lords or *from* a magistrates' court (see further p61 above). In all other circumstances, an amendment to the existing certificate is all that is needed to make or to defend an appeal.

To *defend* an interlocutory appeal no amendment is necessary, because this is regarded as being within the scope of the original certificate.

A new certificate is necessary to conduct an appeal from the magistrates' court, but the existing ABWOR covers the work involved in giving notice of appeal within the six-week time limit and in applying for the case to be stated.[12] The application for legal aid to appeal to the Divisional Court of the Family Division is on Form CLA1.

---

11 Note for Guidance 30 (1989 *Handbook*).
12 Scope Regs Sch para 1 and see *Mawdsley v Mawdsley* (1983) 13 Fam Law 142, CA.

Costs and the statutory charge

The statutory charge poses special problems in matrimonial cases – in the main because the courts do not make orders for costs against the unsuccessful party as a matter of course. Most recent decisions on the statutory charge have been in matrimonial cases, and this subject is discussed separately in chapter 10.

CHAPTER 7

Children Act proceedings

Introduction

The Children Act 1989, which came into force on 14 October 1991, introduced a new legal regime. Its private law provisions govern the ties between parents, children and other relatives, and its public law provisions govern the use by local authorities of child protection and care proceedings.

Amendments to the LAA were introduced at the same time as the Children Act came into force. The main effect was to make 'special' legal aid available to parents, those with parental responsibility, and children in most public law proceedings. They are given legal aid without a means or a merits test.

Other parties to such proceedings – except for local authorities or guardians ad litem – are entitled to legal aid without a merits test but are still required to pass the usual means test.

The normal legal aid rules continue for all other proceedings affecting children, whether or not they are under the Children Act, but if those proceedings are sufficiently closely related to the proceedings attracting free legal aid they may be covered by the free certificate granted for those proceedings.

Subsections (3A) to (3E) were inserted into s15 of the LAA specifically to cover Children Act cases. Regulations 3A and 12A were similarly inserted into the General Regulations, and further information is provided in Note for Guidance 7.

The previous system for legal aid in care proceedings in the magistrates' courts under LAA ss27 and 28 was abolished when the Children Act came into force.

'Special' and other proceedings

A child who is the subject of an application for the use of secure accommodation restricting liberty under s25 of the Children Act is entitled to free legal aid. If the child is not legally represented but wants to be, then, under s15(3B) of the LAA, the Legal Aid Board must grant legal aid without a means test or a merits test.

Similarly, under s15(3C), the Board must grant legal aid without means or merits tests to a child, parent, or person with parental responsibility to be represented in the following proceedings under the Children Act:

- application for a care or supervision order under s31;
- application for a child assessment order under s43;
- application for an emergency protection order under s44;
- application for an extension or a discharge of an emergency protection order under s45.

The proceedings mentioned in the two paragraphs above are defined as 'special Children Act proceedings'.[1]

Parties other than those mentioned above, such as foster parents and grandparents, who are joined or apply to join the proceedings listed in s15(3C), are also entitled to legal aid without having to meet the merits test. But they do have to meet the normal means tests.[2] Local authorities and guardians ad litem are specifically excluded from these provisions (though guardians ad litem frequently sign application forms on behalf of children).

Conversely, when it comes to appeals against care or supervision orders, children, parents or those with parental responsibility who have already been granted legal aid under s15(3C), do not have to meet the means test. But they do have to meet the merits test.[3]

Means- and merits-tested legal aid is available for public law Children Act proceedings other than those listed above, for instance, education and supervision orders.

The normal means and merits tests are also applied to all private law proceedings involving children whether they are 'free-standing' under the Children Act, such as an application for a contact order under s8, wardship or adoption proceedings, or divorce proceedings.

However, sometimes special Children Act proceedings may involve other proceedings for which legal aid is subject to the normal means and merits tests. For example, parents who have been granted legal aid to be

1   General Regs reg 3.
2   LAA s15(3E).
3   LAA s15(3D).

represented in care proceedings under s31 of the Children Act may want to apply in those proceedings for a contact order under s8. In such a case the non-means- and non-merits-tested legal aid would be extended to the s8 application (although the certificate would need to be amended, see below).

The test is whether the additional proceedings are 'sufficiently closely related' to the special proceedings.[4] If, in the opinion of the area office, they are, they can be included on a certificate covering the special proceedings. If they are not sufficiently closely related, a separate application for legal aid will be necessary.[5] Neither the General Regulations nor the Notes for Guidance spell out what is 'sufficiently closely related' but, in accordance with normal administrative law principles, decisions taken by the area office will have to be reasonable. A strong indicator of a close relationship would be, for instance, where applications were being heard together by the same court at the same time.

However, Note for Guidance 7-20 makes clear that the Board will not consider applications for financial orders between the parties to be sufficiently closely related to any public law cases. (It follows that the costs of special proceedings will, in practice, not constitute a statutory charge under s16(6) of the LAA.)

Local authorities, guardians ad litem and 'any other body which falls within a prescribed description', are not entitled to legal aid for any Children Act proceedings, whether means- and merits-tested or not.[6] General Regs reg 3A provides that 'any body acting in a representative, fiduciary or official capacity for the purposes of proceedings under the Children Act 1989' is similarly not eligible for legal aid.

However, it should be noted that these exclusions apply only to legal aid for Children Act proceedings and only to guardians ad litem themselves. Guardians ad litem and bodies acting in a representative, fiduciary or official capacity continue to be eligible for green form, ABWOR and legal aid in all types of proceedings other than those under the Children Act (see p63 above). In addition, individuals continue to be eligible for legal aid even if they are represented in Children Act proceedings through a guardian ad litem, for instance because they are minors or patients.

---

4   Note for Guidance 7–06.
5   Note for Guidance 7–07.
6   LAA s15(3A).

Applications for legal aid

Two special application forms have been introduced as a result of the Children Act:

- Form CLA5A for children, parents or those with parental authority in special proceedings;
- Form CLA5 for other parties, all other free standing Children Act proceedings, and adoption and wardship.

However, if legal aid is needed to take or defend proceedings under the Children Act as part of other family proceedings – such as for divorce or for a matrimonial order in the magistrates' court – then the usual application form for matrimonial proceedings, CLA2A, or for ABWOR, should be used (see pp46 and 102 above).

It should be noted that Children Act proceedings fall within the definition of 'family proceedings' as used in General Regs reg 46(3)(a). This means that one certificate can cover more than one set of proceedings. Therefore, where solicitors act for an adult in respect of proceedings involving several children only one legal aid application is necessary, even where the proceedings are separate. However, each applicant normally needs to apply separately, and so where a solicitor is acting for more than one child, even in the same proceedings, it will be necessary to make separate applications.

The Legal Aid Board has suggested that this can be done without filling in numerous forms.[7] The procedure would be to:

- fill in one form CLA5, leaving blank the applicant's name, signature and other information which differs between applicants, such as date of birth. Leave the form unsigned by solicitor or applicant;
- write 'ORIGINAL APPLICATION' in block capitals in the top right-hand corner of page 1;
- photocopy the application the required number of times so the words 'ORIGINAL APPLICATION' appear on each copy;
- complete the original form for one child and a copy for each of the others with the information particular to each child and have each form signed (original signatures even if the forms are photocopies);
- send the photocopied applications to the area office, attached behind the original application and with one set of accompanying documents.

---

7   *Legal Aid Focus* 4 and 'Multiple Applications – Children and Spouses/Cohabitees', 1992 *Handbook*, p443.

Special proceedings

A solicitor's self-certification scheme has been introduced in respect of the non-merits-, non-means-tested legal aid for special proceedings. Form CLA5A, which is violet with white boxes (see Part V) is a double-sided piece of paper, which, apart from personal details, simply requires the solicitor to state on what date he or she was instructed, to tick a series of boxes to indicate whether the client is a child, parent or person in parental authority, and to state which of the specified proceedings is involved.

In addition, the form has space for the solicitor to indicate that the client also requires legal aid for a related matter, and the reasons it is related.

The form also requires the solicitor to sign a confirmation that he or she has a practising certificate and will continue to hold one, and that it has been explained to the client that the certificate may be discharged if the client requires the case to be conducted unreasonably. The client must also notify the Legal Aid Board of any change of address. Because legal aid in special proceedings is non-means-tested there is no need to send any other forms.

Provided the form is sent to the Legal Aid Board as soon as possible, and within at most three days, the solicitor will be paid by the Legal Aid Board for all work done 'in relation to the proceedings' from the date the form is signed to the date of issue of the certificate.[8]

Some points are worth noting. First, the client does not sign the form; therefore, if, for instance, instructions are received over the telephone the form could be completed, signed and sent off immediately. Secondly, there is no need even to telephone the area office for authority before starting work. Thirdly, there is no requirement that the form should be signed before the Legal Aid Board will pay for work done – the test is whether the work is in relation to the special proceedings. That could be important: if a solicitor is instructed at court or at home without having a form available, he or she could start work immediately and would be paid, provided the form reached the area office in time. The fact that legal aid starts immediately also means that completion of a green form is not necessary.

It is vital, of course, to fill in the Form CLA5A correctly, to ensure that the proceedings are in the special category and the applicant is the child, a parent or a person with parental authority. None of that should be too difficult, but if the solicitor has made a mistake, a free certificate will not be issued, any work already done will not be covered by legal aid, and legal aid will be granted only after the correct forms have been submitted to the

8   General Regs reg 12A.

area office. If the area office does not accept that any additional proceedings included on the Form CLA5A are sufficiently closely related, they will not be included on the certificate and a separate application will be necessary. However, that will not affect payment for work on the special proceedings.

It is also essential that the form should be received at the area office within three working days. If it is not, the work will not be covered from the time of instruction but only from the time when the certificate is issued. This means that if costs are to be covered from the beginning, Form CLA5A must be received as follows:[9]

Instructions received:	Form CLA5A at area office:
Monday	Thursday
Tuesday	Friday
Wednesday	Monday
Thursday	Tuesday
Friday	Wednesday
Saturday	Wednesday
Sunday	Wednesday

If the form is received late it will be treated as an application for emergency legal aid but no work will be covered until an emergency certificate is issued. The area office can extend the time for receipt of Form CLA5A, but will only do so for good reason such as an unexpected postal delay. More specifically, the Board has stated that oversight by solicitors is not a good reason.[10]

Means-tested only legal aid

As noted, it is only children, parents or people with parental responsibility who are entitled to non-means-tested as well as non-merits-tested legal aid for special proceedings. Other parties to proceedings under ss 31, 43 or 45 of the Children Act, or those who want to apply to be parties, must satisfy the means tests, although not the merits tests.

Such parties cannot use Form CLA5A and instead must use Form CLA5 (see Part IV), and that must be completed with the usual means forms: CLA4A with Forms L17 in respect of the applicant and partner, or CLA4B (see p81 above). However, because the merits test does not apply, they do not need to fill out Form CLA5 completely – just pages 1, 2 and 6.

The Board has stated that means-tested only applications under the Children Act will be treated as urgent and the means assessments will be

9   Note for Guidance 7–11.
10   Note for Guidance 7–13.

given priority. Area offices will also deal with them over the telephone as emergency applications and, when the area office is closed, solicitors can make use of General Regs reg 103(6) (see p94) above. If, however, an application is to be dealt with as an emergency, then form CLA3 should be submitted in the usual way.[11]

It should be remembered that the normal rules about emergency certificates apply, and solicitors should carefully explain to their clients the commitments they undertake (see pp94–5 above).

Merits-tested legal aid for Children Act proceedings

All the pages of Form CLA5 should be completed to apply for legal aid for free-standing Children Act proceedings other than those described above. The form should be sent to the area office with the usual means forms and, if necessary, an application for emergency legal aid on Form CLA3.

The area office will apply the merits test in the usual way, but Note for Guidance 7-21 sets out specifically relevant factors:

a) Section 1(5) of the Children Act provides that a court should not make an order unless to do so would be better for the child than making no order at all. The applicant will therefore need to show that the court is likely to intervene and make an order. If there is no dispute between the parties, legal aid is likely to be refused unless there are reasons in the particular case why the court will make an order and representation is justified.

b) Section 1(3) of the Children Act sets out a checklist which the court must consider before making an order under s8 in contested proceedings. In those circumstances the applicant will need to show that he or she is likely to succeed in the light of the checklist.

c) The applicant will have to show that the order applied for will be of sufficient benefit to her or him to justify the grant of legal aid.

d) The applicant will also have to show that he or she needs to be represented having regard to all the circumstances, including the disputed issues between the parties.

The applicant will also have to justify a choice of venue other than the family proceedings court,[12] otherwise legal aid will be limited to that court.

11 Note for Guidance 7-15.
12 Note for Guidance 7-22 and see p96 above.

Applications by children in their own right

From 1 April 1992, r9(2A) of the Family Proceedings Rules 1991 has allowed minors with sufficient understanding and with the leave of the court to conduct proceedings under the Children Act 1989 and the inherent jurisdiction without a next friend or guardian.

From the same date, solicitors are able to accept the signatures of children aged under 16 to green forms, and themselves to sign and make legal aid applications for minors where:

- the child had been given leave of the court to pursue proceedings; or
- the solicitor considers that the child is capable of giving instructions.

In each case the minor will need to give financial information on Form CLA4F. The minor does not need to sign Form CLA5. The solicitor will be considered the minor's agent for all purposes, and should insert his or her own address as that of the client.

Scope of certificates

The certificate will define the proceedings to be covered. As already noted, Children Act proceedings are 'family proceedings' under the General Regs, and so the same certificate can cover more than one set of proceedings. However, where legal aid is granted on a non-merits- or non-means-tested basis, the certificate will only include other merits-tested or means-tested proceedings where those proceedings are sufficiently closely related (see p110 above).

The exact extent of proceedings covered depends on the wording of the certificate. The general rules apply (see p120 below). More specifically in special proceedings, the Board has confirmed in Note for Guidance 7-05 that as well as covering the application for which a certificate has been granted it will also include representation in respect of:

a) an interim order;
b) applying for directions and their variation;
c) applications for a contact order, or the refusal of contact in emergency protection or care order proceedings;
d) an application for a search warrant under s48 in emergency protection order cases;
e) the extension or discharge of an emergency protection order.

Legal aid coverage is not affected just because the proceedings conclude with a different type of order from that for which legal aid was granted – for instance where care proceedings are concluded with a s8 residence order or where an application for a child assessment order is treated as an application for an emergency protection order. However, a specifically stated certificate or amendment is necessary to make (but not to oppose) an application for a s8 order in care or supervision proceedings.

Sometimes one type of proceedings under the Children Act may follow another. For instance, emergency protection order proceedings may be followed by an application for a care order. In most cases that is predictable, and solicitors should cover themselves in the original application for legal aid. Otherwise they should seek an amendment immediately, if necessary over the telephone.

The usual rules apply about appeals (see p62 above), except that in special Children Act proceedings it is not necessary to apply for a new certificate to cover an appeal from a magistrates' court; coverage can be obtained by an amendment.

In public law cases, transfer of proceedings between different courts is covered by legal aid without amendment of the certificate. Similarly, in private law cases, even if the certificate has specified the court where proceedings are to be started, amendments are not necessary for the continued conduct of proceedings if there is a horizontal or vertical transfer. Applying for a transfer is a normal step in proceedings.[13]

The position about authority is the same as in other legal aid cases (see p121). But it should be noted that whereas authority is needed to instruct counsel in the magistrates' court, no such authority will be necessary if a case is transferred, for instance to the county court.

Costs and the statutory charge

The rates of remuneration which can be charged by solicitors and the manner of taxation or assessment depend on the court in which the proceedings took place. Magistrates' court costs will be assessed in the normal way under General Regs reg 104 and are paid at a higher rate than criminal proceedings. County court or High Court costs may be assessed or taxed according to their amount (see p170). The rates are set out in the Legal Aid in Family Proceedings (Remuneration) Regulations 1991. Those which apply to care proceedings are in Sch 1, and those which apply to non-care proceedings and matrimonial proceedings are in Sch 2.

The statutory charge applies to property recovered or preserved in Children Act proceedings. However, they are treated in the same way as matrimonial proceedings, and the £2,500 exemption and power to postpone apply.[14] As already noted, a separate certificate will usually be

---

13 Note for Guidance 7-22.
14 General Regs reg 94(d)(viii) and reg 96(1)(d), and see generally chapter 10.

needed for public and private law proceedings, and therefore the cost of the former should not form part of the statutory charge. Payment is from the Legal Aid Board.

The Law Society has set up a national panel of solicitors who will provide representation and have a measure of expertise in child care cases. A list of solicitors on the panel and further information may be obtained from the Child Care Panel Administrator (see addresses, p327). Applicants for legal aid are, nonetheless, free to nominate any practising solicitor of their choice. Solicitors on the Child Care Panel may receive enhanced payments of between 30 per cent and 100 per cent.[15]

15   Note for Guidance 13–16.

CHAPTER 8

Conduct of legally-aided litigation

Introduction

The certificate defines the extent of the legal aid which has been granted to the applicant.[1] Solicitors will not be paid out of the Legal Aid Fund for work done outside the scope of the certificate.[2] Nor will they be able to charge the client privately. While a certificate is in force in any proceedings, s15(6) provides that the legally-assisted party cannot be obliged to pay more than the assessed contributions due to the Legal Aid Fund, and s31(3) and reg 64 of the Civil Legal Aid (General) Regulations 1989 (hereafter referred to as the General Regs) prohibit solicitors and counsel from being paid, or even being 'a party to any payment', from a source other than the Fund.

In some circumstances solicitors may find that they themselves become liable because they have exceeded the scope of the certificate. They may be liable in negligence to the client who has been unsuccessful in litigation and who, because outside the scope of the certificate, does not have the protection of s17(1) (see p150 below). Or they may be liable to the other side under RSC Ord 62 r11 or s51 of the Supreme Court Act 1981 as amended by s4 of the Courts and Legal Services Act 1990.

Note for Guidance 8-04 emphasises that 'it is up to the solicitor and counsel to make sure that the certificate covers all the work that needs to be done for the assisted person'. However, it should be noted that where the certificate contains an immaterial mistake which has not misled anyone it may be amended retrospectively.[3] Barristers who do work outside the scope of the certificate suffer in the same way as solicitors – they are unlikely to be paid and, because of reg 64, they do not have financial recourse against the solicitor. Therefore a copy of the legal aid certificate, and copies of any authorities (see below p122) should always

1 R & T Thew Ltd v Reeves [1981] 2 All ER 964.
2 LAA s15(7)(b).
3 R v Law Society ex parte Gates (1988) Independent 1 April.

be included with instructions to counsel and where the solicitor is in doubt as to whether contemplated action is within the scope of the certificate, counsel should be asked to advise specifically.

In some circumstances a barrister may be paid although counsel was not authorised under the legal aid certificate. Regulation 63(3) of the General Regs gives a discretion to the court to allow the cost of leading or second counsel for legal aid purposes when it has done so on a standard basis taxation.[4] However, to be safe, practitioners should always obtain authority and only seek to rely on reg 63(3) as a last resort.

Scope

The legal aid certificate contains a description of the proceedings for which it has been granted. Unless those proceedings are matrimonial, the certificate will also specify the opposing party.[5] The description is usually in terms such as: 'to take proceedings against Exploitation Ltd for damages for personal injuries and loss sustained on 11 February 1993'. The certificate will also contain a costs limit (see p121), may be for the whole or part of the proceedings,[6] or may be specifically limited by the Board.[7] A limitation is likely to be expressed along the following lines: 'Limited to all steps up to close of pleadings (and to any pre-trial review or summons for directions and discovery of documents, where applicable) and to the preparation of papers for counsel and obtaining counsel's advice on evidence, merits and quantum. All unaccepted offers of settlement and payments into court not accepted within the prescribed period must be reported to the general committee.'

Certificates in all cases where the costs are likely to exceed £2,500 are likely to contain a condition limiting the certificate to obtaining further evidence and counsel's opinion before proceeding further. Normally a further opinion will be required before trial.

Within the scope of the certificate, the assisted person's legal advisers will be paid for doing whatever is reasonably necessary to bring the proceedings to a successful conclusion.

As Sachs J expressed it judicially:

> the correct viewpoint to be adopted by a taxing officer is that of a sensible solicitor sitting in his chair and considering what in the light of his knowledge

---

4   But see *Din and Another v Wandsworth London Borough Council (No3)* [1983] 2 All ER 841.
5   General Regs reg 47.
6   General Regs reg 46(1) and see further below.
7   LAA s15(4).

is reasonable in the interest of his lay client [who] . . . should be deemed a man of means adequate to bear the expense of the litigation out of his own pocket – and by 'adequate' I mean neither 'barely adequate' nor 'superabundant'.[8]

Thus where it is reasonably necessary the solicitor may, for example, without further authority use enquiry agents and medical and engineering experts and the fees will be paid out of the Legal Aid Fund.

Section 2(7) makes clear that legal aid includes 'so far as necessary' counsel. Section 2(4) provides that representation under legal aid will include:

(a) all such assistance as is usually given by a solicitor or counsel in the steps preliminary or incidental to any proceedings;
(b) all such assistance as is usually given in civil proceedings in arriving at or giving effect to a compromise to avoid or bring to an end any proceedings.

This includes conveyancing work which is necessary to put a compromise into effect.[9]

A certificate which is limited to obtaining counsel's opinion covers the obtaining of only one opinion, which may follow a conference. It could also cover work by the solicitor to clarify an ambiguity in the opinion.[10]

Costs limitations

All certificates are designated in one of three categories on the basis of the actual or expected costs and disbursements of the proceedings exclusive of VAT. The categories are:

– cases costing less than £2,500;
– cases costing between £2,500 and up to £7,500;
– cases costing £7,500 or more.

A condition is attached to the certificates in all cases which fall within the first two categories to the effect that the costs must not exceed £2,500 or £7,500 unless the solicitor first reports to the area office on Form CLA30. Cases in the third category also have an appropriate costs limitation and are allocated to senior Legal Aid Board staff.

The Legal Aid Board considers the requirement to obtain authority to exceed the costs limit to be a request for a report under General Regs reg 70 (see p133). The consequences of failing to comply are serious for

8 *Francis v Francis and Dickerson* [1955] 3 All ER 836 at 839.
9 *Copeland v Houlton* [1955] 3 All ER 178.
10 Note for Guidance 13–09.

the solicitor, but not as serious as failure to obtain specific authority when required by General Regs reg 52. In the latter case the solicitor (and, usually, counsel) will not be paid at all.

Solicitors who fail to report before exceeding the costs limit are liable to have their profit costs deferred under General Regs reg 102 (see p135) or in a particularly gross case may find their conduct referred to the Solicitors' Disciplinary Tribunal.

The Legal Aid Board will consider, and where appropriate grant, applications to extend the costs limit in cases where it has already been exceeded. Deferment will not happen just because the limit has been exceeded. The Board must also decide not to extend the limit, and further decide that had there been a report at the proper time, the limit would not have been extended and the certificate would have been discharged.

If deferment takes place, disbursements and counsel's fees will be paid but solicitors will only be paid the balance within the specified limit. Decisions to defer may be made by area office staff but can be reviewed by the area committee, if the solicitor so requests.

Authorities - obligatory

Nonetheless, there are some steps for which solicitors will not be paid unless they have been specifically authorised by the Legal Aid Board, and there are others for which solicitors may get prior permission in order to ensure that they will eventually be paid for the work and expenses involved.

Some matters are outside the scope of the certificate unless they have been specifically authorised and the certificate amended. Those matters are set out in reg 52 of the General Regs. The most important are:

a) adding another party to the proceedings (including matrimonial proceedings);

b) cross actions and cross appeals. Thus a legal aid certificate to defend proceedings does not include bringing a counter-claim and a certificate to take proceedings does not include defending a counterclaim. In each instance, specific authority in the form of an amendment to the certificate must be obtained.[11] A new certificate rather than an amendment is necessary, however, for appeals to the House of Lords or for appeals from the magistrates' court;[12]

c) work beyond the limitation on a certificate;

d) making an interlocutory appeal (but not defending one);

11   R & T Thew Ltd v Reeves [1981] 2 All ER 964.
12   General Regs reg 46(2).

e) change of solicitor;
f) to bring proceedings in the Court of Justice of the EEC on a reference to that court for a preliminary ruling; and
g) to allow representation by an EEC lawyer.

Application is made on Form CLA 30.

Additionally, under reg 59 of the General Regs, instructing leading counsel or more than one counsel at the same time requires specific authority. However, reg 63(3) of the General Regs (above) should be noted, and *Din and Another v Wandsworth London Borough Council (No 3)* [1983] 2 All ER 841, in which Lloyd J sitting with assessors held that authority to brief leading counsel authorised only the brief itself and necessary consultation after the brief and did not cover consultations or other work done before delivery of the brief.

In all the above instances, authority from the Legal Aid Board is *obligatory*. With the exception of the limited escape for some counsel under reg 63(3) of the General Regs already noted, a failure to obtain authority will result in the work done being outside the certificate and therefore remaining unpaid. Application is made on Form CLA 31.

If authority is granted in these cases, the Legal Aid Board will issue a formal amendment to the certificate under reg 51 of the General Regs. A copy of the amendment must be sent to the court and notice of it must usually be served on the other parties to the proceedings.[13] There are two exceptions to the latter requirement:

– where the amendment relates only to the assisted person's contribution;[14] and
– where the amendment consists of the addition or deletion of a limitation or condition on the certificate.

This latter exception is by necessary implication: since the regulations do not require a condition or limitation on the original certificate to be notified to the other parties, it would be absurd if a later change had to be notified (see p129 below).

The area director's decision to refuse an amendment can be challenged on appeal to the area committee.[15] The procedure is similar to that for appealing against refusal of a certificate except that the appellant has no right to make an oral representation.[16] Where the requested amendment is to remove a limitation on a certificate, reg 55 of the General Regs requires that, before refusing such an amendment, the area director must serve

13   General Regs reg 54.
14   General Regs reg 53.
15   General Regs reg 57.
16   General Regs reg 58.

notice on the assisted person that the request may be refused and the certificate discharged. The assisted person must be given 'an opportunity to show cause why the application should be granted'. This does not apply to emergency certificates.

Authorities – optional

In addition to the matters for which solicitors *must* ask authority under regs 52 and 59 of the General Regs, there are circumstances, set out in reg 61 of the General Regs, where a solicitor *may* ask for authority before incurring expense. Once the Legal Aid Board has given such authority under reg 61, the court taxing officer may not question whether the expense was reasonably necessary – unless the client's authority was necessary also and was not obtained (see below), or the solicitor or assisted person knew or ought reasonably to have known that the purpose for which the authority had been given had failed or become irrelevant or unnecessary.[17] If the expense is within a specific amount authorised by the Board, then the taxing officer may not question the amount.[18]

Prior authority under reg 61 of the General Regs provides protection for the solicitor. It is *not* obligatory: where authority has not been requested, and even where it has been refused, the taxing officer has discretion to allow the expenditure.[19] Application is made on Form CLA 31.

A solicitor *may* apply for authority under reg 61 of the General Regs for:

a) obtaining expert evidence and tendering it: authority should not be necessary to obtain evidence that is normally required as a matter of course, for example a medical report in a personal injuries case or a consultant engineer's report in a case involving machinery where counsel has advised that it is necessary. Excessive caution by solicitors may lead to clients suffering delay and cost. However, taxing officers differ and solicitors must be guided by their local experience;

b) obtaining evidence from non-expert witnesses such as enquiry agents. The comments at a) above apply equally here;

c) unusual steps or unusually large expenses. These might include, for instance, a country solicitor attending a trial in London, although London agents have been instructed (and vice versa), or bringing a witness from abroad;

d) obtaining a transcript.

17 General Regs reg 63(2).
18 Ibid.
19 General Regs reg 63(4).

Where the area director gives authority under reg 61 of the General Regs s/he *must* in all cases, except d) above, specify the number of reports etc. for which permission is given and the fee to be paid for each.[20] Authority would not normally be given to cover expenses personally incurred by the client/litigant in establishing the case. The courts do not usually consider such expenses to be recoverable legal costs. However, it may be possible to recover from the Legal Aid Fund the cost of the assisted person travelling to a doctor to obtain a medical report. The solicitor should first apply for authority under reg 61. A paragraph added to Note for Guidance 40 (1989 *Handbook*) with the agreement of the Chief Taxing Master and the Lord Chancellor's Department states:[21]

> Authority will not normally be granted for the solicitor to meet the costs of the assisted person travelling to obtain a medical report because such costs are not normally recoverable on taxation. However, the Area Committee [now the Area Director] may be prepared to grant prior authority in exceptional circumstances where the report is essential to the conduct of the case and the assisted person cannot afford the cost of travelling to obtain it.

Client's authority

It should be noted, however, that obtaining the authority of the Legal Aid Board under reg 52, 59 or 61 of the General Regs does not remove the need to have the client's agreement before incurring unusual expense. The client, after all, may eventually pay for the expense out of the contribution or as a result of the statutory charge. Therefore, despite the provisions of reg 64(1) and (2) of the General Regs, if the solicitor has not obtained the client's authority as well as that of the Legal Aid Board, the expense may be disallowed by the taxing officer. In *Re Solicitors' Taxation of Costs, Coventry v Coventry* (1982) 126 SJ 173, Megarry V-C (sitting with assessors) said:

> In my judgment, solicitors in legal aid cases are, in all ordinary circumstances, under a duty not to instruct leading counsel even though authorised by the legal aid authorities, unless they have obtained the agreement of their client to this course being taken; and similarly, as to taking some unusual or unusually expensive steps. Further, before this agreement is given, the client must have been fully informed of the probable additional cost involved, and the effect of this additional cost in relation to the client's own assets and the statutory charge on any property recovered or preserved in the proceedings; and the client must have been properly advised on this

20   General Regs reg 61(3).
21   (1985) 82/24 LS Gaz 1854.

Finally, it is advisable, when a solicitor instructs an expert and others, to limit their fees to what will be allowed on taxation unless the Legal Aid Board has specified a maximum, which should then be agreed with the witness; otherwise the solicitor may have to pay the balance. The contractual and professional duties of a solicitor to third parties are not affected by the various legal aid rules about payment.[22]

Charging assisted persons privately

Regulation 64 of the General Regs provides that:

> Where a certificate has been issued in connection with any proceedings, the assisted person's solicitor or counsel shall not receive or be a party to the making of any payment for work done in those proceedings during the currency of that certificate (whether within the scope of the certificate or otherwise) except such payments as may be made out of the fund.

This prohibition seems very wide, but it is nonetheless possible for solicitors and counsel in some circumstances to charge privately for work done in a case for parts of which a legal aid certificate has been granted, while that certificate remains in force.

In *Littaur v Steggles Palmer* [1986] 1 All ER 780, the Court of Appeal held that the word 'proceedings' in reg 64 of the General Regs has a narrow meaning and refers only to the specific proceedings for which legal aid has been granted, although they might be only part of an action. This reflects the fact that legal aid may be granted under reg 46(1) to deal with one issue arising out of an action as a whole.

The plaintiff in *Littaur* had been granted a certificate: 'To apply within proceedings in the Queen's Bench Division 1981 H No 4352 between Hill Samuel Co Ltd Plaintiff and G Littaur Defendant to purge the assisted person's contempt for breach of the order dated 24th July 1981.' The application was not successful and Mr Littaur was sent to prison for contempt. The solicitors were told by the area office that an application to extend the certificate to cover an appeal would be refused, but Mr Littaur asked them to do further work and agreed to pay privately. Eventually he changed solicitors, and when the new solicitors asked for his papers, Steggles Palmer asked for their bill to be paid before handing them over. Mr Littaur argued that nothing was payable because the work had been done while the legal aid certificate was current.

The court rejected his argument. Lord Justice Ackner, with whom the

22   LAA s15(8).

other two judges agreed, said 'after the dismissal of the application, the certificate ceased to have any force; it had served its function and that was the end of it'. He rejected the argument that the certificate was still current because it had not been discharged: 'To my mind this suggests the fallacious proposition that someone cannot be pronounced dead until it is established that he or she has been buried.'

Nonetheless, there are clear limits to the matters for which a solicitor can charge privately while a legal aid certificate remains in force. First, even where, as in *Littaur*, the certificate is spent, solicitors remain under a duty to advise their clients about legal aid.[23] It is only where an application for legal aid has been refused, or it is certain that it will be refused, and where the client after proper advice decides to go ahead privately, that the solicitor can ask the client to pay.

Secondly, the client must agree clearly and unambiguously to pay privately; until then the contract is that the solicitor should be paid on legal aid. If the solicitor fails to get such agreement before proceeding privately, s/he may not get paid at all.

Thirdly, it is only where the work is outside the bounds of the legal aid certificate by reason of being outside the proceedings for which legal aid has been granted, that private payment is permitted. Thus, a solicitor could, in the right circumstances, charge privately for work done in connection with a counter-claim where legal aid was only granted to defend the action, or for work defending a petition for divorce where legal aid had only been granted for ancillary proceedings. However, it can never be permissible for a solicitor to charge privately during the currency of a certificate for work which is within the proceedings for which legal aid has been granted but outside the scope of the certificate, because it is an expense for which authority has not been asked or has been refused, or which has been disallowed on taxation. The judgment in *Littaur* does not allow 'top-up payments' from assisted persons or on their behalf, for example, to instruct leading counsel or to pay for solicitors to go abroad to collect evidence.

Following *Littaur*, the legal aid authorities gave advice to solicitors which is now published as Note for Guidance 13-02. Where legal aid was given only for a specific step in proceedings, solicitors should apply promptly for the certificate to be discharged or extended when that step had been completed, said the guidance, and continued:

> Before acting privately for a client in any steps in an action in which the client is legally aided his solicitor should first either:

---

23   See Principle 9.17 of the *Guide to the Professional Conduct of Solicitors*, Law Society 1990; 1992 *Handbook*, p446 and chapter 1, above.

   (a) Ensure that an appropriate application for legal aid had been made and refused; or

   (b) Have his client's consent either – (i) not to apply for legal aid or for an amendment to cover the step or steps; or (ii) to act prior to the application being determined–

and in either case should ensure that he (a) has his client's instructions to act privately, (b) explains what this will mean, and (c) advises his client that the Legal Aid Area Office will have to be informed (see para 9 below).

Whenever a solicitor is instructed to act privately for a client in an action in which the client is legally aided, he should inform the appropriate area office in writing, as soon as possible, explaining the reason. The very fact that an assisted person is also instructing his solicitor in a private capacity may be a matter which the area committee should take into account when considering whether it is reasonable for the assisted person to continue to receive legal aid.

A corollary of the decision in *Littaur* is that solicitors are expected to attend court appointments as long as an undischarged certificate keeps them on the court record; and they are at risk of being ordered to pay costs if they fail to attend appointments, even though they are not authorised under the certificate to carry out further work.[24]

Action following issue

When satisfied that the certificate is adequately worded, the solicitor must take the following action.

File a copy

A copy of the certificate must be filed with the court. If proceedings have not yet begun the copy should be filed when proceedings are commenced.[25]

Serve notice

A notice of issue of the legal aid certificate must be served on all other parties. If proceedings have not yet begun, a notice of the issue of the legal aid certificate must be filed with the court for service by the court when it issues proceedings, and in each case an additional copy must be filed for retention by the court.[26]

The notice provides important information for the other parties. It tells them that, even if successful, they may not obtain an order for costs

---

24   *Castleton v Anglian Windows Ltd* (1989) *Times* 14 December.
25   General Regs reg 50(4).
26   General Regs reg 50(1) and (2).

(see chapter 9). Failure to serve a notice promptly puts the assisted person's solicitors at risk of having to pay costs under RSC Ord 62 r11 if other parties are prejudiced. The Court of Appeal ordered the assisted person's solicitors to pay costs incurred unnecessarily by the opposing party in *Sinclair-Jones v Kay* [1988] 2 All ER 611. In that case the defendant was granted legal aid on 10 March 1987. On 3 March the plaintiff had entered judgment in default and 1 May had been fixed for assessment of damages. It was not until 29 April, two days before that appointment, that the defendant's solicitors gave notice of issue of the certificate.

In its decision, the Court stated that earlier decisions could no longer necessarily be regarded as applicable since the coming into effect of Ord 62 r11. In particular, it was no longer necessary that solicitors should be guilty of 'gross misconduct' before an order for costs was made against them (see further p157).

The 1989 Regulations do not specify a form for the notice of issue, or even what it should contain. Forms of notice of issue and of amendment, discharge or revocation of certificate were, however, specified in Schs 1 and 2 to the Legal Aid (General) Regulations 1980. Although the 1980 Regulations were repealed by the 1989 Regulations, the 1980 forms contained all the information which is obviously needed – details to identify the proceedings and the certificate – and they have continued in general use. It is good practice to use them and, suitably brought up to date with references to the current regulations, they are shown in Part V.

When a certificate is issued subject to a condition or limitation, as in the example in Part V, the question arises whether details of that condition or limitation should be included in the notice of issue. Doubt arises because the Court of Appeal held in *Scarth v Jacobs-Paton* (1978) *Times* 2 November, that notice of a limitation should be given in the notice of issue. It is submitted that that decision was clearly wrong. It was made at a time when the regulations specified the use of a form like that in Part V, which clearly makes no provision for giving notice of a limitation. Also, the decision refers only to appeals. Following it, the legal aid authorities, as a matter of policy, include any restriction on the certificate for an appeal in the description of the proceedings for which legal aid has been granted. It is therefore automatically included in the notice of issue if the form in Part V is used. In any other type of case, the notice of issue should *not* contain any reference to a condition or limitation imposed on the certificate. To do so would be a breach of the general duty of confidentiality which solicitors owe to their clients and might be actionable – release of the information could clearly be helpful to opposing parties and prejudicial to the assisted person; see also Notes for Guidance 4-17 and 8-02.

Money on account

The solicitor must consider how much money to ask for on account of disbursements from the Legal Aid Board under reg 101 of the General Regs. This provides for payment not only of disbursements actually incurred but also of those which are to be incurred in the future. There are very few, if any, cases in which it cannot reasonably be said that disbursements will be incurred in the future: court fees, experts' fees, fares etc. Solicitors should therefore make sure that they have funds in hand at all times. Application is made on Form CLA28.

Payment on account of fees, a matter which arises later, is considered separately below.

Change of solicitor

The legal aid certificate names a solicitor and a firm to act for the assisted person. Anyone in the firm may carry out work under the certificate because of General Regs reg 65(2), which provides that a solicitor may entrust the case 'to a partner of his or to a competent and responsible representative of his employed in his office or otherwise under his immediate supervision'. However, the case can only be taken over by another firm if the certificate is amended. This may take place, therefore, only with the agreement of the Legal Aid Board. That is so even if the reason for the change is that the named solicitor has moved to the other firm.

In those circumstances, or where a client has lost confidence in a solicitor or has moved some distance from the office, the Board is unlikely to refuse a change. But an amendment may be refused – and the Board may even consider discharge of the certificate – where the reason for the change is simply that the client is dissatisfied with sound advice from the existing solicitors and wants a second opinion.

A client should always be very cautious, and be carefully advised, before changing solicitors. A change will usually lead to delay. If the case is one where the statutory charge is likely to come into operation, a change of solicitors could also cost the client a lot of money. The fact that new solicitors will have to spend time becoming familiar with a case which is already known to the existing solicitors is almost certain to increase costs, and it is unlikely that any of those costs will be recovered from the other party to the proceedings in the event of a successful outcome. Those increased costs will therefore inflate the statutory charge should the client recover or preserve any property. The amounts involved will obviously vary in each case, and especially according to the extent to which a case is advanced. It should need very strong reasons before a client changes solicitors near the end of a case. (These considerations do not apply, of course, if the change of firms is to follow an individual solicitor who has moved.)

If the client does decide to change solicitors, the first step is to write to the Legal Aid Board and ask for the certificate to be amended to show the name of the new solicitors. The area office will need to be told the name of the individual solicitor in the new firm whose name is to be put on the certificate. The letter should also explain why the client wants to change and describe the stage which the case has reached. It is good practice and common courtesy to send a copy of the letter to the existing solicitors, who will normally be asked for their comments by the area office before it agrees to the amendment.

If and when the amendment is made, the new solicitors will write to the previous solicitors and ask for the papers. The new solicitors should undertake either to include the costs of the previous solicitors in a final comprehensive bill when the case is concluded, or to make the papers available to the previous solicitors at that stage to enable them to prepare a bill.

Unless the previous solicitors are owed pre-legal aid certificate costs by the client, they must hand the papers over. The usual solicitors' lien over clients' papers does not apply to unpaid legal aid costs. The reasons were set out in a Note for Guidance first prepared by the Law Society but adopted by the Legal Aid Board as Note for Guidance 29 in the 1990 *Handbook*. It is inadequately replaced by a note on page 447 of the 1992 *Handbook* and explains that a solicitor's lien arises in respect of work which the client has a personal responsibility to pay. That is not so with legal aid costs, since the solicitor has a statutory right to be paid out of the Legal Aid Fund under s15 of the LAA 1988 and is prohibited from accepting payment from any other source under General Regs reg 64. Therefore, when offered an undertaking by the new solicitors which safeguards their legal aid costs the previous solicitors must hand over the papers. If they do not, the client and the new solicitors have three options, all of which may be exercised at the same time: complain to the Legal Aid Board, complain to the Law Society, or sue.

In some circumstances it might even be possible to argue that the lien does not stand in respect of pre-certificate costs which the previous solicitors left outstanding while they proceeded with the legal aid work. It might be possible to infer that they had agreed to defer payment of those costs to the end of the case, and that they should hand the papers over because their interests would be safeguarded under General Regs reg 103 which provides for payment by the Legal Aid Board of pre-certificate costs out of the client's contributions or monies covered by the statutory charge.

However, it should normally be possible for the previous solicitors to have a bill drawn in respect of the legal aid costs before they hand the papers over, and they would probably be sensible to do so even though they have the undertaking of the new solicitors. There are two reasons for this. First, they retain immediate control of drawing the bill for the work they have done. Secondly, they can use that bill as the basis for a claim on account of fees under General Regs reg 100(6), although a properly drawn bill is not essential for such a claim. General Regs reg 100(6) provides that a firm of solicitors may be paid on account of its fees when its retainer is terminated and it appears unlikely that the costs will be taxed within six months of the date of termination of the retainer.

It will still be necessary, of course, for the fees to be taxed or assessed at the end of the case (see chapter 9), and at that point the fees paid on account will be debited against the final amount which is found to be due to the previous solicitors.

Solicitors' duties

Duty to report to the Legal Aid Board

The general principle is that a legally-aided person's solicitor and counsel must conduct the case in the same way as they would if the client were paying privately. The relationship between them and the legally-aided client is the normal professional one with the usual rights and duties attached. There are, however, certain duties imposed on lawyers by legislation and regulations arising out of the fact that they and the legally-aided client have a triangular relationship with the Legal Aid Fund, which may be paying some or all of the cost of the litigation.

Thus solicitors and counsel are under an obligation to supply the Legal Aid Board with information. Under the General Regs, they must report to the Board:

a) where they have reason to believe that the assisted person requires the case to be conducted unreasonably (reg 67(1)(a));

b) where they have reason to believe that the assisted person has failed to supply information required by the regulations or has supplied false information (reg 67(1)(b));

c) where they are uncertain whether it would be reasonable for them to continue acting (reg 67(2));

d) where they have given up the case (reg 69);
e) as and when required by the area director (reg 70(1), certifying, if requested, the grounds on which it is reasonable for the assisted person to continue to receive legal aid (reg 70(2));
f) when the assisted person refuses to accept a reasonable offer of settlement or payment into court (reg 70(1)(a));
g) when a legal aid certificate has been issued to another party to the proceedings (reg 70(1)(b));
h) where the assisted person has died or been made the subject of a receiving order (reg 71);
i) where the case has been completed or for any reason cannot be completed (reg 72);
j) when money or property is recovered for the assisted person and, if recovered in matrimonial proceedings, whether it includes land or money to be used in purchase of a home (reg 90);
k) where the statutory charge is postponed, as soon as money is released to the assisted person and with sufficient information to allow a charge to be registered (reg 96(6));
l) if the assisted person's solicitor has reason to believe that an attempt may be made to circumvent reg 87 (see below), s/he must inform the Legal Aid Board (reg 87(2)).

Counsel is under no duty to report under the circumstances set out in paragraphs e) to l) above: the duty in those circumstances rests solely on solicitors.

Some of the duties to report listed above are new to the 1989 regulations: e), f), g), h), k) and l). However, they apply to certificates issued under the old regulations. The report by solicitors under e) above is on a standard form issued by the Board. If they fail to report within 21 days of the anniversary, the assisted person and solicitors will be given notice that the certificate may be discharged and the assisted person will be asked to show cause why this should not happen.[27]

Regulation 73 of the General Regs makes clear that the normal privileges between client, solicitors and counsel are not to prevent disclosure.

Although they are placed under no specific duty to do so, solicitors should also inform the Board if the estimated cost of the proceedings on which an actual contribution has been based is likely to be inaccurate. Failure to do this could cause hardship to the client, who unexpectedly has to pay a large sum in arrears, and loss to the Legal Aid Fund.

---

27   General Regs reg 70(3).

Other duties

Regulation 87 of the General Regs effectively imposes a duty not only on the assisted person's solicitor, but on third parties generally – including, therefore, opposing parties' solicitors – to pay all monies due to the assisted person to his or her solicitor or, if a solicitor is no longer acting, to the Legal Aid Board. The regulation provides that only the solicitor or the Legal Aid Board can give a valid receipt for the money, so any third party who hands the money over to anyone else (including the assisted person) may find that s/he has to pay it a second time. Solicitors for third parties who have paid money over in breach of reg 87 could find themselves liable in negligence to their own clients.

The assisted person's solicitor must pay to the Board all monies received for the assisted person under an order or agreement.[28] Partial exemptions from this requirement are possible, however. The Board may give the assisted person's solicitor permission to hand over any money which it is satisfied does not need to be retained to safeguard the Legal Aid Fund.[29] This enables solicitors to account to their clients for at least the main part of any money due without having to wait for the sometimes lengthy process of taxation and accounting (see further p144). Under regs 90(4) and 96 of the General Regs, the area director can postpone payment to the Board of money which has been recovered or preserved in matrimonial proceedings and is required for the purchase of a home (see further p190).

Under reg 110 of the General Regs, the solicitor is under an obligation to safeguard the interests of the Fund on any taxation on a standard basis under an order for costs in favour of the assisted person, although the latter may not have any interest in the taxation. This includes taking any necessary steps to obtain a review of taxation.

Assisted persons' duties

Assisted persons are under an obligation to pay their contributions and to comply with the statutory charge. If they fail to do so, the courts can enforce compliance.

Under reg 44 of the General Regs, the Legal Aid Board may require that an assisted person undertake to inform the Board if, in addition to the contribution, s/he receives any money from a body, such as a trade union, which might reasonably be expected to be used towards the costs of the proceedings.

28   General Regs reg 90(1)(b).
29   General Regs reg 90(2).

An assisted person is, in any event, under a general duty to inform the solicitor of:[30]

> any change in his circumstances, or in the circumstances of his case, which he has reason to believe might affect the terms or the continuation of his certificate.

This covers not only a change in means which might lead to a reassessment, but also any change in the merits, such as the possible disappearance of a vital witness.

There is, in addition, a specific duty on the assisted person, or anyone else whose resources have been brought into assessment, to inform the Legal Aid Board:[31]

> of any change in the financial circumstances under which the original determination was made which he has reason to believe might affect the terms or continuation of the certificate.

On signing the legal aid form, the applicant promises to inform the Legal Aid Board immediately if his or her means change and, as already noted, the solicitor should explain the client's obligations at the time the application form is signed.

Sanctions

The sanctions against solicitors who fail in their duty to the Fund may be severe. If a solicitor's failure to observe the regulations results in loss to the Fund, the payment of the solicitor's fees may be deferred until s/he has complied with the regulations.[32] In Note for Guidance 15-23, the legal aid authorities state that they have advice from leading counsel that the solicitor for an assisted person is under a 'clear statutory duty to pay over monies recovered in an action' and that solicitors who breach that duty may be ordered by the court to make good the resulting loss to the Fund.

Under reg 109 of the General Regs, a solicitor's costs may be disallowed or reduced where they have been 'wasted by failure to conduct the proceedings with reasonable competence and expedition'. In addition, a solicitor may be ordered to pay the costs of opposing parties and of the client under RSC Ord 62 r11 where they have been incurred unreasonably or improperly, or wasted by failure to conduct the proceedings with

---

30 General Regs reg 66.
31 Resources Regs reg 11.
32 General Regs reg 102.

reasonable competence and expedition. Section 51 of the Supreme Court Act 1981, as amended by s4 of the Courts and Legal Services Act 1990, is in virtually the same terms as RSC Ord 62 r11, but also imposes liability on counsel (see further p162).

Assisted persons must supply the information required by the regulations. If they fail to do so they may find that their legal aid certificates are discharged. If they *intentionally* fail to do so or knowingly furnish false information, their certificates may be revoked, with all the severe consequences that brings (see p139). They may also be prosecuted by the Board, and if found guilty are liable to a fine not exceeding level 4 or up to three months' imprisonment under s39(1). The Legal Aid Board may also sue them for any loss to the Legal Aid Fund.[33]

Finally, assisted persons should be made aware of the court's powers to refer cases of abuse to the Legal Aid Board under reg 68 of the General Regs. Cases may be referred where, at any time during the hearing, the court considers that the assisted person has made an untrue statement or failed to disclose a material fact about means, intentionally has failed to supply other material information to the Legal Aid Board or to his or her solicitor, or knowingly has made an untrue statement.

Reassessment of means

The legal aid authorities have the power to reassess or 'further assess' (see below) the assisted person's means, and in some circumstances to require an increased maximum contribution. This is recognised on the legal aid form where the applicant signs an acknowledgement to that effect.

The position of the assisted person depends on whether he or she applied for legal aid before 12 April 1993 (because in that case the period of computation would have begun before that date) and whether the certificate was issued before 12 April 1993 (Civil Legal Aid (Assessment of Resources) (Amendment) Regulations 1993 reg 3).

Certificates issued before 12 April 1993

During the original computation period in respect of certificates issued before 12 April 1993 'reassessment' may take place if it appears that the assisted person's income has increased by more than £750 or decreased by more than £300. The same applies where the assisted person's capital has increased by £750 or more. Any improvement in financial circumstances as a result of an award which is subject to the statutory charge is

---

33   LAA s39(4).

disregarded. Thus awards of damages or capital in the legally-aided proceedings will make no difference, whereas an order for periodical payments might.

The result of a reassessment during the period of computation may be both altered contributions and/or the discharge of the certificate.[34]

In addition, at any time, the assessment officer 'may' carry out a new assessment if it appears that there was an error in the original assessment and it would be 'just and equitable' to correct it. Such a new assessment takes the place of the original assessment in all respects and therefore may also lead to higher contributions and/or discharge of the certificate.[35]

Outside the computation period, but during the currency of the certificate, a 'further assessment' of the assisted person's means may be made where the area director thinks that they are such that he or she could afford to proceed without legal aid. It is important to note, however, that, unlike a reassessment or a new assessment, a further assessment will, at worst, lead to the discharge of the certificate – it cannot increase the assisted person's contribution.[36]

Reassessments, new assessments and further assessments in respect of certificates issued before 12 April 1993 will all take place using the allowances, eligibility criteria and scales of contribution in force before 12 April 1993 (Civil Legal Aid (Assessment of Resources) (Amendment) Regulations 1993 reg 3).

Sometimes the assisted person has a degree of control over the exact timing of the event which triggers reassessment, for instance where s/he is moving into rented accommodation and receiving capital from the sale of a dwelling-house which had been disregarded in the original assessment. In those circumstances it might be in the assisted person's interest to delay matters until the expiry of the computation period 12 months from the date of the application for legal aid.

Certificates applied for on or after 12 April 1993

Assisted persons who applied for legal aid on or after 12 April 1993 may be reassessed or have new assessments made in the same circumstances as those whose certificates were issued before that date. Just to confuse matters a little, however, what is called 'reassessment' in respect of a certificate applied for before 12 April 1993 is called 'further assessment' in respect of a certificate applied for after that date (Resources Regs reg 12 as amended by Civil Legal Aid (Assessment of Resources) (Amendment)

---

34   Resources Regs reg 12.
35   Resources Regs reg 14.
36   Resources Regs reg 13.

Regulations 1993 reg 8). But the possible consequences are the same: altered contributions and/or discharge. What is more, this type of re-assessment or further assessment may take place at any time and it no longer makes any difference that the original period of computation has expired. (Original Resources Regs reg 13 modified by Civil Legal Aid (Assessment of Resources) (Amendment) Regulations 1993 reg 9).

As far as new assessments are concerned, a change in wording now means that the assessment officers 'shall' carry out the new assessment, not only in the circumstances set out above but also where new information has come to light (Resources Regs reg 14 as amended by Civil Legal Aid (Assessment of Resources) (Amendment) Regulations 1993 reg 14).

Further assessments and new assessments in respect of certificates issued after 12 April 1993 will, of course, take place using the allowances, eligibility criteria and scales of contribution in force after 12 April 1993 (Civil Legal Aid (Assessment of Resources) (Amendment) Regulations 1993 reg 3).

Certificates applied for before but issued on or after 12 April 1993

The period of computation in respect of certificates applied for before 12 April 1993 will naturally have a computation date which also begins before that date.

Re-assessments and new assessments take place using the allowances, eligibility criteria and scales of contribution which came into force on 12 April 1993. (Civil Legal Aid (Assessment of Resources) (Amendment) Regulations 1993 reg 3).

However, as far as any changes of means outside the contribution period are concerned, assisted persons whose certificates are issued on or after 12 April 1993 are all treated the same irrespective of when they applied. In other words the separate category of 'further assessment', where the certificate may be discharged but a higher contribution cannot be required, is not available in respect of any certificate issued on or after 12 April 1993. (Civil Legal Aid (Assessment of Resources) (Amendment) Regulations 1993 regs 3 and 9).

Discharge and revocation

Effect of discharge and revocation

The area director may discharge or revoke a certificate.[37] The

37   General Regs reg 74(1).

consequences of each are different. For the assisted person revocation is very undesirable.

When a certificate is discharged, legal aid simply ceases from the date of discharge.[38] This normally happens when a case is concluded. Revocation, on the other hand, may be a severe sanction on the assisted person. When a certificate is revoked, the assisted person is treated as though s/he had never received legal aid.[39] Solicitors and counsel will still be paid out of the Legal Aid Fund,[40] but the assisted person may be made liable for the full costs, rather than the assessed contribution. In addition, the solicitor has the right to recover from the former assisted person the difference between the legal aid costs and the full solicitor and own client costs on a private basis.[41] The assisted person also loses any protection against orders for standard basis costs otherwise provided by s17(1), but the opposing party's rights to an order for costs against the Legal Aid Fund under s18 are not affected.[42]

Neither discharge nor revocation affects the operation of the statutory charge.[43]

Discharge or revocation brings the retainer between client, solicitor and counsel to an end, although if proceedings have started, the solicitor must first file the notice of discharge or revocation from the Legal Aid Board and serve notice on any other parties.[44] Until that has been done the solicitor remains on the court record. This was affirmed in *Wood v Young* (1981) 125 SJ 609; (1981) 122 NLJ 758. After the defendant's emergency certificate had been discharged his solicitors wrote to the plaintiff's solicitor that they could take the matter no further because they were without instructions. Imbedded in other information was the erroneous statement that the certificate had been 'revoked'. When the plaintiff's solicitor subsequently served a notice of motion on them, the defendant's solicitors contended that it was invalid because they were no longer acting. Goulding J held that the notice of motion had been validly served. The departure from the prescribed form was not immaterial and omissions left the real substance of the information incomplete. Read as a whole, the letter gave the plaintiff insufficient information about the defendant's representation to enable the plaintiff to know what his position was and to act upon it.

---

38 General Regs reg 74(2).
39 General Regs reg 74(2).
40 General Regs reg 84.
41 General Regs reg 86(1)(b).
42 General Regs reg 74(2).
43 General Regs reg 85.
44 General Regs regs 82 and 83.

Clearly, however, this decision does not mean that only a notice in the prescribed form will take the assisted person's solicitors off the record. If the defendant's solicitors' letter in *Wood v Young* had set out the required information accurately and clearly, the result would have been different.

Discharge or revocation will be authority for the costs to be taxed or reassessed.[45]

Grounds for discharge and revocation

Grounds for discharge are also in some circumstances grounds for revocation but, because of the serious consequences of the revocation, where there is an option the Legal Aid Board should use revocation only where the assisted person has shown some wilful culpability.

Emergency certificates

Emergency certificates are treated differently from full certificates. An emergency certificate *must* be revoked where the assessment shows the assisted person has not satisfied the means tests.[46]

An emergency certificate *may* be revoked or discharged, on the other hand, where:

a) the assisted person has failed to attend for an interview or to provide information or documents as required by the regulations; or has failed to accept an offer of full legal aid in time;[47] or

b) when the time allowed for the duration of the emergency certificate, and any extension, has expired.[48]

Before revocation under ground a) above, the Legal Aid Board must serve the assisted person and the solicitor with notice of its intention and give the assisted person 'an opportunity to show cause why his certificate should not be revoked'.[49] Where the Board serves such a notice, no further work may be done under the certificate without specific authority.[50]

Full certificates

A full certificate *may* be revoked or discharged, under the General Regs, where the assisted person:

45   General Regs reg 84.
46   General Regs reg 75(1) and (2).
47   General Regs reg 75(3).
48   General Regs reg 75(4).
49   General Regs reg 75(5).
50   Ibid.

a) has made an untrue statement or failed to disclose material facts about his or her resources;[51] or
b) has not provided the Legal Aid Board or his or her solicitor with material information as required by the regulations;[52] or
c) has knowingly made a false statement in supplying such information;[53] or
d) has failed to attend for an interview or to provide information or documents as required by the regulations.[54]

The certificate may not be discharged or revoked on ground a) if the assisted person shows that s/he used 'due care and diligence'.[55]

Provision is made for the discharge of a full certificate on financial grounds[56] and on the merits.[57] Thus a full certificate *must* be discharged, under the General Regs, where:

a) the assisted person's means have changed (see p136 above) so as to make him or her ineligible for legal aid;[58] or
b) the assisted person's means have changed to the extent that the area director considers that s/he 'could afford to proceed without legal aid' and asks for a reassessment;[59] or
c) the assisted person no longer has reasonable grounds for taking, defending or being a party to proceedings;[60] or
d) the assisted person has required the proceedings to be conducted unreasonably so as to incur an unjustifiable expense to the Fund;[61] or
e) it is unreasonable in the particular circumstances that the assisted person should continue to receive legal aid.[62]

In addition, under reg 80 of the General Regs, the area director *may* discharge a certificate where:

a) the assisted person consents; or
b) the assisted person is more than 21 days in arrears with a contribution; or
c) the assisted person has died; or

51 General Regs reg 78(1)(a).
52 General Regs reg 78(1)(b).
53 General Regs reg 78(1)(c).
54 General Regs reg 79.
55 General Regs reg 78(2).
56 General Regs reg 76.
57 General Regs reg 77.
58 General Regs reg 76(1) or (2).
59 General Regs reg 76(3).
60 General Regs reg 77(a).
61 General Regs reg 77(b).
62 General Regs reg 77(c).

d) the assisted person has been the subject of a bankruptcy order; or
e) the proceedings have been disposed of; or
f) the work authorised by the certificate has been completed.

The assisted person has no right to be heard where discharge is on the grounds of means under reg 77, or where it is under reg 80 of the General Regs, apart from bankruptcy. Where it is on the grounds of bankruptcy under reg 80, and in all other instances, the Legal Aid Board must serve a notice on the assisted person and give him or her 'an opportunity to show cause why his certificate should not be revoked or discharged'.[63] In addition, there is a right of appeal against the decision to the area committee.

It should be noted that a legal aid committee has power to rescind the revocation of a legal aid certificate where the revocation was based on a mistake of fact. A rescission has retroactive effect so that the assisted person is treated as though the legal aid certificate had continued in existence without interruption.[64]

Payment on account

Solicitors may always ask to be paid money on account of disbursements incurred or to be incurred under reg 101 of the General Regs (see p128 above).

Regulation 100 of the General Regs makes provision for solicitors and counsel to be paid part of their fees on account for the work they have done. The scheme works almost automatically. The legal aid computer sends claim forms to solicitors who must return them completed. The first payment can be made after the certificate has been in force for 12 months and further payments after 24 and 36 months from the date of issue. Claims can only be made in the period from two months before to four months after the payment has fallen due. The same rules apply to counsel. The maximum payment depends on the financial year in which it is made:

Financial year	Maximum payment %
1993/94	62
1994/95	70
1995/96 onwards	75

As already noted (p132 above), where there has been a change of solicitors, reg 100(6) of the General Regs authorises an area committee to

---

63 General Regs reg 82.
64 See *Langford v Gibb* (1984) *Times* 26 January.

pay fees on account to the original solicitors if it appears that taxation will not take place for at least another six months.

In addition, under reg 101(1)(b) of the General Regs, an area committee may pay solicitors' or counsel's fees on account where:

- the proceedings have continued for more than 12 months; and
- it seems unlikely that an order for taxation will be made within the next 12 months; *and*
- the delay will be such as to cause hardship to solicitors or counsel.

In most cases falling within the hardship provisions of reg 101(1)(b) it would also be possible to make a routine claim for payment under reg 100. Reg 101(1)(b) could, however, still be useful in two respects. First, it may be used to top-up payments received under reg 100. Secondly, where proceedings have been begun before the issue of the certificate, it will be possible to make a claim under reg 101(1)(b) before it is possible to do so under reg 100.

Standards published in Note for Guidance 13-08 indicate how reg 101(1)(b) is normally interpreted. Solicitors must show that the delay in taxation will, rather than may, cause hardship. If the amount of outstanding costs is substantial it will be easier to do so and it is possible to submit claims in respect of a number of cases and ask for the cumulative effect to be taken into account.

It is necessary to produce some evidence, such as a letter from the firm's bank or information about the overdraft, to show that non-payment would have a serious effect on the practice. That must go beyond the general, such as pointing to high interest rates or the economic climate of the time, although general factors such as high interest rates, coupled to specific ones, such as a large overdraft, would be relevant.

Whatever form a payment on account takes, solicitors and counsel will still need to have their fees taxed or assessed at the end of the case. Payments received on account are deducted from the final payment made – and, if they have received more on account than is finally due, they must repay the balance to the Legal Aid Fund.

Interim costs orders are, strictly speaking, not payments on account of fees but they can be equally welcome. Where interlocutory proceedings, such as applications for injunctions, have taken place, it is possible to ask the court to order taxation of legal aid costs. Such an order will be authority for the taxation of an interim bill which will be paid in the normal way (see chapter 9).

The provision for payment on account also applies to barristers; those struggling in their first years of practice may find it particularly useful.

The end of the case

As far as lawyers are concerned a case is not finished until they have been paid – which in a legal aid case usually means several months, at least, after a trial or settlement because of the requirements to have costs taxed or assessed and reporting to the Legal Aid Board.

However, in order to give a proper service to their clients, they must consider two questions as soon as a case has been settled or decided by the court, and they must do so without waiting to sort out the costs, unless that is done almost immediately. First, should the certificate be discharged? Yes should be the answer if the certificate was applied for after 12 April 1993 and all that remains is taxation of costs and collection will not be a problem. Otherwise the client will continue to be liable to pay contributions out of income. Second, if the solicitor is holding money recovered on behalf of the assisted person, should authority be obtained from the Legal Aid Board for that money to be paid to the assisted person? Because of the statutory charge, solicitors must pay any money recovered on behalf of the client to the Legal Aid Board, unless the postponement provisions apply (see p190) or the area director agrees otherwise under General Regs reg 90(2). The Legal Aid Board will eventually account to the assisted person for the money but that process may take some time.

It may not even begin until the costs have been taxed – which is also frequently a lengthy process. The assisted person might therefore wait for months or even years to receive the fruits of the litigation. This is very frustrating and can lead to friction between clients and their legal advisers. However, there is no reason or excuse in most cases for making clients wait for the bulk of their money.

Regulation 90(2) of the General Regs provides that the area director may authorise the solicitor to pay the Board, instead of the whole amount recovered or preserved, only such sum as will safeguard the interests of the Legal Aid Fund. The solicitor is then authorised to pay the balance to the assisted person on account until the final sum due can be ascertained. Before the area director gives such an authority s/he will require an undertaking from the solicitor on Form CLA 29 that the amount which the Legal Aid Fund will be asked to pay will not exceed an amount equal to the contributions paid and the money retained and paid into the Fund. If solicitors underestimate the amount required to be paid, the Legal Aid Board will normally refuse to pay any shortfall under reg 102 of the General Regs. However, a reasonably competent solicitor should be able to give an estimate of the difference between costs recovered from the opposing party on the one hand and legal aid costs on the other and, with a margin for safety if necessary, assess what the likely impact of the statutory charge will be. Solicitors who fail to use reg 102, and therefore fail to pay even part of the money due to their clients until after taxation, are in most cases in breach of their professional obligations.

See also final accounting, p171.

CHAPTER 9

Costs

Introduction

Sorting out the money at the end of a legal aid case seems to cause many unnecessary problems. On the one hand, legal aid practitioners complain about delay in payment and unnecessary bureaucracy, whereas the Royal Commission on Legal Services found a major cause of delay in payment for legal aid work to be the tardiness of solicitors in submitting their claims. Assisted persons suffer the most of all if they have to wait an unnecessarily long time before being able to enjoy the fruits of successful litigation. Further, in some instances, their gains are rendered illusory by the workings of the statutory charge, of which they may not have been made fully aware when they began litigation or agreed to a settlement (the statutory charge is discussed in chapter 10). Undoubtedly, the organisation of and payment for legal aid work, as well as the system for taxing costs, needs thorough reform. However, there is little doubt that solicitors make insufficient use of the opportunities offered by the regulations to obtain prompt and proper payment and to expedite payments and accounting to the client.

This chapter is concerned with costs:

- when and how one party may be ordered to pay them to the other, where either or both are legally-aided;
- when and how the Legal Aid Fund may be ordered to pay costs to an unassisted party;
- and how solicitors and counsel are paid for the work they have done for an assisted person out of the Legal Aid Fund.

Legal aid costs must be either taxed by the court or assessed by the Legal Aid Board (see p169 below). In the absence of agreement costs payable by one party to another must always be taxed. Therefore, when a legally-aided party succeeds in an action two forms of taxation may be taking place at the same time: a taxation between the Legal Aid Board and the losing party to decide what the losing party should pay, and a taxation between the Legal Aid Board and the winning assisted party's legal representatives to decide what they should be paid out of the Legal Aid Fund.

It is important to remember that there are time limits for the taxation of costs: three months in the High Court and the county court[1] and, normally, six months in matrimonial cases. Solicitors who delay in sending in their bills may find them reduced or disallowed altogether.[2]

The taxation process is normally initiated by the successful assisted party's solicitors presenting a bill (see Part V). Where legal aid and inter-party taxation is taking place at the same time, the bill is drawn up with two sets of columns: one setting out the amounts claimed against the opposing party – all of which will be payable to the Legal Aid Fund, and through it ultimately to the assisted party's solicitors – and the other the additional amount claimed from the Legal Aid Fund, consisting of items which cannot be claimed against the opponent (for examples see below). There are three columns in each set, containing the solicitor's costs, disbursements (including counsel's fees) and VAT claimed. Where only a legal aid taxation is taking place, the bill would, of course, consist of only three columns.

The fees and disbursements payable by one party to another and by the Legal Aid Board to the assisted person's representative are both paid on what is known as the standard basis. This provides for a reasonable amount in respect of all costs reasonably incurred.[3] The accepted approach was set out in the judgment of Sachs J in *Francis v Francis and Dickerson* [1956] P 87:

> When considering whether or not an item in a bill is 'proper' the correct viewpoint is that of a sensible solicitor sitting in his chair and considering what in the light of his then knowledge is reasonable in the interests of his lay client . . . It is wrong for the taxing officer to adopt an attitude akin to a revenue official called upon to apply one of those Income Tax rules as to expenses which have been judicially described as 'jealously restricted' and 'notoriously rigid and narrow in their operation'. I should add that . . . the lay client in question should be deemed a man of means adequate to bear the expense of litigation out of his own pocket – and by 'adequate' I mean neither 'barely adequate' nor 'superabundant'. It may save misapprehension too, if one remembers that neither in an unassisted case nor in an assisted case has a solicitor any implied authority to take steps which are extravagant or over-cautious.

1   RSC Ord 62 r29 and CCR Ord 38 r20.
2   General Regs reg 109.
3   RSC Ord 62 r12.

Few solicitors would draw their own bills for taxation, most would either employ specialist costs drafters or engage a firm of costs drafters, who charge a percentage of the bill as drawn or as taxed. However, solicitors need to be aware of the rates allowed in their local courts and their own expense rates in order to tell the bill drafters what rate to charge. The solicitors should also point out any special features, such as the weight, complexity or urgency of the case, or the fact that it was undertaken without counsel so that a substantial mark-up of 100 per cent or more would be justified. Equally, solicitors should remember, throughout the case, not just when it comes to taxation, that they will not be paid properly unless they have kept proper records to substantiate the amount of time they have spent on the case.

A copy of the bill is sent to the opposing party and lodged with the court, together with the relevant papers. Unless the costs are agreed at that stage there will be a hearing in front of the taxing officer or district judge. If the assisted party has an interest, s/he may attend (see p166 below). The paying party's representative will try to reduce the amount s/he has to pay, and frequently any reductions made in those columns will be added to the claim against the Legal Aid Fund (thus increasing the statutory charge).

When the bill has been taxed, it will be totalled up by the winning party's solicitor and returned to the court with the taxing fee (5 per cent of the amount claimed). The court issues an order for costs against the paying party and an allocatur showing the amount payable out of the Legal Aid Fund. The costs order is enforceable like any judgment, and unless it seems likely that payment will not be forthcoming, solicitors should ensure that it is paid immediately and the proceeds sent to the Legal Aid Board with the report on case and other relevant documents, otherwise the client will not be paid that part of his or her winnings (see chapter 10).

Orders between parties

Orders for costs in favour of the assisted person

It is a general rule that costs follow the event: effectively, that the loser is ordered to pay the costs of the winner. It is just as important for an assisted party to recover costs from the other side, whether by way of an order or by agreement where the case has been settled, as it is for a privately paying client to do so. The reason, as already pointed out, is that any part of the costs paid to the assisted person's solicitors which is not recovered from the other side will be taken out of the assisted person's contributions and, if the contributions are not sufficient, out of the proceeds of the litigation through the application of the statutory charge.

In addition, an assisted person's solicitor is under a duty to protect the interests of the Legal Aid Fund.[4] That, however, does not place him or her under an obligation to claim an order for costs where it is not in an assisted person's own interest to make such a claim and where a privately paying client would not, in the same circumstances, do so.

Costs between parties are assessed or taxed on the standard basis like legal aid costs. However, it does not follow that a succesful legally-aided party will recover all his or her legal costs from the opposing party. For example, in the course of the litigation the court might have ordered that the assisted party should pay the costs of one or more interlocutory applications, or ordered that the opposing party should not be obliged to pay them whatever the final outcome of the case. Further, it is likely that on the taxation the court will disallow the costs occasioned by the fact that the assisted person was on legal aid, such as opinions from counsel required by limitations on the certificate and correspondence between the assisted person's solicitors and the Board. On a taxation on the standard basis between parties, any doubts are resolved in favour of the paying party.[5]

Normally, therefore, the Legal Aid Fund must pay out more to the assisted person's solicitors and counsel than is recovered from the unsuccessful party. The debit balance will be recouped either from the contributions paid by the assisted person before they are returned to him or her, or, if necessary, by the application of the statutory charge. In this respect the assisted person is in a similar position to someone who has been paying privately: it is quite normal for privately paying parties who have been successful in litigation, and who have recovered costs on the standard basis from the other side, to recover only a portion of what they have to pay to their own solicitor.

Therefore, whenever there is a possibility that the statutory charge will arise, legal representatives must treat the question of costs exactly as they would in a case involving privately paying clients. In general litigation, such as personal injuries or housing actions, where costs normally follow the event, the statutory charge is unlikely to be large if the assisted person has been reasonable and the lawyers competent.

It is in matrimonial cases that the charge has caused most controversy, and that is largely because an order for costs against the unsuccessful party is much less likely to be made. The costs imposed on a property or lump

---

4   Reg 110 of the Civil Legal Aid (General) Regulations 1989 (hereafter referred to as the General Regs).
5   RSC Ord 62 r12(1).

sum are also inflated by the costs of proceedings which have nothing to do with obtaining that property or money: namely, injunctions, committals, custody and access. A respondent husband may inflate costs by making injunction and committal proceedings necessary; and increase costs further by failing to produce evidence in ancillary proceedings when required to do so. In such a case, where, at the conclusion of the proceedings, the judge orders that each side bear its own costs, the operation of the statutory charge will mean that the wife petitioner is paying for the husband's misconduct.

There appear to be two main reasons which account for the too frequent failure of lawyers to ask for, and of judges to make, orders for costs in matrimonial cases. The first may be a general misunderstanding about the extent of the protection against an order for costs enjoyed by the unsuccessful assisted party. Matrimonial cases have a higher proportion of assisted parties on both sides than any other category of litigation. Many lawyers, especially barristers, and judges apparently believe that no order for costs may be made against an assisted person – or that if an order is made its amount must be restricted to the size of the maximum contribution. That is, of course, wrong. Section 17(1) provides that the assisted person's

> liability . . . under an order for costs made against him with respect to the proceedings shall not exceed the amount (if any) which is a reasonable one for him to pay having regard to all the circumstances, including the financial resources of all the parties and their conduct in connection with the dispute.

Therefore, behaviour which increases the costs to the other side, will, clearly, be relevant under s17(1).

It is the financial resources at the time that the order is made that are relevant (see further below). Therefore, if, as not infrequently happens, the husband is given a lump sum when the house is transferred to the wife, that lump sum may be taken into account, and indeed should be taken into account.[6]

On interlocutory hearings, where the assisted person's costs cannot be assessed, the order, where appropriate, should be for 'petitioner's costs in cause' or 'costs reserved'. In the latter instance the successful party's representatives must make sure that the judge deals with the reserved costs at the final hearing.

The other reason that costs orders have been made too infrequently in matrimonial cases has been the courts' general reluctance to make orders for costs in such cases. In *Povey v Povey* [1970] 3 All ER 612, it was held

---

6   This is confirmed in *McDonnell v McDonnell* [1977] 1 All ER 766, CA.

that costs do not follow the event as in other areas of litigation. That decision must now, however, be considered in the light of the more recent decision in *Gojkovic v Gojkovic* [1992] 1 All ER 267, CA. In that case the Court of Appeal held that in Family Division cases, *prima facie* the normal indemnity rule of costs following the event should apply as in other types of cases, although it might be more easily displaced and should be unusual in cases involving children. The court in *Gojkovic* also considered the use of *Calderbank* offers.

A *Calderbank* offer (after *Calderbank v Calderbank* [1975] 3 All ER 333, CA) is, in tactical terms, the same as a payment into court but is made in circumstances where, because of the nature of the dispute, a payment into court is not appropriate. One party makes a compromise offer 'without prejudice' to the general issues at the hearing but, if it should turn out that the award made is less advantageous, reserving the right to refer to it on the specific issue of costs.

In *Gojkovic* the court held that where there were substantial assets and a *Calderbank* offer was made, *prima facie* the party refusing the offer was liable for costs after the date of the offer if he or she failed to be awarded an amount in excess of the sum offered. If the *Calderbank* offer was less than the amount awarded in ancillary relief, costs should, *prima facie*, follow the event.

However, a normal order for costs between parties to be taxed on the standard basis, is still likely to leave a shortfall between what can be recovered from an opponent and the costs which are payable to the legal representatives of a successful party. In privately paying cases that shortfall can in a suitable case be covered by an order for costs on an indemnity basis. The difference between the standard basis and the indemnity basis is that on the former any doubts about the reasonableness of a claim or its amount will be resolved in favour of the paying party, ie, the unsuccessful opponent. On the indemnity basis, doubts are resolved in favour of the receiving party, ie, the successful party.

Indemnity costs are payable only in exceptional cases, such as where a party is in contempt of court or has been guilty of conduct which is oppressive or wholly unmeritorious, or if the case is a major test case.

It has been suggested that indemnity costs cannot be ordered to be paid to an assisted party.[7] The argument is that courts have no power to order indemnity costs in legally-aided cases because General Regs reg 107(3)(b) requires all costs to be taxed on the standard basis only. General Regs reg 107 provides:

---

7   See, for instance, Mr Registrar Michael Segal, 'Legal aid and indemnity costs' [1990] Fam Law 417.

(3) Where in any proceedings to which an assisted person is a party: . . .
  (b) the court gives judgment or makes a final decree or order in the
  proceedings, the judgment, decree or order shall include a direction
  (in addition to any other direction as to taxation) that the costs of
  any assisted person shall be taxed on the standard basis.

Section 31(3) of the 1988 Act and General Regs reg 64 preclude the
assisted person's legal representatives from being paid except by the Legal
Aid Board, and therefore they must be paid on the standard basis. It is
further argued that the Legal Aid Board would make a profit if it was paid
on the indemnity basis while paying only on the standard basis, and that
would offend against the general principle that a receiving party is not to
make a profit out of costs. That, however, would appear to be an incorrect
view. First, General Regs reg 107(3)(b) refers to an order on the standard
basis 'in addition to any other direction as to taxation'. Therefore, its
wording does not rule out an order for indemnity costs between the parties
in addition to the normal order for taxation on the standard basis of the
costs which are to be paid out of the Legal Aid Fund to the assisted
person's solicitors. Secondly, this is consistent with the wording of RSC
Ord 62 r3(4) which provides:

The amount of his costs which any party shall be entitled to recover is the
amount allowed after taxation on the standard basis where:
(a) an order is made that the costs of one party to proceedings be paid by
    another party to those procedings; or
(b) an order is made for the payment of costs out of any fund (including the
    Legal Aid Fund)
unless it appears to the court to be appropriate to order costs to be taxed on
the indemnity basis.

Thirdly, there is nothing contrary to principle in the Legal Aid Fund
making a profit out of costs orders. It did so frequently during the 40 years
or more when legal aid High Court profit costs were liable to a 10 per cent
deduction while no such deduction applied to party and party costs.
  Fourthly, General Regs reg 107 (3)(b) is concerned only with orders for
the taxation of costs payable out of the Legal Aid Fund, not with
payments into it. This is indicated not only by the reference, already
mentioned, to 'any other direction as to taxation'; it is also made clear by
the 1988 Act, s31 of which states:

(1) Except as expressly provided by this Act or regulations under it -. . .
  (b) the rights conferred by the Act on a person receving advice, assistance
    or representation under it shall not affect the rights or liabilities of

other parties to the proceedings or the principles on which the discretion of any court or tribunal is normally exercised.

(2) Without prejudice to the generality of subsection (1)(b) above, for the purpose of determining the costs of a legally assisted person in pursuance of an order for costs or an agreement for costs in his favour . . . the services of his legal representative shall be treated as having been provided otherwise than under this Act . . .

Put at its highest, General Regs reg 107(3)(b) could not be said expressly to contradict this provision, and therefore an assisted person is as entitled to an order for indemnity costs as anyone else.

If, despite these arguments, a court remains reluctant to make an order for indemnity costs on the ground that the Legal Aid Board would make a profit, it could provide that the amount of costs payable by the losing party should be limited to the amount which the Fund is required to pay to the assisted person's legal representatives.

A similar argument has arisen where a bill for taxation between parties, whether on the standard or the indemnity basis, includes pre-certificate costs in respect of work done while a green form was in force. This may be in circumstances where either the green form has been submitted for payment, or where that has not yet happened and the solicitors intend to make no claim for payment to the Board if they recover the costs from the other party. In either instance there should be no overpayment, because if payment has been made by the Board the solicitors will have to account for it.

Some courts take the view that they will allow only as much against the paying party as could be claimed against the Legal Aid Fund. They therefore require to know the amount of work authorised on the green form and will not allow more costs against the paying party. This is said to be in accordance with the indemnity principle laid down in *Gundry v Sainsbury* [1910] 1 KB 645, CA, which provides that receiving parties cannot be paid more costs than they are liable for to their own legal representatives. That decision, however, was with reference to privately paying clients and is contrary to s31(1)(b) and (2) above. An argument under s31(1)(b) is supported by the recent judgment of Hirst LJ to the effect that 'the proper approach under this section [s31(1)(b)] is to ask whether the position of a non-legally aided plaintiff would have been different' and he cited in support two earlier cases reversed on appeal since 'but for legal aid the discretion [of the trial judge] would clearly have been exercised the other way'. (*Advanced Technology Structures Ltd v Cray Valley Products Ltd and another* (1992) *Times* 29 December citing *Re Saxton* [1962] 3 All ER 92 and *Blatcher and another v Heaysman and another* [1960] 1 WLR 663.) The 'legally assisted person' referred to in s31(2) includes someone receiving advice and assistance under the green form scheme.[8] Assisted persons' solicitors should therefore argue that the amount authorised under the green form is irrelevant. Nonetheless, the safer course is to make sure that all the work done is covered by green form extensions.

Orders for costs against the assisted person

Where the assisted person has lost a civil action, it is possible for orders for costs to be made in favour of the successful party against the assisted person, or against the Legal Aid Fund, or both.

The court must first consider whether, in accordance with the normal principles, an order for costs should be made against the assisted person. However, if an order is made, s17(1) provides that any liabilities thereunder must not exceed 'the amount (if any)' which it is reasonable for the assisted person to pay 'having regard to all the circumstances, including the means of all the parties and their conduct in connection with the dispute'. The assessment of how much the assisted person has to pay is made by the judge, the registrar or other person before whom the trial or hearing took place (unless there is a direction to the contrary). It may take place either at the time of the hearing, or at an adjourned later date. It may not, however, take place until after the proceedings are concluded.[9] 'Proceedings' in this context has the narrow meaning adopted by the Court of Appeal in *Littaur v Steggles Palmer* [1986] 1 All ER 780 (see p126 above). Therefore, where the certificate has authorised representation in part only of an action, the assessment may take place when that part has come to an end. In other circumstances, where the certificate authorises representation in an entire action, the assessment may take place only when the action is concluded and, therefore, not in respect of costs which have been ordered on an interlocutory application. However, the courts seem to have achieved the same object by ordering that interlocutory costs be set off against any damages or costs to which the assisted party might become entitled later in the proceedings.[10]

On an assessment under s17, all the factors set out in s17(1) must be taken into account. The liability is not necessarily restricted to the amount of the assisted person's legal aid contribution. Thus where an assisted person, for example, has recovered damages which are less than a payment into court, and as a result has to pay costs, the amount of the

8   LAA s2(11).
9   General Regs reg 117.
10   *Lockley v National Blood Transfusion Service* [1992] 1 WLR 492, CA.

damages awarded may be taken into account in assessing liability under s17(1). Similarly, lump sums awarded in matrimonial proceedings may be highly relevant when considering the liability of an unsuccessful assisted party.[11] It must be borne in mind that where the successful party was also legally-aided, the effect of the statutory charge is that any costs not ordered against the unsuccessful party will be borne by the successful party.

There are special rules concerning those acting in a representative, fiduciary or official capacity, or as next friend: their personal means are not taken into account.[12]

A person's house, clothes, household furniture and tools and implements of trade are not taken into account, to the same extent that they are left out of account in determining a person's disposable capital and income on a legal aid means assessment. They are also protected from execution in respect of any order for costs made, although not from execution in respect of, for example, an award of damages.[13]

It is usually worthwhile to obtain an order for costs against an assisted person, even if it is clear that he or she cannot pay at the time. A person for whose benefit an order has been made under s17(1)(e) may apply within six years for the order to be varied on the grounds either that new information which was not reasonably available at the time the order was made has become available, or that there has been a change in the assisted person's circumstances.[14]

It should be noted that s17 is normally of little use in protecting assisted persons against orders for costs in mortgage actions. The section does not prevent the mortgagee adding its costs to the security under the type of provision which is found in most mortgage deeds.[15]

Persons receiving ABWOR (see chapter 3 above) enjoy similar protection.[16]

Orders for costs against the Legal Aid Fund

Where proceedings have been 'finally decided in favour of an unassisted party', in the event that that successful party has been unable to obtain an order for all of his or her standard basis costs against the unsuccessful

---

11 *McDonnell v McDonnell* [1977] 1 All ER 766, CA.
12 General Regs reg 135.
13 LAA s17(3) and General Regs reg 126.
14 General Regs reg 130.
15 *Saunders v Anglia Building Society (No 2)* [1971] 1 All ER 243, HL.
16 LAA s12(1); Legal Advice and Assistance Regulations 1989 (hereafter referred to as Advice and Assistance Regs) reg 34 and Sch 5.

assisted person, it may be possible for that party to obtain an order against the Legal Aid Fund under s18. (Some area offices will agree to pay costs under s18 without the need for a formal order). To obtain such an order, however, it is first of all necessary that the successful party is unassisted in the sense that s/he does not have legal aid (or ABWOR).[17] Persons who have been unassisted for part of the proceedings but are in receipt of legal aid at the time of making an application against the Fund under s18 may be awarded costs against the Fund in respect of that time when they were unassisted. However, whatever they receive could be caught by the statutory charge.[18]

In all cases an order against the Fund may be made only if:

a) the proceedings have been finally decided in favour of the unassisted party;[19]

b) the court has first considered what order should be made against the assisted person under s17(1);[20]

c) the court is satisfied that it is just and equitable in all the circumstances that provision for the costs should be made out of public funds.[21]

If costs are sought against the Fund after proceedings at first instance, the applicant must satisfy two further requirements:[22]

d) the proceedings must have been instituted by the assisted party;

e) the court is satisfied that the unassisted party will suffer severe financial hardship unless an order is made.

The s18 requirements are considered in turn below.

'Proceedings . . . finally decided in favour of an unassisted party' (s18(1))

This phrase means that the unassisted party must have been substantially successful in the proceedings. In *General Accident Limited v Foster* [1972] 3 All ER 877, an assisted person had appealed against an interlocutory judgment against him for £650 where he had been granted leave to defend for the balance of a total of £818. The Court of Appeal reduced the amount for which judgment was given to £450 and gave leave to the assisted person to defend the balance of the claim provided that he paid

17   LAA s18(1); see *Almond v Miles* (1992) *Times* 4 February and *Awad v Pillai and Nathanielse* [1982] RTR 266, CA as illustrations of how a successful defendant may be disadvantaged by being on legal aid.

18   *Re H and another (minors) (No 2)* (1992) 142 NLJ 1004 HL.

19   LAA s18(1).

20   LAA s18(3).

21   LAA s18(4)(c).

22   LAA s18(4)(b).

£341.50 into court. In considering whether an order should be made against the Legal Aid Fund under the identical predecessor legislation to s18, the Court of Appeal held that the unassisted party had been substantially successful and that accordingly an order should be made. The assisted person had asked for unconditional leave to defend and the unassisted party had successfully resisted.

Similarly, in *Kelly v London Transport Executive* [1982] 2 All ER 842, it was held that the proceedings had been finally decided in favour of the defendant where the plaintiff had been awarded damages of £75 but the defendant had paid £750 into court.

Any proceedings in respect of which a separate certificate could be issued are treated as separate proceedings for the purposes of s18.[23] Therefore, an unassisted party can apply under s18 when successful in interlocutory proceedings although the assisted person is finally successful in the action as a whole.[24]

'Just and equitable in all the circumstances' (s18(4)(c))

In *Hanning v Maitland (No 2)* [1970] 1 All ER 812, the Court of Appeal held that the words 'just and equitable' were not a term of 'art' or capable of precise definition: the court has a wide discretion and may consider the conduct of the party before and during the litigation. The fact that the unassisted party has been successful is a most important consideration, and in some circumstances may be sufficient to make it just and equitable that an order should be made.[25] The financial position of the party applying for the order is relevant only to the extent that it may show that it would be just and equitable to make the order; it may not be regarded as a contrary consideration.[26] The fact that the successful unassisted party may not be personally responsible for paying his or her costs, because, for example, an insurance company or an organisation such as the Automobile Association has undertaken to indemnify, is irrelevant.[27] It may be just and equitable to make an order in favour of a large, wealthy limited company, a public enterprise or a public authority such as a chief constable.[28]

---

23 General Regs reg 134(2).
24 See, for example, *O'Sullivan v Herdmans Ltd (No 2)* [1988] 1 WLR 1373.
25 *Davies v Taylor (No 2)* [1973] 1 All ER 959.
26 *General Accident Ltd v Foster*, above.
27 *Davies v Taylor*, n24 *supra* and *Lewis v Averay (No 2)* [1973] 2 All ER 231.
28 *General Accident Ltd v Foster*, above; *Kelly v London Transport*, above; *Maynard v Osmond (No 2)* [1979] 1 All ER 483.

'What order for costs should be made against the assisted party'
(s18(3))

Before an order may be made under s18, the court must consider the personal liability of the assisted person to pay costs under s17(1). The order will be made against the Fund only for the balance over and above what the assisted person may be ordered to pay.

'Proceedings were instituted by the assisted party' (s18(4)(b))

This is a test of substance, not of form. Regulation 134(2) of the General Regs provides that any proceedings in respect of which a separate legal aid certificate might properly be issued must be treated as separate proceedings for the purposes of s18. This means that, for example, a counter-claim may be treated as separate proceedings, and therefore an unassisted party's costs of successfully defending a counter-claim will be recoverable from the Fund. Where the counter-claim has been the main or only substantive issue, those costs might, of course, amount to most or all of the costs of the action.[29]

In *Landau v Purvis* (1986) *Times* 12 August, the first defendant, who was legally-aided and had lost the action, was ordered to pay the costs of the third defendant, who had been successful and who was not legally-aided. The plaintiff, who had been successful against the first defendant, was also legally-aided. When the third defendant was unable to recover his costs from the first defendant under s17, he applied for an order against the Fund under s18. Mr Gerald Godfrey QC, sitting as a deputy High Court judge, refused the application. He held that in order to satisfy the requirements of s18(4)(b) the order for costs must be against the 'assisted party' who instituted the proceedings. In this case, although the proceedings had been instituted by an assisted party, that was not the party against whom the order for costs had been made. It is worth noting that the consequences would have been different if the judge had made a different type of order for costs initially. In cases with one successful and one unsuccessful defendant the court has a discretion as to costs. The usual order is that the plaintiff should pay the costs of the successful defendant and be reimbursed by the unsuccessful defendant (called a *Bullock* order after *Bullock v London General Omnibus Co* [1907] 1 KB 264). The alternative, adopted in *Landau v Purvis*, is that the unsuccessful defendant is ordered to pay costs direct to the successful defendant (called a *Sanderson* order after *Sanderson v Blyth Theatre Co* [1903] 2 KB 533). In

29   As in *R & T Thew v Reeves* [1981] 2 All ER 964.

deciding which course to follow, the judge should try to spread equitably the hardship caused by an impecunious unsuccessful defendant.[30]

Had the judge in *Landau v Purvis* made a *Bullock* order for the legally-aided plaintiff to pay the third defendant's costs, the plaintiff's means, including any damages and costs recovered from other defendants, would have been assessed under s17. If he were found to have had insufficient resources to meet the order in favour of the third defendant, the latter would have been able to claim against the Legal Aid Fund under s18.

'Severe financial hardship' (s18(4)(b))

Earlier decisions on the words 'severe financial hardship' were criticised by Lord Denning in *Hanning v Maitland (No 2)* [1970] 1 All ER 812, on the ground that they had construed the words:

> so as to give emphasis to the word 'severe'. But in the light of experience, I do not think they should be construed so strictly. In future, the words should be construed so as to exclude insurance companies; and commercial companies who are in a considerable way of business; and wealthy folk who can meet the costs without feeling it. But they should not be construed so as to exclude people of modest income or modest capital who find it hard to bear their own costs.

In *Hanning*, decided in 1970, the successful party, a single man earning £936 a year, had capital of about £2,700 and had incurred costs of about £325 in defending the action. By way of comparison the upper limits for disposable income and capital were in that year £700 and £500 respectively.

A company may suffer severe financial hardship.[31] In principle, a local authority or any other large body may also claim to suffer 'severe financial hardship'. However, it must produce evidence to show real impairment of the ability to function normally.[32]

It is not only extreme wealth which may disqualify an applicant from obtaining an order. So may extreme poverty. Thus, in *Kelly v London Transport* (above) the defendant did not obtain an order against the Fund. There was evidence that, even after a grant from the Greater London Council of £179 million, the defendant's financial deficit for the relevant financial year would be about £100,000. Therefore, payment by it of some £8,000 in costs would not make 'any appreciable difference'.

Successful parties to whom s18(4)(b) applies will not necessarily be

---

30   *Bankamerica Finance v Nock* [1988] 1 All ER 81, HL.
31   *R & T Thew Ltd v Reeves*, n29 *supra*.
32   *R v Greenwich London Borough Council ex parte Lovelace* [1991] 3 WLR 1015, CA.

paid the full amount of their costs. They are entitled to be paid only as much out of the Fund as will remove the severe financial hardship. The means of a spouse are relevant, but only to the extent that someone with a financially self-supporting spouse is better off than someone whose spouse is entirely dependent.[33]

An order may be obtained under s18 against the Fund only to the extent that the unsuccessful party was legally-aided. Thus no order will lie against the Fund in respect of costs incurred before the issue of a certificate to the unsuccessful party, or after the certificate has been discharged or revoked. Similarly, where the assisted party had legal aid only to defend an action, no order may be made in favour of an unassisted person who successfully defends a counter-claim the bringing of which was not authorised by the certificate.[34]

Assistance by way of representation (ABWOR)

Section 13 applies provisions to ABWOR which are practically identical to those of s18.

First instance or not?

It is important to determine for the purposes of ss13 and 18 whether costs have been incurred in a court of first instance or in an appeal, because in the former case the applicant must satisfy the two additional tests ((d) and (e) above). This question was considered in *Megarity v The Law Society; Gayway Linings Ltd v The Law Society* [1981] 1 All ER 641, where the House of Lords held that all proceedings, including interlocutory proceedings, on appeal to an appellate court, such as the Court of Appeal, were separate from the proceedings of the court of first instance and therefore not subject to the additional tests. Whether or not an appeal to a judge in chambers from a master or registrar would be separate from the proceedings at first instance would depend on whether or not the order by the registrar or master would finally decide an action by giving judgment for one party.

Megarity arose out of a personal injuries action in which the plaintiff had been ordered by a High Court judge to submit unconditionally to an examination by the defendant's medical adviser, pending which all further proceedings were stayed. The legally-aided plaintiff unsuccessfully appealed to the Court of Appeal. The Legal Aid Fund was ordered to pay the costs although the main suit had not been concluded and the possibility remained, therefore, that the legally-aided plaintiff would be ultimately successful. The House of Lords held that proceedings in

33 *Adams v Malcolm Riley Associates* [1988] 1 All ER 89.
34 As in *R & T Thew Ltd v Reeves*, n29 *supra*.

separate courts, such as the High Court and the Court of Appeal, were separate proceedings and that, since the Court of Appeal was by definition an appellate court, those proceedings could not be of first instance.

In *Gayway Linings*, the appeal by the legally-aided defendant was to a judge in chambers from an order of a registrar striking out the defence and entering judgment for the plaintiff. The appeal was unsuccessful. The House of Lords held that, although the original appeal had been heard by a judge in chambers rather than by the Court of Appeal, it did not fall within the definition of 'first instance' because the order appealed against was one which finally disposed of the action. The position would, otherwise, have been different. As Lord Diplock made clear:

> Nothing that I have said should be taken as encouraging the making of orders under section 13(1) [now s18(1)] in respect of an unassisted party's costs in an appeal from the registrar or master to a judge in chambers from any other kind of interlocutory order than one that finally disposes of the action.

The Divisional Court is a court of first instance for the purposes of s18, although it may not be when reviewing the decision of an inferior court or tribunal.[35]

Procedures under ss17 and 18

The procedures to be followed on the assessment of an assisted person's liability for costs to the opposing party or to obtain an order against the Legal Aid Fund are set out in regs 123 to 133[36] and regs 134 to 147 of the General Regs.[37] In *Din v Wandsworth London Borough Council (No 2)* [1982] 1 All ER 1022, the House of Lords held that orders for costs should not be made provisionally, as a matter of course, against the Legal Aid Fund subject to the legal aid authorities being given an opportunity to make representations, since that would place the onus on the legal aid authorities of showing why an order should not be made. Nonetheless, that has continued to be the practice.

Procedures under ss12 and 13

The procedure for assessing an ABWOR client's liability to an opposing party for costs is set out in Advice and Assistance Regs reg 34 and Sch 5. Regulation 35 provides that, before a court makes an order against the

---

35 *R v Greenwich London Borough Council ex parte Lovelace (No2)* [1991] 3 WLR 1015 overruling *R v Leeds County Court, ex parte Morris and another* [1990] 1 All ER 550.
36 LAA s17, costs against an assisted person.
37 LAA s18, costs out of the Fund.

Legal Aid Fund, it shall give the area director an opportunity to make representations. However, apart from that, no specific procedure is set out in respect of s13. Courts will no doubt adapt the procedures laid down for civil legal aid in regs 134 to 147 of the General Regs.

Recovery by the Legal Aid Fund from the assisted person

Any costs which the Legal Aid Fund is ordered to pay to an assisted person's opponent cannot be recovered by the Fund by using the mechanism of the statutory charge.[38] However, in *R v Leeds County Court ex parte Morris and another* [1990] 1 All ER 550, the Divisional Court achieved the same object by ordering that monies paid out by the Fund under what is now s18 should be set off against compensation which the Fund was holding on the assisted person's behalf. Watkins LJ stated:

> It surely cannot be right that public funds should be resorted to for payment of an assisted person's liability for costs when that person has the means to do so herself.

The Divisional Court's decision was made on the application of the Legal Aid Board, but it seems to be contrary to the wording and the scheme of the 1988 Act (and its predecessors) and is logically absurd. As mentioned previously, s18(3) requires the court to consider what order for costs should be made against the assisted person under s17 before it makes an order against the Fund. Having made the order against the Fund, the court cannot then remove the basis on which it was made and evade the protective provisions of the Act and General Regs, by ordering the assisted person to pay more than it has already decided is the correct liability under s17.

Orders against solicitors and barristers

Solicitors may be ordered to pay costs under the court's inherent jurisdiction if they have shown gross misconduct, or under s51 of the Supreme Court Act 1981 as amended by s4 of the Courts and Legal Services Act 1990 or under RSC Ord 62 r11 in a wider range of circumstances. The last-named provision states that a solicitor who in any proceedings incurs costs unreasonably or improperly, or wastes costs by failing to conduct the proceedings with reasonable competence and expedition, may:

a) have the costs due to him or her from the client disallowed;

---

38   *O'Sullivan v Herdmans Ltd (No 2)* [1988] 1 WLR 1373, HL.

b) be directed to repay to the client any costs which the client has paid to the solicitor or other party; or
c) be directed personally to indemnify the other party against costs payable by him or her.

Ord 62 r11, which is also followed in the county court, applies whether or not the party for whom the solicitor is acting is legally-aided. It replaced the previous provision, Ord 62 r8, on 28 April 1986. The old Ord 62 r8 was substantially different, and in particular contained a reference to 'any other misconduct or default', which is not found in the present Ord 62 r11. The effect of the change was considered by the Court of Appeal in *Sinclair-Jones v Kay* [1988] 2 All ER 611. The Court held that it was no longer necessary, before an order could be made, to show that the solicitor was guilty of gross misconduct: it was sufficient if the court was satisfied, in accordance with the wording of r11, that the costs had been 'incurred unreasonably or improperly . . . or wasted by failure to conduct proceedings with reasonable competence and expedition'. In *Sinclair-Jones*, the solicitors, who had been late in serving notice of issue of a legal aid certificate, were ordered to pay the costs wasted by the opposing party.

A differently constituted Court of Appeal challenged the correctness of *Sinclair-Jones* in *Holden & Co v CPS* (also known as *Re Crown Court at Lewes* [1990] 1 All ER 368) but its decision was obiter. In any event, the Court of Appeal Civil Division confirmed the correctness of *Sinclair-Jones* in *Gupta v Comer* [1991] 1 QB 629, CA, and the matter was put beyond doubt by s4 of the Courts and Legal Services Act which amended s51 of the Supreme Court Act 1981 so as effectively to repeat, with minor changes, the provisions of Ord 62 r 11 as interpreted in *Sinclair-Jones*, and to extend the liability of solicitors to cover counsel.

The test is now a simple one of negligence. This means, first, that because it is much easier to establish liability under s51 and Ord 62 r11, the court's inherent jurisdiction over solicitors is of little practical importance. Secondly, a number of decisions made under either the court's inherent jurisdiction or the old Ord 62 r8, holding that solicitors must be guilty of gross misconduct before orders for costs can be made against them, can no longer be relied on. Thus, the former leading case of *Myers v Elman* [1939] 4 All ER 484, which held that solicitors must be guilty of 'serious misconduct' before an order can be made, is at most authoritative only on the effect of the court's inherent jurisdiction. The decision in *Mauroux v Sociedade Comercial Abel Pereira da Fonseca SARL* [1972] 2 All ER 1085 – that failure to serve notice of issue of a legal aid certificate is not sufficient to justify an order for costs against the solicitors – can no longer be relied on. The same can be said of *Currie and*

Co v The Law Society [1977] QB 990, in which the court held that in order to incur liability the solicitor must be shown to be guilty of 'a serious dereliction of duty'.

In R & T Thew Ltd v Reeves (No 2) [1982] 3 All ER 1086, Lord Denning held, following Myers v Elman (above), that the conduct of the solicitor must be 'inexcusable and such as to merit reproof' before an order could be made. Again, that no longer represents the law, but it is possible that on the facts, as found by the court, the result would be the same under Ord 62 r11.

The plaintiff had been unable to recover from the Legal Aid Fund the costs of successfully defending a counter-claim because the unsuccessful defendant's certificate had only granted legal aid to defend the plaintiff's claim and had not included bringing a counter-claim. The court considered whether the defendant's solicitors should be ordered to pay the plaintiff's costs under the old Ord 62 r8. The solicitors had stated on the application form that legal aid was merely required to defend the plaintiff's claim. However, the application and accompanying documents showed clearly that the only substantive issue was over a possible counter-claim. The area office file disclosed that it was on that basis that legal aid was granted, and everybody involved in the case went ahead on that basis.

It is also unlikely that on the facts, as found in Orchard v South Eastern Electricity Board [1987] 1 All ER 95, that case, again under the old Ord 62 r8, would be decided differently today. The defendants applied for costs against the plaintiff's solicitors, who had obtained legal aid for their clients and pursued a claim which turned out to be a fiction. The trial judge had refused an order for costs against the solicitors. The Court of Appeal upheld his decision. The jurisdiction to order costs against solicitors should be exercised with great care and discretion and only in clear cases, the Court held. It should not rest solely on inference without evidence, and it was not for solicitors or counsel to impose a screen through which a litigant had to pass before bringing a claim before the court. The Master of the Rolls, Sir John Donaldson, accepted that:

> the plaintiff's solicitors had a duty not to further a claim which could be characterised as an abuse of the process of the court. It was contended that no competent counsel, solicitor or expert could possibly have supported the plaintiff's claim. In the end what mattered was what the judge had thought. He had unrivalled opportunities for hearing the plaintiff's case put and knowing what it was like before it was destroyed by cross-examination and the deployment of the Board's evidence. None of the Board's submissions caused the slightest doubt about the unassailability of the judge's conclusions.

Other cases also continue to give useful guidance. To initiate or continue an action unreasonably when it has no or substantially no chance of success constituted sufficient conduct for an order under Ord 62 r8. In *Davy-Chiesman v Davy-Chiesman* [1984] 1 All ER 321, CA, an order was made under this provision against the solicitor although he had followed counsel's advice. The circumstances were, however, unusual. Mr Davy-Chiesman, a criminal bankrupt, had legal aid, limited to obtaining counsel's opinion, to be represented in ancillary proceedings and an application for access to his child. Counsel advised that the limitation should be removed but that Mr Davy-Chiesman should not apply for a lump-sum order because any money would be taken by his trustee in bankruptcy. After the limitation had been removed counsel changed his mind and conducted a lengthy application for a lump sum, which was dismissed. At no time did the solicitor inform the Law Society that the proceedings were being conducted upon a basis different from that on which legal aid had been granted. The solicitor was ordered to pay his own client's costs and those of the other side under the old Ord 62 r8. His duty to inform the legal aid committee was independent of counsel's, and his failure was 'a serious dereliction of duty'.

Lord Justice Dillon observed:

> the solicitor's duty is not just to pass on any views expressed by counsel; he has to consider for himself the effect of the change of circumstances, to use his own common sense and to form his own opinion, though obviously in doing that he will take the view expressed by counsel into account.

A further example of solicitors being ordered to pay costs is found in *Novoth v Tanner* [1984] 5 CL 199 ((1983) 12 October (Stroud County Court), which concerned a dispute over a house in joint names. Both sides were legally-aided. When counsel exchanged authorities the day before the hearing it was clear that A had no claim to an equity in the house. A's counsel offered to settle for £250 with no order for costs. B's counsel offered £100, with the same order. After negotiation, B's counsel met A's counsel's original offer: £250 with no order for costs. A's counsel refused to accept. The case started and was adjourned. B's counsel wrote to A's counsel pointing out, with reference to *Kelly v London Transport Executive*, that A must be unreasonable in rejecting an offer identical to the first offer he himself had proposed and asking for comment on the legal aid position. No formal reply was received to the letter or to a subsequent reminder. B paid £250 into court, which A did not accept within the time limit. On the afternoon before the resumed hearing, A's solicitor served notice of application to accept the money in court out of time. At the resumed hearing this application was granted and a further application made for A's costs. B's counsel applied for B's costs, citing *Kelly* and *R & T Thew v Reeves (No 2)* [1982] 3 All ER 1086, and reading the letter written to A's counsel. The deputy county court registrar held that the failure to appreciate the effect of the Court of Appeal decision was an error by A's solicitors but justifiable until this was made clear at the original hearing. Carrying on the action after that date was not justified. Legal aid taxation of the costs of A and B was ordered. No order for costs was made up to and including the original hearing, but A's solicitors were ordered personally to pay B's costs from that date.

In *Kelly*, Lord Denning indicated a long list of duties which were owed by lawyers in the conduct of legally-aided litigation. His remarks, however, were obiter and merely factual illustrations of the circumstances in which an order might have been made under RSC Ord 62 r8. To the extent that those illustrations implied wide general duties on the part of solicitors and counsel for legally-aided litigants, they are not a correct statement of the law.[39] Lord Denning's remarks have not been given greater authority by the changes introduced by Ord 62 r11 and s4 of the Courts and Legal Services Act 1990.

In addition to RSC Ord 62 r11, there is specific provision in reg 109 of the General Regs for the disallowance of solicitors' legal aid costs (see above). Costs may be disallowed or reduced where the taxing officer considers that they have been wasted by 'failure to conduct the proceedings with reasonable competence and expedition' or 'where the solicitor has without good reason delayed putting in his bill for taxation'. Regulation 109 also applies to counsel's fees. Notice must be served on the solicitors or counsel in question before such a reduction may take place.

Taxation by the court

The position of the assisted person

The assisted person has the right to take part in the taxation process if s/he has an 'interest' in the taxation. The circumstances in which the assisted person has an interest include where the statutory charge is likely to arise or where the outcome of the taxation is likely to affect the amount of contribution which is returned.

Under reg 119 of the General Regs, solicitors must explain to legally-aided clients the extent of their financial interest in the taxation and advise them what steps they can take.

---

39   See discussion at January 1983 *LAG Bulletin* 8 and March 1983, 14.

Courts will return bills unless solicitors certify in writing:

- either that the assisted person has no financial interest in the bill; or
- that s/he has an interest and why (contribution and/or statutory charge), has been supplied with a copy of the bill, and has indicated whether or not he or she wants to be heard on the taxation.

Costs due to the assisted person's involvement in the taxation process are covered by the original legal aid certificate, even where it has been revoked.[40] The full costs of a legal aid taxation, however, are borne by the Legal Aid Fund. Neither an assisted person's contribution, nor the statutory charge may be used to recover the costs of a legal aid taxation.[41]

In each case the court taxing officer must have authority to carry out the taxation. The authority is usually in the form of a court order for legal aid taxation, which may be an order made in the course of interlocutory proceedings, so giving solicitors effectively an opportunity to be paid on account (see above). The authority to tax may also be a notice of discharge or revocation of the legal aid certificate. Therefore, if a case has come to an end and the solicitors have forgotten to obtain an order for taxation, authority to tax may be obtained by having the certificate discharged.

Taxation of costs to be paid out of the Legal Aid Fund is made on the standard basis. This requires payment of a reasonable amount in respect of all costs reasonably incurred.[42] Any doubts are resolved in favour of the paying party, in this case the Legal Aid Fund. It is the same as the basis on which costs are taxed between winners and losers of litigation. However, it should not be assumed from this that the costs which a successful legally-aided litigant will recover from his or her opponent will therefore be the same as the costs payable out of the Legal Aid Fund. Some costs attributable, for example, to satisfying queries or special requirements of the Legal Aid Board may be recoverable from the Legal Aid Fund but not from an opponent. That is how the statutory charge normally arises.

There are also some special features of legal aid taxation which should be noted:

a) costs for which prior authority has been obtained from the Legal Aid Board must be allowed;[43]
b) an assisted person attending court to give evidence may be allowed the normal expenses payable to a witness, whether successful or not, but not any other allowances or expenses;
c) counsel may supply a memorandum to the court setting out any factors

---

40 General Regs reg 120.
41 General Regs reg 119(2).
42 Ord 62 r12(1).
43 General Regs reg 63(1) and (2).

which influence the fee; if the solicitor does not feel that counsel's fees can be supported at the taxation he or she should inform counsel in advance;

d) where there are joint parties and only some are legally-aided, the costs must be apportioned;

e) if an assisted person's solicitor employs a solicitor agent, that agent's costs should be included as part of the profit costs of the principal, who should account to the agent by private arrangement;

f) if a foreign lawyer is instructed, those fees should be shown as disbursements.

If solicitors are unhappy with the result of the taxation they should appeal – or 'carry in objections to the taxation'. This may be done under reg 113(2)(a) of the General Regs where an assisted person is dissatisfied with the costs allowed against another party on taxation; or in the case of the assisted person's solicitor, under reg 113(2)(b) of the General Regs in respect of the costs allowed against another party or in respect of the taxation of costs payable out of the Legal Aid Fund. In either event, before the objections may be made, the assisted person's solicitor must obtain authority from the area committee.[44] If the Legal Aid Board refuses authority, that may, in an appropriate case, be challenged by judicial review. However, unless the assisted person has a financial interest in the appeal such proceedings must be brought in the name of the solicitors alone.[45]

Barristers have the right, with the agreement of the area committee, to appeal against the results of a taxation – and solicitors must inform barristers' clerks in writing of the results of a taxation within seven days and are under a duty to report counsel's objections to the area committee or the Board.[46] If an appeal is authorised the solicitor must conduct it.[47]

When the taxation has been completed, the court issues a taxing officer's certificate or allocatur (the jargon varies with the type of court), which sets out the amounts allowed for profit costs, counsel's fees and disbursements, together with the VAT. The solicitor sends this to the Legal Aid Board, together with the appropriate form of report on case and necessary documentation. If the solicitor is holding any money which has been recovered or preserved in the proceedings and which has not yet been paid over to the Board, as it should have been in accordance with reg 90 of the General Regs, a cheque should accompany the report on case. Eventually, payment will be made to the solicitor through the banking

44   General Regs reg 114.
45   R v Legal Aid Board ex parte Bateman (1992) 142 NLJ 347.
46   General Regs reg 112.
47   General Regs reg 116.

clearing system, BACS, or as part of a composite cheque which the Legal Aid Board sends to firms every two weeks in respect of monies due to them out of the Legal Aid Fund. Counsel will be paid separately.

Assessment by the area director

In some circumstances it is not possible to have the costs taxed by the court and they *must* instead be assessed by or on behalf of the area director. In yet other circumstances it is possible for the solicitor to short-circuit the process of getting payment by using assessment by the area director as an alternative to taxation.

On an assessment, the director allows those costs which would be allowed by the court on a taxation on the standard basis.[48]

Assessment by the area director is mandatory where the solicitor or counsel has ceased to act before the proceedings are begun and there has been no subsequent change of solicitor under the certificate.[49]

In the following circumstances, under the General Regs, solicitors may elect assessment by the area director instead of taxation by the court:

a) where the case has been brought to an end by judgment, decree or final order, the costs to be paid by an opposing party to the assisted person have been agreed and the assisted person's solicitor and counsel are prepared to accept these in full satisfaction of their claim against the Legal Aid Fund.[50] Solicitors and counsel may choose to accept the costs from the opposing party although these may be lower than those otherwise payable from the Legal Aid Fund because such costs will probably be paid more quickly if the process of taxation is avoided. Area offices may shorten the process even further by discharging the certificate on receipt of a letter from the solicitors asking for this to be done and stating that they have no claim against the Legal Aid Fund. The solicitors then retain the costs they have been paid by the other party (any payments they have received on account of disbursements or profit costs will be deducted from future payments from the Legal Aid Board);

b) where the solicitor considers that the total amount which s/he and counsel would receive under a taxation would be less than £1,000;[51]

c) where proceedings have been settled without any direction of the court as to costs, on terms that include an agreed sum in respect of standard

48 General Regs reg 105(1).
49 General Regs reg 105(2).
50 General Regs reg 106(1).
51 General Regs reg 105(3)(a).

basis costs which the solicitor and counsel are willing to accept in full satisfaction of the work done;[52]

d) where there are special circumstances in which taxation is against the interests of the assisted person or would increase the amount payable from the Fund;[53] or

e) where the solicitor's claim is for costs incurred in recovering sums payable to the Fund after a direction or order has been made for legal aid taxation.[54]

Regulation 105A requires that the assisted person must be sent a copy of the bill at least 21 days before it is sent for assessment. The Legal Aid Board suggests a signed certificate to be sent with the bill in the following terms:[55]

> I certify that the copy of the attached bill has been provided to the assisted person pursuant to Regulation 105A of the Civil Legal Aid (General) Regulations 1989, with an explanation of his/her financial interest in the assessment of the bill and his/her right to make written representations on the bill and thereafter on any subsequent review to the area committee or appeal to the Legal Aid Board's Costs Appeals Committee. I confirm that 21 days have passed since the copy bill was provided to the assisted person.

Where a solicitor or counsel is dissatisfied with an amount allowed on an assessment by the area director, s/he may make written representations within 21 days to the area committee.[56] The Legal Aid Board has recommended to area committees that they should allow solicitors and/or counsel to attend on a review as well as to make written representations. If they want to do so, they should make their request at the same time they make their written representations, and if the assisted person has an interest s/he should also be given an opportunity to attend.[57]

If they are dissatisfied with the area committee's decision, solicitors or counsel may ask the committee, within 21 days, to certify that a point of principle of general importance is involved.[58] If the committee does so certify, the solicitor or counsel may then, within a further 21 days, appeal to a committee of the Legal Aid Board.[59]

---

52   General Regs reg 105(3)(b).
53   General Regs reg 105(3)(c).
54   General Regs reg 105(3)(d).
55   Legal Aid Focus 4th issue and Note for Guidance 13-07.
56   General Regs regs 105(4) and 106(3).
57   (1992) 89/9 LS Gaz 19.
58   General Regs reg 105(5).
59   Reg 105(6).

Checklist

Claims for payment should be made as promptly and efficiently as possible. At the end of a case solicitors must consider which is the most advantageous way to deal with the question of costs. Might it be done by assessment rather than by a full taxation? If taxation is necessary, the solicitor must:

a) immediately after judgment etc. ask counsel's clerk for a fee note and ask witnesses for details of their expenses;

b) forward all papers to the cost draftsperson, unless the bill can be prepared in the office;

c) when the bill is returned, check the entries and submit the bill and papers to the taxing authorities;

d) if the court makes a provisional taxation, check and return this quickly or attend an appointment;

e) if counsel's fees have been reduced, so inform counsel in writing,[60] ask counsel's clerk if there are any objections, and, if not, amend the fee note;

f) if the assisted person, solicitor or counsel is dissatisfied, ask the area committee for authority under reg 113 or 116 of the General Regs, notify the taxing officer and, if appropriate, the opposite party;

g) complete the bill, prepare the summary, return it to the court with the taxing fee, keep a made-up copy of the bill on the file;

h) when the taxing officer's certificate or allocatur arrives, send it to the area committee immediately together with a completed form of report on case and any other necessary documents;

i) wait for payment and ensure that office procedure requires that individual caseworkers are notified of the contents of the periodic legal aid cheque in order that they may close the file.

Final accounting

The solicitor is under a number of duties in relation to the statutory charge and final accounting to the client. These duties include:

a) informing the area director and sending a copy of an order or agreement by which property is recovered or preserved;[61]

b) paying any money received to the Board unless the area director agrees otherwise or the postponement provisions apply;[62]

60   General Regs reg 112(1).
61   General Regs reg 90(1)(a).
62   General Regs reg 90(1)(b).

c) if the postponement provisions apply:
   (i) providing the area director with sufficient information to register
       a charge or sending a copy of an undertaking to that effect from
       other solicitors or a registered conveyancer;[63]
   (ii) if the purchase has not been concluded within a year from the
       order or agreement, sending the money to the Legal Aid
       Board.[64]

These duties have also been referred to in chapter 8, together with the
sanctions that may be applied to solicitors who are in breach.

Where costs or monies have been recovered or preserved, practitioners
should send the following documents to the area office:

a) Form CLA 16 claim for costs;
b) taxation certificate or allocatur;
c) orders for inter partes costs;
d) where money was awarded a copy of the judgment;
e) separate completed Costs 1 forms for each debtor;
f) any costs, or judgment debt already recovered and not previously sent
   (but see reg 90(2) and p144).

A Costs 1 form is only required where the money is still to be collected
and therefore not where costs or monies have been recovered in full by the
solicitor before the final accounting.

Where the enforcement of the order for costs is the only outstanding
item of work, solicitors should file a notice of change with the court in
favour of the Legal Aid Board, Debt Recovery Unit, Greencroft House, 12
Roger Street, London WC1N 2JL. (*Legal Aid Focus* 8).

The Legal Aid Board must account for any money it has received on the
assisted person's behalf and pay any balance due after deducting:[65]

a) any part paid to it in respect of standard basis costs;
b) any money due to it under the statutory charge provisions; and
c) any costs incurred enforcing orders in favour of the assisted person
   under reg 91(1) of the General Regs.

The Legal Aid Board must pay the balance to the assisted person unless it
has been notified under reg 103(2) of the General Regs that pre-certificate
costs are outstanding (see p144 above).

63   General Regs reg 96(6).
64   General Regs reg 96(7).
65   General Regs reg 92.

Payment from the Legal Aid Board of pre- and post-legal aid costs

Solicitors may be paid for work done before the issue of an emergency certificate in the limited circumstances where reg 103(6) of the General Regs applies (see p93).

Regulation 103(6) is the sole exception to the general rule that costs may only be paid out of public money in the Legal Aid Fund in respect of work done before the issue of a legal aid certificate. However, in some circumstances a solicitor may recover costs incurred before the issue of a certificate out of money standing to the assisted person's credit with the Legal Aid Fund. Regulation 103(2) of the General Regs provides that where a person receives legal aid after proceedings have been begun, any solicitor who has acted on behalf of the assisted person in those proceedings and who has by law a lien on any documents necessary for the proceedings, which s/he has handed over subject to that lien, may give notice of the fact to the appropriate area committee. In that event, if any money is recovered on behalf of the assisted person, the Legal Aid Board must pay the solicitor's costs out of that money, or divide it pro rata if the money is insufficient to cover the costs incurred before and after the grant of legal aid.[66]

Where the pre-legal aid costs have not been taxed, there is provision for an assessment to be done by the area committee on a solicitor and own client basis and for the client to be heard.[67]

66 General Regs reg 103(4).
67 General Regs reg 103(5).

CHAPTER 10

Statutory charge

Introduction

The Legal Aid Fund has first call on any money or property recovered or preserved for the assisted person as a result of the legally-aided proceedings, up to the amount which the Fund has paid out in legal costs to solicitors and counsel (including VAT) on behalf of the assisted person and which the Fund has not otherwise recovered either through an order for costs made against the other side or through the contribution which the assisted person has previously paid.[1] The same general rule applies, with necessary modifications, in respect of charges or fees payable out of the Fund under the green form scheme.[2]

Effect of the charge

Generally

The amount of legal costs which a successful party recovers from the other party is likely to be less in most cases than the amount of the costs which s/he will have to pay to his or her own lawyers (see further chapter 9). In the case of an assisted person, it is likely to be less than the Legal Aid Fund has to pay out. The effect of the statutory charge is that the Fund recovers this deficiency out of the fruits of the litigation, unless it has already been covered by the assisted person's contribution.

Example

Anne Brown has won an action for damages for personal injuries suffered at work through the negligence of her employer. She is awarded £10,000 damages and costs. The costs payable by the defendant are taxed at £2,000, the costs payable by the Legal Aid Fund are taxed at £2,450 and Anne Brown

---

1 LAA s16(6).
2 LAA s11(2).

has previously paid a contribution of £250. The defendant pays the taxed costs. The statutory charge is calculated by deducting the total of the costs recovered from the other party and of the contribution, from the costs payable by the Legal Aid Fund, as follows:

	£
recovered costs from other party	2,000
contribution	250
total (to be deducted)	2,250
payable out of Legal Aid Fund	2,450
less total from above	2,250
total deficiency	200

The statutory charge will be, therefore, £200. This £200 is deducted from the damages award of £10,000, leaving £9,800. (Of course, the Fund will also retain Anne Brown's contribution of £250.)

The example highlights the importance of obtaining orders for costs against the opposing party wherever possible at all stages of the legally-aided proceedings, even where the client has a nil contribution, and the importance of enforcing any such orders. If successful in the litigation, the client will have to pay out of the fruits of that litigation any costs which are not recovered from the other party. The effect of the statutory charge is to place an assisted person who is successful in litigation in almost the same position as a party who is paying privately. When the statutory charge bites, legal aid works as though it is a loan to the assisted person to finance litigation which must be repaid when the litigation is over. This is shown clearly when there is a payment into court.

Example

Again Anne Brown has recovered damages of £10,000. But the defendant had paid £11,000 into court three months before the trial. Ms Brown's costs up to the payment in and payable by the defendant are £800. The defendant's costs from the date of the payment in are £1,800, which Ms Brown is ordered to pay under s17(1) (the award is taken into account in making the assessment under s17(1)). Ms Brown's legal aid costs are £2,450. She has paid a contribution of £250.

	£
payable out of Legal Aid Fund	2,450
less contribution	250
	2,200

The statutory charge will therefore be £2,200 and, in addition, Ms Brown will have to pay the balance of £1,000 to the defendant, leaving her with £6,800 out of the total of £10,000 awarded or, if her contribution is taken into account as well, with a net balance of £6,550.

Advisers must always bear this in mind, particularly when negotiating a settlement, and when considering a payment into court, an open offer or whether to appeal. They should also make their clients fully aware of how the statutory charge works, remind them when necessary and keep them informed about the costs being incurred as they would their privately paying clients. Failure to take these steps could be negligence if the client suffers damage and could also result in disciplinary action.[3]

'Proceedings'

The amount of money which is imposed as a charge on property recovered or preserved is the balance of the costs of the proceedings in which that property has been recovered or preserved. What is meant by 'proceedings' in this context? The question arises most frequently in matrimonial proceedings, where orders may be made for the payment of lump sums or transfers of property in a suit which may have included also, for instance, a non-molestation and an ouster injunction and custody and access hearings. In such cases, the question arises as to whether the amount of the statutory charge includes the costs of all the other parts of the proceedings, or just that part in which the property was recovered or preserved.

In *Hanlon v Law Society* [1980] 2 All ER 199, Ms Hanlon obtained legal aid to prosecute a suit for divorce and to apply for an injunction. She was granted a decree of divorce, given custody of the two daughters of the marriage and, under the Matrimonial Causes Act 1973 s24, the husband was ordered to transfer to her the matrimonial home. After deducting the amount of the outstanding mortgage, the matrimonial home was worth about £10,000. The costs payable out of the Legal Aid Fund were £8,025, made up of £925 for the decree and applications for an injunction, £1,150 for custody and access, and £5,950 in respect of the s24 property adjustment proceedings. The court made no orders for costs against the husband in respect of any part of the proceedings because he was also legally-aided (but see further below p185).

On appeal, the House of Lords held that the charge under s9(6) of the 1974 Act (now s16(6)) was in respect of the costs of the totality of the proceedings covered by the legal aid certificate and not merely in respect of the costs of the particular proceedings under the 1973 Act s24 about the property. Since Ms Hanlon's certificate covered the divorce suit and the ancillary proceedings arising out of it, the cost of the divorce proceedings and the proceedings for custody and access were included in the charge. It

---

3 See *Client Care – A Guide for Solicitors*, The Law Society, 1991.

followed, therefore, that the whole sum of £8,025 (less a £1,015 contribution) was a charge on the house.

However, *Hanlon* must be read in the light of *Richards v Richards* [1983] 2 All ER 807. In that case, which was not concerned with legal aid, the House of Lords held that:

a) an ouster injunction required proceedings under the Matrimonial Homes Act 1967 s1 or the Domestic Violence and Matrimonial Proceedings Act 1976 to be brought separately from any existing matrimonial proceedings (for divorce or judicial separation, for example); and

b) separate proceedings were also necessary for a non-molestation injunction unless the application arose out of or in connection with the cause of action, for instance a divorce petition alleging violence.

Where separate proceedings are necessary as a result of the decision in *Richards v Richards*, the cost of those proceedings should not be included in calculating the amount of the statutory charge on a lump sum order or property transferred in matrimonial proceedings. This is the case even though it is the practice of area offices to include such proceedings on one certificate together with other matrimonial proceedings. Regulation 46(3) of the Civil Legal Aid (General) Regulations 1989 (hereafter referred to as the General Regs), which provides specifically that 'a certificate shall not relate to more than one action, cause or matter', makes an exception to that general rule in respect of, among others, 'matrimonial proceedings'. It is because of this exception that the Legal Aid Board is able to include with matrimonial proceedings other proceedings which should be separate under the principle in *Richards*.

This practice, however, does not result in the costs of the injunction proceedings being included in the statutory charge on matrimonial property transferred. In *Hanlon*, Lord Scarman was the only judge to consider the ambit of the charge where a legal aid certificate included more than one set of proceedings. Although he did so in ignorance of the exceptions in reg 46 of the General Regs and on the basis that if two sets of proceedings were included in one certificate that would have been done in error, his statement is clearly correct:[4]

> In most cases a reference to the legal aid certificate will determine the extent of the charge. If, however, there should be included in the certificate proceedings which ought not (under the statute or regulations) to be so included, the charge would not cover the cost of such proceedings . . . an error would be the inclusion in one certificate of two sets of proceedings for which separate

4   [1980] 2 All ER 199 at 213.

certificates ought to have been granted. I would not think it right to subject property recovered or preserved in the one set of proceedings to meet the costs incurred in the other.

The legal aid authorities take the same view in their administration of the scheme. It is advisable, nevertheless, for practitioners to prepare two separate bills in respect of the two sets of proceedings in such cases.

Finally, two points should be noted. First, where the assisted person has also received green form help 'in connection with those proceedings or any matter to which those proceedings relate', the cost of that help forms part of the statutory charge.[5]

Secondly, the statutory charge does not include the amount of any costs which the Legal Aid Fund has been ordered to pay to an assisted person's opponent under s18.[6] Yet, in R v Leeds County Court ex parte Morris and Another [1990] 1 All ER 550, the same effect was achieved by an order that the Legal Aid Fund should be able to set off the amount of a s18 order against monies that it was holding for an assisted person. That decision, however, is highly questionable (see p162 above).

'Property recovered or preserved'

The statutory charge applies to any property which has been recovered or preserved in the proceedings for which the assisted person has received legal aid.[7] The 'property' will include any rights under any compromise reached to bring an end to proceedings.[8]

The charge also applies to any costs which the assisted party obtains, even if they relate to a period when the party was not legally aided. In Re H and another (minors) (No 2) (1992) 142 NLJ 1004 HL the respondent had been unassisted for part of the proceedings but had been in receipt of legal aid at the time of making an application against the Fund under LAA s18. The House of Lords held that while he might be awarded costs against the Fund in respect of the time when he was unassisted, whatever he was paid would be caught by the statutory charge.

The ambit of s16 is therefore very wide. The charge may attach to any money, property or rights which have been obtained or retained as a result of the litigation. Although the first test is always whether the property in question has been in issue in the proceedings, that test is not necessarily conclusive (see s16(7), considered further below).

5   LAA s16(9)(b).
6   O'Sullivan v Herdmans Ltd (No 2) [1988] 1 WLR 1373, HL.
7   LAA s16(6).
8   LAA s16(7).

The question of what property has been recovered or preserved is especially difficult to decide in matrimonial cases. As Donaldson LJ stated in *Hanlon* in the Court of Appeal:[9]

> In exercising its powers under s24 of the 1973 Act the court looks at the whole financial position of the parties jointly and severally during the marriage and at the whole financial position of the parties severally after the breakdown of that marriage. It notionally pools all the assets and redistributes them in such a way as to produce as little change in real terms as possible. Every individual asset of each of the parties is at risk even if . . . calamity in the form of a transfer to the other party to the marriage is unlikely to strike at all such assets.

Affirming the Court of Appeal's decision, the House of Lords held that whether or not a particular asset had been in issue was to be decided by looking at the pleadings and evidence in the case. Lord Simon of Glaisdale said:[10]

> It is a question of fact not of theoretical 'risk'. In property adjustment proceedings, in my view, it is only property the ownership or transfer of which has been in issue which has been 'recovered or preserved' so as to be the subject of the legal aid charge.

He went on to describe how this question of fact is decided:

> What has been in issue is to be collected as a matter of fact from pleadings, evidence, judgment and/or order.

In *Hanlon*, both parties had claimed the whole beneficial interest in the former matrimonial home and therefore the entire value was caught. The other judges agreed. Lord Scarman said:[11]

> A person recovers or preserves in legal proceedings only what is in issue between the parties; and one discovers what is in issue by looking to the pleadings and the evidence. Had there been in this case a clear concession or admission that, *as a matter of prior entitlement*, ie before the exercise of the court's discretion under ss24 and 25 of the 1973 Act, the husband's beneficial interest in the house was limited to a half share, I would have agreed that by her proceedings the appellant 'recovered', ie got, his half share, but was not engaged in 'preserving' hers, which was not in dispute. But I am satisfied that

9   [1980] 1 All ER 763 at 781.
10   [1980] 2 All ER 199 at 203.
11   Ibid. at 214.

no such concession or admission was made by the husband. The whole house was in issue. (Emphasis added).

Assets may be caught by the statutory charge although their *ownership* has not been in issue – it is sufficient, for example, that possession or whether the asset should be sold has been in dispute in the proceedings. This is well illustrated by *Curling v The Law Society* [1985] 1 All ER 705. Ms Curling had been the respondent in matrimonial proceedings. The petition had contained a prayer for a property adjustment order in respect of the matrimonial home. It was eventually agreed that the home should be sold and Ms Curling receive £15,000. The Court of Appeal accepted that, despite the prayer, at no material time had the ownership of the matrimonial home been in issue. However, the charge still attached to the £15,000. Lord Justice Oliver said:

> Where, even though the title to property might not be in issue, the pro-ceedings were necessary in order to reduce it into or restore it to the possession of the owner, it seemed that, quite literally, the property had been 'recovered'.

Although the plaintiff's interest had been undisputed in the matrimonial proceedings, he pointed out, it was 'effectively locked away from her' until she obtained an order of the court or prevailed on the petitioner to pay her the monetary equivalent to her interest.

It cannot be said that these remarks were *obiter*, and the implications of the judgment therefore clearly go beyond the matrimonial sphere. It makes clear, for example, that a legally-aided landlord who recovers possession from a tenant may find the property subject to the statutory charge. On the wide wording of the Act, that would be correct. A periodic or statutory tenant who retained possession would not find that the statutory charge applied to the property because the tenancy would not be a chargeable interest. (On the other hand, a tenant who accepted a lump sum in return for giving up possession in a negotiated settlement would find the lump sum caught by virtue of s16(7).)

However, *Curling* shows that a prayer in the divorce petition does not necessarily put ownership of the property in issue. It will depend on the facts. In *Curling* the Court of Appeal accepted that, despite the prayer, on all the evidence, the ownership of the matrimonial home had never been in issue. In the earlier case of *Jones v Law Society* (1983) *Times* 27 January, Arnold P, sitting at first instance, had made the opposite finding on almost the same facts. He held that in the absence of any other evidence, the prayer for a transfer of property order was sufficient to put the ownership of the matrimonial home in dispute. This was so although the petitioner had not filed and served the notice under the Matrimonial Causes Rules 1977 r73, which was essential if her claim was to proceed. Although the Court of Appeal in *Curling* did not overrule *Jones*, the latter decision is no longer (if it ever was) authority for the proposition that a prayer is sufficient to put property in issue.

Following *Curling v The Law Society*, the Law Society (then the administrators of the scheme) took counsel's opinion and issued guidance to its area offices, which was published in (1985) 82/16 LS Gaz 1214. This guidance went further in its detail than an explanatory leaflet for practitioners about the charge published subsequently and reprinted in subsequent editions of the *Legal Aid Handbook* (although not the 1993 edition).

The guidance in the *Gazette*, which continues to be followed by area offices, states that a prayer in the petition asking for a 'transfer of property order' or 'property adjustment order' in respect of a named specific property raises a *prima facie* inference or presumption that the property is in dispute. A prayer which does not specify any property is not sufficient to put a specific property in issue. But where it is clear from correspondence or other evidence that the prayer referred to a specific property, then that property will be caught by the statutory charge.

The inference, where a property is specified, is *prima facie* and not conclusive. But area offices are told that if, in such cases, they consider on a preliminary view that the charge arises, it should be necessary to peruse all the pleadings, evidence and correspondence 'only in exceptional cases'. It is for solicitors, therefore, to argue the point, and the guidance makes clear that if solicitors maintain that the charge does not arise they should be asked for their reasons and for copies of relevant papers to rebut the presumption.

On the other hand, the absence of a prayer altogether may not save the assisted person. In such cases the guidance states that 'it may be necessary to peruse pleadings, correspondence and other evidence before coming to a view'.

Property can be recovered or preserved and the assisted person be liable to the statutory charge even though, financially, s/he may be worse off as a result of the outcome of the litigation. This is most likely to be the case where the assisted person has been partially successful in resisting a claim and has therefore 'preserved' part of the matter in dispute, as happened in *Till v Till* [1974] 1 All ER 1096. However, it can also happen where the assisted person has recovered less than the amount to which s/he is entitled. That was what happened in *Jones v Law Society* (above). The value of Mr Jones' share in the matrimonial home was about £5,000. He agreed to accept £4,000. Arnold P held that, since he had received the money under a compromise to bring to an end the proceedings, it was caught by the statutory charge under s16(7) (then s9(7)). On the basis of the subsequent ruling of the Court of Appeal in *Curling*, it would also have been caught under s16(6) (then s9(6)).

The wide scope of s16(7) is vividly illustrated by the case of *Van Hoorn v Law Society* [1984] 3 All ER 136, where the statutory charge was held by Balcombe J to attach to property which had not been the subject of the original dispute.

The plaintiff in *Van Hoorn* was granted legal aid to appeal against the dismissal of her application to pass over the executors of her deceased former husband and to grant to herself and her eldest daughter letters of administration with the will annexed. Under a compromise, her appeal was dismissed by consent. The terms of the compromise included that she should take absolutely the former matrimonial home in which she had been living but of which the executors were the legal owners. Balcombe J held that the former matrimonial home was clearly within the statutory charge as a result of s16(7). This was so even though the application of the tests in *Hanlon* (above) would indicate that the property had not been in issue.

It has not been decided by the courts whether property which has been the subject of a mortgage possession action is subject to the statutory charge if a defendant on legal aid successfully avoids a possession order. Some area offices, at least, take the view that the mortgagees are seeking mortgage arrears and therefore no property is preserved.[12] Nonetheless, on the wording of the Act and the General Regs, and particularly the decision in *Curling*, there must be a danger that area offices will seek to impose the charge in mortgage possession actions. It is quite clear that some of the statutory charge cases came to the courts in the 1970s and 1980s as a result of changes of policy by legal aid officials applying the rules more strictly. Clients in mortgage possession actions should be warned that the charge might apply and therefore, given also that effectively they have no s17 protection against orders for costs, that legal aid may be of only marginal benefit in their case. (Green form help is, of course, another matter.)

Exemptions

Generally

Provision is made under the regulations for certain property recovered or preserved to be exempt from the statutory charge. These exemptions are

---

12   See, for example, letter in November 1991 *Legal Action* 25.

set out in full in the Legal Advice and Assistance Regulations 1989 (hereafter referred to as the Advice and Assistance Regs) Sch 4 and the General Regs reg 94.

The main exemptions in respect of both schemes are:

a) any periodical payment of maintenance and various magistrates' courts payments;

b) the first £2,500 of:
   (i) property preserved or recovered under the Matrimonial Causes Act 1973 ss23(1)(c) or (f) or (2), 24, 27(6)(c) or (f) or 35;
   (ii) orders made under the Inheritance (Provision for Family and Dependants) Act 1975 ss2, 5 and 6; or
   (iii) orders under the Married Women's Property Act 1882 s17;
   (iv) orders made or deemed to be made under Sch 1 to the Children Act 1989;
   (v) orders made in various other family proceedings;
   (vi) any sum, payment or benefit – such as social security benefits – which cannot by statute be assigned or charged.

The following exemptions apply only to civil legal aid:

a) payments of money under an order made by the Employment Appeal Tribunal or an agreement which has the same effect;

b) orders for interim payments of damages.

There are two exemptions which apply only to the advice and assistance scheme (including ABWOR). They are dealt with below (p178).

The £2,500 exemption

In the family cases specified, the amount which is recovered or preserved will not fall below a protected minimum of £2,500 despite the statutory charge (see above). It should be noted, however, that the effect of the exemption is not to limit the amount of the charge to £2,500.

Hanlon v Law Society (above p170) provides a good illustration, if her contribution is ignored. After deducting the outstanding mortgage, the matrimonial home was worth about £10,000. The statutory charge amounted to £8,025 and, were it not for the exemption, Ms Hanlon would have been left with £1,975. However, because £2,500 of the £10,000 was exempt, only £7,500 could be deducted and the Legal Aid Fund was left out of pocket for the balance.

It is also necessary to reaffirm that the £2,500 exemption applies to lump sums in matrimonial proceedings, in view of dicta by Purchas LJ (affirmed by Eveleigh LJ) in *Simmons v Simmons* [1984] 1 All ER 83. The dicta were to the effect that such lump sums are not exempt due to the requirement under reg 90 (then reg 91) of the General Regs for a solicitor to pay any monies received on behalf of a client forthwith to the Law Society. The dicta are inconsistent with the plain wording of the legal aid regulations, and as the remarks were *obiter*, they need not be followed. The legal aid authorities, while following other parts of the judgment at the time, ignored the part which referred to the £2,500 exemption and lump sums.

Exemptions specific to the green form scheme

There are two exemptions from the statutory charge which are available only under the green form scheme, ie, they do not apply to the civil legal aid scheme. They are both important in practice.

First, the green form statutory charge does not attach to the client's dwelling, household furniture or tools of trade which have been recovered or preserved as a result of help being given under the scheme.[13] That means that where possible, for example, help should be given in some types of housing cases and in all cases involving trespass to goods under a green form rather than the legal aid certificate. The types of housing cases where it would make a difference are those where the client will preserve or recover possession of a chargeable interest – a freehold or long leasehold. Examples of cases where use of a green form rather than a legal aid certificate would avoid the statutory charge are mortgage possession proceedings (but see above at p183) and acting for a landlord in possession proceedings.

Secondly, under Advice and Assistance Regs reg 33, any property may be exempted from the charge by the area committee where, in the opinion of the solicitor, it would cause grave hardship or distress to the client to enforce the charge or where the charge could only be enforced with unreasonable difficulty because of the nature of the property. Since it is the solicitor who enforces the statutory charge it is for the solicitor to make the application. The Legal Aid Board has given advice on the factors which are taken into account.

About 'grave hardship' the Board says:[14]

– if the client is on low income, authority to waive will normally be given where compensation has been received to remedy financial loss but not where there is an element of profit;
– the lower the value of the money or property involved the smaller the

13   Advice and Assistance Regs Sch 4 para (b).
14   Note for Guidance 2-29.

chance of grave hardship being suffered, although authority might be given if grave hardship is shown when the personal or financial circumstances of the client are considered in relation to the value of the money or property;
- grave hardship might also be shown if the value is so low as to extinguish or substantially diminish the benefit to the client – although the area office might consider disallowing the solicitor's costs on the ground that the client should have been advised that the work would not be cost-effective;
- authority to waive the charge will be given in respect of essential items such as a cooker, refrigerator or furniture. Authority will usually be refused in respect of 'luxury' items which, as far as the Board is concerned, includes not only jewellery and video recorders but also television sets. If possible the charge on furniture and items of that type should be avoided under Advice and Assistance Regs Sch 4 para (b) (see above).

'Grave distress'[15] depends on the circumstances in which the property was recovered or preserved, or whether it has any special meaning for the client. For instance, if the circumstances have been distressing to the client, perhaps because the property was acquired following death, then authority to waive the charge will probably be given. The same applies to property of sentimental value such as a wedding ring.

Solicitors should be careful about applying for a waiver of the charge on the grounds of difficulty of enforcement.[16] Authority will be given only where there is real difficulty such as the property being outside the jurisdiction, but this will raise the question whether the solicitors were right to do the work in the first place. If payment has been made to the client by mistake it is not appropriate to apply under Advice and Assistance Regs reg 33. It is something to be taken into account by the area office when it considers the solicitors' claim for costs.

Mitigation and avoidance

Orders for costs

The one sure way of mitigating the statutory charge is to obtain an order for costs against the other party whenever possible. Solicitors and barristers must treat costs in legal aid cases where chargeable property is at stake in exactly the same way as they would treat costs if the client were paying

15   Note for Guidance 2-30.
16   Note for Guidance 2-31.

privately – and encourage judges and registrars to do the same (see pp148 to 153 above).

It must be remembered, however, that obtaining an order will not by itself be enough. The order must be enforced and the costs collected and paid to the Legal Aid Board. Only 'sums recovered' serve to reduce the statutory charge.[17]

Leaving property out of dispute

In some cases the charge may be avoided altogether by leaving property out of dispute. It is clear from the decided cases, and most particularly from *Hanlon* and *Curling*, that only where it is necessary should property be brought into dispute. If property is to be left out, in the words of Lord Scarman in *Hanlon* (quoted on p173 above), it must be 'a clear concession or admission . . . as a matter of prior entitlement'. It is preferable in such circumstances that the petition should not contain a prayer for a transfer of property order or, if it does, that it should not specify a property unnecessarily. If this is not done, the assisted person will be faced with the 'prima facie presumption' which legal aid official guidance has suggested would exist on the basis of *Curling* (see p181).

However, practitioners should bear in mind that in some cases it might not be to the assisted person's advantage to have property taken out of dispute – where to do so might make the property subject to assessment or reassessment from which it would be otherwise exempt (see p67 and 136 above). This might result in the assisted person becoming ineligible for legal aid or in increasing the contribution payable out of capital.

The applicant's dwelling-house will cause no problems at the time of assessment, but it may become a serious problem in any subsequent reassessment. Thus, if the assisted person sells the house after assessment and either does not buy another with the capital, or buys a cheaper house so as to release some capital, that capital will be the subject of reassessment and may be taken in contribution and/or lead to the discharge of the certificate. (It should be noted, incidentally, that property may not be the subject of both the statutory charge and assessment/reassessment. It may be subject to the charge only if it has been in dispute, and disputed property is exempt from assessment.)[18] On a reassessment, the £2,500 exemption does not apply and payment of further contributions cannot be postponed for many years as can payment of the statutory charge.

If it is a choice between possible liability under the charge or property being subject to assessment, the former is preferable. Assessment may

17   LAA s16(9).
18   Civil Legal Aid (Assessment of Resources) Regs 1989 reg 6.

result in the applicant not being eligible or having to pay contributions in advance. The statutory charge must be paid at the earliest when the assisted person realises assets from the litigation, and may be avoided altogether by an order or agreement for costs.

Two certificates

In some circumstances where an assisted person has two certificates, it may be possible to avoid some costs being imposed on the property by carrying out most of the work under the other certificate. For example, where an assisted person has certificates to be represented in wardship and matrimonial ancillary proceedings, contested custody proceedings should be brought in wardship to avoid their cost forming part of the statutory charge.

Similarly, wherever possible successive applications for ancillary relief should be brought under different certificates rather than one amended certificate. Normally a certificate to take ancillary proceedings is limited to one substantive application. To make a further application that certificate must be amended or application made for a fresh certificate. If the existing certificate is amended, the costs incurred under it will constitute part of the statutory charge if any property or money is recovered or preserved as a result of an application for ancillary relief made under the amendment. If, however, that new application had been made under a fresh certificate, then the costs incurred under the old certificate would not form part of the statutory charge.

Whether to amend an existing certificate or discharge it and apply for a new one depends first, on the size of the contribution that the client would have to pay under a new certificate and, secondly, whether whatever is recovered or preserved will be subject to the statutory charge. The answer to the second question will not always be clear, but solicitors must consider the options very carefully. Otherwise, following *Watkinson v Legal Aid Board* [1991] 2 All ER 953, they might find themselves liable in negligence. In that case Lord Donaldson, the Master of the Rolls, stated:

> The moral of this forensic tale is two-fold. First, solicitors should never apply for a certificate to be amended if they could equally well apply for a fresh certificate . . . Second, in matrimonial proceedings where there is likely to be what might almost be described as an 'annual pay round' in the form of succeessive applications for a revision of the amount of periodical payments, solicitors should use every endeavour to procure the discharge of a legal aid certificate once its purpose has been fulfilled (see reg 80(c)(ii) of the 1989 regulations) and before any new step is taken in the proceedings for which legal aid will be required.

Lord Donaldson's observations should be read subject to two points. First, he did not consider the possibility of an additional contribution in respect of the fresh certificate and, secondly, the Legal Aid Board will not carry the costs from one certificate onto another even if the second certificate has not been discharged, and indeed, as we shall see, if the statutory charge has already arisen under a certificate, discharge makes no difference.

Discharge of the certificate or ceasing to receive green form help?

It does not help the client to have a legal aid certificate discharged before reaping the fruits of the proceedings. Section 16(6) means that the charge applies in respect of any deficiency on a person's account which exists at the time costs are payable or property is recovered or preserved. Any doubts are removed by reg 85(1) of the General Regs, which states:

> Where a certificate has been revoked or discharged, section 16(6) of the Act . . . shall apply to any property recovered or preserved as a result of the person whose certificate has been revoked or discharged continuing to take, defend, or be a party to the proceedings to which the certificate related.

The position is different in respect of advice and assistance, including ABWOR, as a result of new wording in the 1988 Act, which requires that the client should be in receipt of assistance at the time when the charge arises.

Section 11(2) imposes the statutory charge on costs payable to or property recovered or preserved for 'the legally assisted person'. That expression is defined in s2(11) as 'any person who receives under this Act, advice, assistance or representation'. The important word, 'receives', is in the present tense. If Parliament had intended the definition to encompass those no longer in receipt of green form help, they could have said so, for example by including the words 'or has received'.

The same end could also have been achieved by simply using the word 'person', as in s16(6), in respect of civil legal aid or keeping the wording in the previous legislation. The Legal Aid Act 1974 s5(1) referred to 'a client'. 'Client' was defined, in s4(1), as a person 'given' advice and assistance.

Further support for the view that the charge does not apply when green form assistance has ceased may be gleaned from the Advice and Assistance Regs. They have nothing to say on the subject, which may be construed as significant given that, as mentioned above, it was thought necessary to specify in reg 85(1) of the General Regs that the charge applied after revocation or discharge of the certificate. Therefore, this is another reason for solicitors to apply promptly for green form payments. When the claim for payment is made the client ceases to be in receipt of green form assistance. For the purpose of avoiding the statutory charge, that must be done before an order or agreement is made under which money or property is recovered or preserved.

Artificial devices

Lastly, the court will disregard artificial devices created to avoid the charge. In *Manley v The Law Society* [1981] 1 All ER 401, CA, the assisted person was offered £40,000 in settlement of proceedings he had brought against a company. His own solicitor's costs payable out of the Legal Aid Fund were £17,000 and therefore, as a result of the statutory charge, if he accepted the offered settlement he would receive only £23,000. He had incurred debts of more than £23,000 in developing the invention which was the subject of the litigation. Both parties' legal advisers devised a scheme of compromise under which the £40,000 was paid to the parties' solicitors jointly. Out of that sum the solicitors, acting as the company's agent, were to buy the plaintiff's debts for the company. The company would then write off the debts. The balance, if any, after deduction of expenses, was to be paid to the plaintiff (although it was expected that his debts would exhaust most of the £40,000). It was intended that the charge would be avoided because the plaintiff would not *recover* the £40,000 under the compromise, but merely be given the right to have the terms of the compromise enforced – the Legal Aid Fund's charge would attach only to the balance (if any) paid to the plaintiff, and his solicitors would recover their costs from the Fund.

The Court of Appeal held that, looking at the reality of the compromise, the assisted person had recovered £40,000 and that the statutory charge would, therefore, come into operation. Lord Denning observed:

> it is clear beyond doubt that the object of David Manley and his solicitors was to deprive the Legal Aid Fund of any charge on the £40,000. That was the be all and end all of this elaborate transaction. The solicitors wanted to make the Legal Aid Fund pay all their costs, and at the same time deprive the Legal Aid Fund of any charge in respect of those costs. I do not think they should be permitted to succeed in this. I do not think the settlement itself can be set aside. It has gone too far to do that. But I think that equity can intervene so as to hold that, if and in so far as the solicitors had intentionally deprived the Legal Aid Fund of the charge on their costs, they are themselves precluded from making any claim on the Legal Aid Fund for those costs.

In *Draskovic v Draskovic* (1980) 11 Fam Law 87, Balcombe J refused to accede to one party's request that his interest in the former matrimonial home be given to the children on trust, because to have done so would have affected the statutory charge.

In *Griffiths v Griffiths* [1984] 2 All ER 626, however, a lump sum representing a proportion of the proceeds of sale of the former matrimonial home was set aside for the children where that setting aside affected the statutory charge. The Court of Appeal upheld this order because the husband had not met his obligations towards the children since leaving the home and had spent all of his share of the proceeds on durables for himself.

There are circumstances, therefore, where the courts will consider it proper to make orders for capital sums to the children. Furthermore, by s3 of the Matrimonial and Family Proceedings Act 1984, the courts are required to give 'first consideration' to the welfare of children of the family when making property orders. It is arguable that 'first consideration' means first before everybody and everything, including the Legal Aid Fund and the statutory charge.[19]

Postponement

In family cases the Legal Aid Board may agree to postponement of the statutory charge. The provisions differ according to when the property was recovered or preserved. The Law Society issued guidance which is also followed by the Board[20] and some of which is retained in Notes for Guidance 15-11 to 15-14 in the 1993 *Handbook*.

Money or property recovered or preserved on or after 1 December 1988

The power to postpone enforcement is set out in regs 96, 97 and 98 of the General Regs. They came into force on 1 December 1988 – earlier than the rest of the 1989 regulations – by virtue of the Legal Aid (General) (Amendment) (No 2) Regulations 1988 SI No 1938. They apply to money or property recovered or preserved under a court order or agreement made on or after that date.

The power to postpone exists only in respect of proceedings under:
- the Matrimonial Causes Act 1973; or
- the Married Women's Property Act 1882; or

19   See September 1984 *Legal Action* 101.
20   (1989) 86/3 LS Gaz 12.

- the Inheritance (Provision for Family and Dependants) Act 1975; or
- the Children Act 1989.

The Legal Aid Board has no discretion to postpone the enforcement of the statutory charge in any other cases (although it will always be very slow to take enforcement proceedings over a dwelling-house) and the power applies only to property or money which, by the express terms of a court order or the terms of an agreement, is to be used as, or to buy, a home for the assisted person or his or her dependants. That is an important point for practitioners to note: the power to defer does not arise in the absence of specific terms in the order or agreement. A Family Division *Practice Direction* [1991] 3 All ER 896 sets out a form of words which has been agreed with the Legal Aid Board:

> And it is certified for the purpose of the Civil Legal Aid (General) Regulations 1989 [that the lump sum of £X has been ordered to be paid to enable the Petitioner/Respondent to purchase a home for himself/herself (or his/her dependants)][that the property (address) has been preserved/recovered for the Petitioner/Respondent for use as a home for himself/herself (or his/her dependants)].

Before the Legal Aid Board can agree to the postponement:

a) the area director must be satisfied that the proposed property offers sufficient security;
b) the assisted person must agree to execute a legal charge over the property in favour of the Legal Aid Board; and
c) the assisted person must agree that interest will accrue from the date the charge is registered.

The rate of interest from 1 January 1992 is 10.5 per cent but it is varied from time to time by regulation. The interest is calculated on a simple, rather than a compound basis, on the amount which would have been retained in respect of the statutory charge. In other words, interest is not charged on unpaid accumulated interest. Interest accrues from the time the charge is registered,[21] whether or not the legal costs have been paid out of the Legal Aid Fund by that time. However, no interest is actually payable until the charge is redeemed.[22]

When the Board has agreed to defer enforcement of the statutory charge, the assisted person's solicitor may release money to the vendor of the property.[23] As soon as the area director has agreed that the proposed

21   General Regs reg 97(4).
22   General Regs reg 99(1).
23   General Regs reg 96(4).

property offers adequate security, the assisted person's solicitor may release money to another solicitor or to a registered conveyancer acting for the assisted person in the purchase, provided they undertake to comply with the obligations of the assisted person's solicitor.

The obligations of the assisted person's solicitor in this context are either to provide the area director with sufficient details to register the charge on the property, or to send the area director a copy of the undertaking from the other solicitor or the licensed conveyancer. It should be noted that the assisted person can only instruct another solicitor or a registered conveyancer *before* the agreement is made to defer enforcement.

If the deferment of enforcement is in respect of money rather than property, it must be used for the purchase of a home within one year from the making of the relevant order or agreement.[24] However, the Legal Aid Board has an overriding discretion to grant an extension. Unless an extension is granted, the solicitor must immediately pay the money into the Legal Aid Fund when the year has expired.

Where a charge has been registered under reg 96 or 97 of the General Regs, the Legal Aid Board may agree to the property being sold and, instead of being paid the outstanding statutory charge, accept a charge over the new property.

The Board has no power to postpone enforcement except as set out in regs 96, 97 and 98.[25] This means that the passages in *Hanlon* and other cases referring to a general power based on trusteeship of the Legal Aid Fund and the aims of the legal aid system no longer apply in respect of statutory charges arising on or after 1 December 1988.

The Legal Aid Board has prepared standard forms for the various agreements and undertakings required by regs 96, 97 and 98 of the General Regs.

Money or property recovered or preserved before 1 December 1988

Where property was recovered or preserved in legally-aided proceedings before 1 December 1988, the new regulations do not apply. Instead the Legal Aid Board has a discretion, as set out in the judgments in *Hanlon v The Law Society* [1980] 2 All ER 199, HL, to postpone enforcement of the charge or to transfer the charge to a replacement home, provided that it can do so without endangering the security.

---

24   General Regs reg 96(7).
25   General Regs reg 95(2).

The main differences in practice in respect of property recovered or preserved before 1 December 1988 are:

- the power to postpone enforcement applies only to property which consists of an interest in land – no power exists to postpone enforcement of the statutory charge if it applies to money;[26]
- interest is *not* payable on the original or any substituted charge (including a substituted charge entered into after 1 December 1988);
- the power to postpone is not limited to the proceedings listed in reg 96(1) of the General Regs, and in particular is available in respect of property recovered or preserved in proceedings under the Law of Property Act 1925 s30;
- the power to postpone enforcement is not limited to cases where an agreement or court order specifies that a property is to be used as a home;
- the provisions about substitution of property are more stringent.

In *Hanlon* (above) the House of Lords considered how the discretion to postpone enforcement should be exercised. The decision continues to apply in respect of property recovered or preserved before 1 December 1988. The Legal Aid Board should consider not solely its duties towards the Legal Aid Fund. In the words of Lord Simon of Glaisdale:[27]

> But I venture to think that it is too narrow to hold that the prime, if not exclusive, duty of the respondent in exercising its discretion is to the legal aid fund. Certainly the well-being of the fund is one of the matters which the respondent would weigh in the exercise of its discretion in relation to the charge. I think, however, that the duty of the respondent is rather to the whole legal aid scheme, and that this would not exclude consideration, among other factors, of the assisted litigant and of the purpose and the result of the litigation . . . the respondent, weighing all the relevant factors (those I have mentioned not purporting to be exhaustive), has a discretion to accept an alternative charge on a replacement home.

Lord Scarman agreed:[28]

> The Law Society [now the Legal Aid Board] is not merely the guardian of the fund. Its function is to secure that legal aid is available as required by the statute: see s15(1) of the 1974 Act [now ss1 and 3(2) of the 1988 Act]. If, therefore, in its judgment it is able, without endangering its security, to defer

---

26   *Simpson v Law Society* [1987] 2 All ER 481.
27   [1980] 2 All ER 199 at 211.
28   Ibid. at 214.

the enforcement of the charge or to switch it to another property, both of which would be options open to a person owning a charge, reg 19(1) enables it to do so, provided always that the security is not thereby endangered.

Following *Hanlon*, the Law Society issued a leaflet to solicitors to explain the statutory charge and Law Society practice when exercising its discretion about postponing enforcement. The last edition of the leaflet, issued in August 1985, included the 'Guidelines for Exercising the Law Society Discretion Relating to the Statutory Charge on Dwelling-houses', which are followed by the Legal Aid Board in respect of property recovered or preserved under orders or agreements made before 1 December 1988. The Guidelines (also set out as Note for Guidance 46 in the 1989 *Handbook* but not included in the current edition) state broadly that:

a) an area committee must not initiate proceedings to enforce the charge by an order for possession against an assisted person without the consent of the legal aid committee (now the Legal Aid Board);

b) when a dwelling-house subject to the statutory charge is sold, the sum due to the Fund must be paid unless the area committee gives prior authority for substitution by means of a charge in a form approved by the Board on another dwelling-house. It will do so if:

   (i) there is sufficient equity in the second dwelling-house; and

   (ii) the second or subsequent dwelling-house is to be occupied as the sole residence of the assisted person together with at least one unmarried child of his or hers under 18 or in full-time education at the date of purchase; or

   (iii) it is necessary for the assisted person or his or her dependants to move for reasons of health, disability or employment; and

   (iv) it appears to the area committee that substitution is just and reasonable and a refusal to make it would cause hardship to the assisted person;

c) the area committee will authorise more than one substitution only in exceptional circumstances.

Redemption and substitutions

Note for Guidance 15-18 sets out the procedure to be followed when the assisted, or former assisted, person wants to redeem the statutory charge. Requests for redemption figures, and vacation of charges, are dealt with by the Land Charge Section (Room 313), Legal Aid Accounts Department, Legal Aid Board (see Appendix). The same department deals with substitutions and further advances. The minimum information required is the assisted person's full name at the time of the registration of the charge and the title number or land charge reference. If the certificate number is also quoted, the request will be dealt with more quickly.

Part III

Criminal legal aid

CHAPTER 11

Green form and duty solicitor schemes

Introduction

Most of the work done by lawyers in connection with criminal cases is paid for under the criminal legal aid scheme. But, in general, that only provides help to defendants, and only after they have been charged and granted legal aid by a court.

Other parts of the legal aid scheme can be used where criminal legal aid is not available. The green form scheme can provide help to defendants and prospective defendants before they are granted criminal legal aid, as well as to others, such as witnesses or victims, who are involved in the criminal legal process.

Even more important are the advice at police station scheme, the duty solicitor schemes in magistrates' courts and ABWOR, which is provided specifically for those who are the subject of a police application to a magistrates' court for a warrant of further detention.

Use of green form and 'limited' ABWOR

The same rules apply to the green form scheme when it is used in criminal cases as when it is used in civil cases. Therefore chapter 2 should be consulted and read with what follows. Unlike criminal legal aid (see next chapter), coverage of the green form scheme is not confined to defendants. So solicitors can be paid under the scheme to advise and help clients whether they are, for example, defendants, prospective defendants, the relatives of defendants, witnesses, the owners of property seized by the police, victims or prosecutors.

The scheme may also be used in connection with complaints against the police, and advising on civil suits. Such matters would usually be separate, under Advice and Assistance Regs reg 17, from a prosecution in which the client was the defendant and was also receiving green form help or, more likely, criminal legal aid (see p40 above). Therefore, the advice and assistance could be given under a separate green form and/or the client would not be disqualified from green form help by reason of already having a legal aid order.

A green form may also be used, with extensions if necessary, to prepare prosecutions, for which legal aid is usually not available. Solicitors and other advisers may find it particularly helpful in bringing private prosecutions for assault or harassment, or for statutory nuisance under s82 of the Environmental Protection Act 1990. It is worth remembering that the green form scheme can cover disbursements such as fees for expert reports from doctors, surveyors or environmental health officers.

Most commonly, however, the green form scheme will be used to help defendants or potential defendants. By using the green form where no legal aid order is in force, solicitors can, for example, advise suspects, prepare an application for legal aid, attend identification parades, negotiate police bail, contact sureties, begin preparation of a defence (including interviewing witnesses), provide notes for a client to use in court, and advise on an appeal.

It should be noted, however, that much of the work which can be done under the green form, and of which examples are given above, can also be done under the advice at police station scheme, which also covers the services of 'own' solicitors. Where there is a choice it is always in the interests of the client, and of the solicitor, for the work to be done under the advice at police station scheme (see p203 below) because it is not means-tested, the solicitor will be paid more for doing it, and it is a 'separate matter' under Advice and Assistance Regulations reg 17.

Although solicitors providing advice at police stations will also normally be available to help defendants in court, it is worth remembering the extent to which the green form can be used in court. First, to pay for the help of a '*McKenzie* adviser'. The rights of all parties in court to have someone, whether legally qualified or not, with them to take notes and give advice was recently confirmed in the context of a civil case, involving a poll tax defendant, in the magistrates' courts in *R v Leicester Justices ex parte Barrow* (1991) *Times* 5 August. The green form scheme can pay for a solicitor or a member of solicitors' staff to sit in court with the client and provide help under the *McKenzie* principle (but see p23 above).

Secondly, the green form scheme may be used in the magistrates' courts to provide what in chapter 3 we called 'limited ABWOR'. Under Scope Regs reg 7(1)(b), a magistrates' court can authorise representation under the green form scheme to a party to proceedings before the court. It is important to note the preconditions, however. The court can only author-ise representation where:

a) the client is not receiving and has not been refused legal aid;
b) the court is satisfied that the hearing should proceed that day;
c) the court is satisfied that the client would not otherwise receive legal representation;
d) representation is provided by a solicitor who is already within the precincts of the court for a purpose other than giving ABWOR under this provision.

Duty solicitor schemes in magistrates' courts mean that reg 7(1)(b) is little used, but where a duty solicitor is not available or appropriate and legal aid has not yet been granted it should be invoked. The need is most likely to arise in connection with bail applications or the representation of fine defaulters, who are not normally granted legal aid by the courts but are the largest single growth sector in the prison system. However, practitioners should ensure that magistrates' courts do not use the regulation to provide, in effect, representation by 'dock briefs' rather than by legal aid orders.

It should be remembered that payment will be made only up to the prescribed limit. For the procedure for recording authority to represent and obtaining payment see p53 above.

'Full' ABWOR is, of course, available to provide representation in magistrates' courts in applications for warrants of further detention (see below, p206) and before prison governors (see chapter 3).

Lastly, it should be pointed out that the use of the green form scheme, including limited ABWOR, in criminal cases is means-tested in the normal way. References in Advice and Assistance Regs regs 6, 7 and 8 to help 'without reference to the client's financial resources' apply only to police station and court duty solicitor schemes and to representation on applications for warrants of further detention.

Duty solicitor schemes in general

Duty solicitor schemes in police stations and magistrates' courts are set up under Advice and Assistance Regs regs 6, 7 and 8. The Legal Aid Board Duty Solicitor Arrangements 1992 (the 'Arrangements') set out for both schemes the administrative structure, how duty solicitors are selected and their duties. Payment of solicitors is dealt with under the Legal Advice and Assistance (Duty Solicitor) (Remuneration) Regulations 1989 – for the court schemes – and the Legal Advice and Assistance at Police Stations (Remuneration) Regulations 1989. The latter also cover own solicitors.

A common feature of both schemes is that they are non-means-tested and non-contributory. If clients require the type of legal help available under the schemes, they qualify whatever their income or capital.

Duty solicitor schemes are run by a national network set up by the Legal Aid Board through its duty solicitor committee, and regional and local duty solicitor committees. The committees interview and select solicitors to serve on the schemes. Paragraphs 34 and 35 of the Arrangements set out the selection criteria for solicitors to serve respectively on magistrates' court and police station schemes. The criteria include requirements about expertise and availability – basically that the solicitor regularly practises in criminal defence work; has experience of it, including advocacy, during the previous 12 months, and practises in the area. Similar conditions, set out in para 47, govern the approval of duty solicitors' representatives.

The local duty solicitor committees are responsible for making the detailed arrangements for schemes in their area, and it is their duty to ensure adequate coverage of both magistrates' courts and police stations. That is normally ensured by drawing up a rota of solicitors to cover the courts – although some less busy courts have 'call-in' schemes and either a rota or a panel, where solicitors are contacted in rotation but are under no obligation to accept calls. Some police station schemes, in particular, have run a panel scheme during office hours and a rota outside office hours.

The Arrangements contain provisions designed to prevent duty solicitors poaching the clients of other solicitors. Duty solicitors are obliged to inform prospective clients that they have the right to instruct someone else and must ask them if they have a solicitor whom they wish to instruct. If the answer is in the affirmative, the next step differs according to whether the duty solicitor is in the police station or in the magistrates' court.

In the police station, if the named solicitor is not available the duty solicitor may act for the suspect only if specifically asked to do so by him or her in writing and provided those instructions are filed within seven days with the local duty solicitor committee.[1]

In the magistrates' court, if the named solicitor is not available the duty solicitor may, with the defendant's agreement, act for him or her on the particular occasion. The duty solicitor is not allowed to continue to act after that unless specifically asked to do so in writing.[2] There is no requirement for those instructions to be filed with the local committee.

1   Arrangements para 60.
2   Arrangements para 51.

Advice at police stations

Who can use the service

Solicitors will be paid by the Legal Aid Board for giving advice and assistance to:

- anybody who has been arrested and is held in custody in a police station or anywhere else; or
- is being interviewed in connection with a serious offence under the armed services' legislation; or
- is attending the police voluntarily to assist with an investigation, which may include victims of crime.[3]

As already mentioned, the non-means-tested, non-contributory help available under the scheme may be given either by a duty solicitor under the Arrangements set up by the Legal Aid Board, or by solicitors who have been instructed direct (or through friends or relatives) by the prospective client – so-called 'own solicitors'.

An 'own solicitor', who is not subject to the selection conditions mentioned above, is simply defined as 'a solicitor who gives advice and assistance to a person arrested and held in custody or to a volunteer otherwise than as a duty solicitor'.[4]

How to apply

Suspects at the police station who want help from the duty solicitor will inform the custody officer, who in turn contacts a central telephone service covering the whole country. The telephone service will contact the solicitor who is on duty on the local rota, or the solicitor on the panel whose turn it is. The client does not complete a green form or any other legal aid form.[5] Advice and Assistance Regs reg 6(2) provides specifically that the request for assistance can be made by telephone and, given the nature of the case, it usually will be. If the client requests his or her own solicitor, the police will contact that solicitor direct.

A rota solicitor must accept the case unless already engaged at a police station or with a warrant for further detention.[6] A panel solicitor is under no such obligation. Neither is an 'own' solicitor under any obligation to help if contacted by a suspect in a police station, unless that solicitor had already agreed to take on the case.[7]

---

3   Advice and Assistance Regs reg 6(1).
4   Legal Advice and Assistance at Police Stations (Remuneration) Regs 1989 reg 2.
5   Advice and Assistance Regs reg 9(2)(a).
6   Arrangements para 55(1).
7   *The Guide to the Professional Conduct of Solicitors*, principles 9.01 and 9.18.

It should be noted that under the advice at police station scheme there is special provision for children – in this context meaning persons aged under 16. A solicitor may accept an application for advice and assistance direct from a child if satisfied that the application 'cannot reasonably be made' by a parent, guardian, or other person with parental authority or the area director's authority.[8]

The service provided

There is a prescribed financial limit to the amount of work which can be done. A solicitor will not be paid more than £90 in respect of work done for a client, including charges for time spent advising and assisting, on the telephone, travelling and waiting and any expenses (see below for the method of charging and payment). The costs taken into account in respect of each client, however, do not include anything charged by a duty solicitor as a stand-by payment.[9]

This limit may, however, be retrospectively extended by the Legal Aid Board, if its determining officer is satisfied that 'the interests of justice' required further advice and assistance to be given 'as a matter of urgency'.[10] The considerations that will be taken into account in deciding whether further work was justified include:

- whether the offence involved was an arrestable offence under s24 of the Police and Criminal Evidence Act 1984;
- the client's age, physical or mental capacity, and any language difficulties;
- whether the work was necessary;
- if the costs have been increased by an unusually large claim for travelling time or travelling expenses, whether a local agent or duty solicitor should have been used.[11]

A rota solicitor, or a panel solicitor who has accepted the case, must, at the very least, give initial advice to the client over the telephone – unless the client is incapable of speaking due to drunkenness or violent behaviour, in which case the duty solicitor must make arrangements to give initial advice as soon as possible.[12]

8 Advice and Assistance Regs reg 14(2).
9 Advice and Assistance Regs reg 4(1)(a) and Legal Advice and Assistance at Police Stations (Remuneration) Regs 1989 reg 5(5).
10 Legal Advice and Assistance at Police Stations (Remuneration) Regs 1989 reg 5(6).
11 Note for Guidance 17-34, and see p246 below.
12 Arrangements para 55(2).

Duty solicitors have been criticised for being reluctant to go to police stations and therefore, although it is generally speaking for the solicitor to decide after receiving the telephone call whether it is necessary to attend, his or her discretion is severely circumscribed. Paragraph 57 of the Arrangements says that the solicitor must decide whether it is in the suspect's interest that the solicitor, or a representative, goes to the station. In making that assessment the solicitor must consider whether advice and help can be given over the telephone 'with sufficient confidentiality to deal adequately with the matter'.[13] Where the suspect is a juvenile or 'person at risk', ie, mentally disordered or mentally handicapped, it is presumed that the solicitor will decide to attend at the police station.[14]

In some circumstances the duty solicitor must go to the police station if asked to do so by the suspect.[15] That is the case where:

- the police intend to interview the suspect and s/he has been arrested in connection with an 'arrestable offence' as defined in s24 of the Police and Criminal Evidence Act 1984;
- the police intend to hold an identification parade, group identification or confrontation;
- the suspect complains of serious maltreatment by the police.

If there are exceptional circumstances which justify non-attendance at the police station the solicitor must say so on the costs claim form (see below); and if an interview is postponed to a time when the solicitor is no longer on duty, he or she must make arrangements to make sure that someone attends.

A duty solicitor may send a representative to a police station if:

- the use of representatives has been authorised by the regional duty solicitor committee;
- the representative has been approved by the local duty solicitor committee; and
- the duty solicitor thinks it is appropriate to send a representative; and
- the police are prepared to allow a clerk the same rights of access as a solicitor.[16]

The suspect must be informed about the status of the representative. Any representatives giving advice to armed forces personnel must be solicitors. None of these requirements applies to an 'own' solicitor (see p203).

13   Arrangements para 57(1).
14   Arrangements para 57(2).
15   Arrangements para 56(1).
16   Arrangements para 59.

Getting paid

The three-month time limit for submitting a claim for payment applies to police station work as to criminal legal aid, and is dealt with below at p251.

The claim is made on a separate Form APS 3 in respect of each client. The same form is used by duty solicitors and 'own' solicitors. Section 2, which specifies the amount of work done and the amount claimed, must be signed by the 'conducting solicitor', which may be the solicitor who attended or, if a clerk went to the station, a supervising solicitor. If the prescribed costs limit has been extended it is important to specify the reason in section 3.

In addition to claiming for the work done, rota solicitors may also claim at an hourly rate for the period when they are 'on standby'. Any fees charged for attending clients will, however, be deducted from the standby claim, up to half of its amount. For example, if the total standby claim comes to £84.00 and the claim for attendances is £60, then £42 will be allowed for the standby claim. If, however, the claim for attendances had been £30, then £54 would have been allowed for the standby claim, and so on.

The rates are set out in the Schedule of the Legal Advice and Assistance at Police Stations (Remuneration) Regs 1989 and are regularly amended – usually annually. Announcements of changes are made in the *Law Society's Gazette* and *Legal Aid Focus*. The rates from 1 April 1992 are as follows:

Standby (per hour)	£3.50 to £84.00 max
	(£3.55 to £85.20 max)
Duty solicitor (unsocial hours)	£57.50
Duty solicitor (other hours)	£43.50 (£46.50)
Own solicitor (all hours)	£43.50 (£46.50)
Own solicitor (travelling and waiting)	£24.25
Telephone (advice) per item	£19.75 (£20.50)
Telephone (routine) per item	£2.25 (£2.40)

(Rates in brackets are for London—Legal Aid Area 1)

Duty solicitors may charge the same rate for travel and waiting as they do for advice.

If a duty solicitor remains in the police station beyond the period of duty, he or she can continue to charge at the duty rate.

'Unsocial hours' are between 5.30pm and 9.30am on weekdays and any time on a day which is not a business day.[17]

---

17   Legal Advice and Assistance at Police Stations (Remuneration) Regs 1989 reg 2 as amended.

ABWOR for warrants of further detention

If the police want to hold a suspect for more than 36 hours they must apply to a magistrates' court for a warrant of further detention under s43 of the Police and Criminal Evidence Act 1984, and for an extension of the further warrant under s44.

Non-means-tested and non-contributory ABWOR is available to provide representation for a suspect when such applications are made.[18] Again, the applicant has no need to complete a form.[19]

The solicitor makes the claim for payment in section 5 of Form APS 3. Although the solicitor providing ABWOR on an application for a warrant of further detention would normally be the same solicitor who was giving advice and assistance in the police station, there is no requirement for this to be the case.

The rates allowed are the same as for ABWOR generally (see chapter 3). However, where representation is by a duty solicitor during unsocial hours (as defined above), the relevant rates are increased by one-third.[20]

Duty solicitors in the magistrates' court

The scope of the service

Duty solicitors in the magistrates' court provide a first aid service to criminal defendants. It is non-means-tested and non-contributory, and therefore there is no need for applicants to complete a form.

In this context, 'duty solicitors' means just that. 'Own' solicitors cannot be paid for work done under this scheme. However, 'own' solicitors can provide advice, assistance, and sometimes even representation under normal green form and ABWOR rules as described at the beginning of this chapter.

The services duty solicitors are allowed to provide and the clients they can represent are restricted to ensure that they are not used as a cheap, and inferior, alternative to full legal representation on criminal legal aid, or to provide state-funded help in cases which are relatively unimportant. The work they can undertake, and which will be paid for by the Legal Aid Board, is set out in Scope Regs reg 7(2) and (4) and Arrangements para 52. Duty solicitors can:

a) give advice to any defendant in custody;

b) make a bail application on behalf of a defendant;

---

18   Scope Regs reg 7(1)(c) and Advice and Assistance Regs reg 5.
19   Advice and Assistance Regs reg 9(2)(b).
20   Advice and Assistance Regs reg 30(2).

c) represent a defendant in custody who is pleading guilty – unless the duty solicitor thinks the case should be adjourned in the interests of justice;
d) where necessary, give advice and representation to a defendant who is at risk of going to prison as a result of failing to pay a fine or other money due to the court, or breaking a court order;
e) provide advice and, if necessary, representation to a non-custody defendant who, in the opinion of the duty solicitor, needs such help;
f) help a defendant to apply for legal aid, although they must give the defendant an option of nominating another solicitor.

In all cases, except for d) above, in order to qualify for representation by a duty solicitor, as opposed to advice, a defendant:

– must not be or have been in receipt of legal aid in connection with the same proceedings;[21]
– must not be or previously have been in receipt of ABWOR, in connection with the same proceedings;[22]
– must not have received advice or assistance from the same solicitor or any other duty solicitor at any previous hearing in connection with the same case.[23]

Lastly, while acting as duty solicitor, a duty solicitor must not:

– represent anyone at committal proceedings or on a not-guilty plea;
– normally provide advice or representation to a defendant in connection with an offence which is not imprisonable.[24]

Getting paid

The claim should be made within three months on Form DSC, which is self-explanatory. Payment is on an hourly basis for the time spent in court at an average of the rates payable for advocacy and attendance under the criminal legal aid scheme.[25] The rate, as at 1 April 1992, and not increased in 1993, which is the same inside and outside London, is £48.88. That rate is increased by 25 per cent for duty solicitor sessions on days which are not business days.

Solicitors may not charge for time spent travelling to and from office and court unless they were called in from the office to act as duty solicitors. However, they may charge travelling time and expenses from

21 Scope Regs reg 7(2).
22 Scope Regs reg 7(2).
23 Arrangements para 53(2).
24 Arrangements para 53(1).
25 Legal Advice and Assistance (Duty Solicitor) (Remuneration) Regs 1989 reg 5(2)(a).

home to court when acting as duty solicitors on a Saturday, Sunday or bank holiday. In that event the rate is the normal criminal legal aid rate of £24.25 per hour.

CHAPTER 12

Obtaining criminal legal aid

Introduction

Criminal legal aid, like civil legal aid and the green form scheme, has its legal basis in the Legal Aid Act 1988 (LAA) and the details of its working is set out in regulations. The relevant provisions are found in Part V (ss19–26) of the 1988 Act and in the Legal Aid in Criminal and Care Proceedings (General) Regulations 1989 (the Criminal Regs). Rules about payment of fees are found in the Legal Aid in Criminal and Care Proceedings (Costs) Regulations 1989 (the Criminal Costs Regs). (Despite the title of the regulations, they are not relevant to care proceedings since the Children Act 1989 came into effect on 14 October 1991.)

Unlike civil legal aid, however, the administration of criminal legal aid is mainly through the criminal courts. The magistrates' courts, and sometimes the Crown Court, decide who should be granted legal aid, and the Crown Court assesses the costs of work done in that court. The role of the Legal Aid Board is largely confined to considering appeals against some of the decisions of the courts and assessing the costs of magistrates' court work. That also means that the Lord Chancellor's Department has a more direct concern with criminal legal aid, and sometimes it will be necessary to refer to circulars from the Lord Chancellor's Department. Only one Note for Guidance from the Legal Aid Board, Note for Guidance 17, is concerned with criminal legal aid, and occasionally reference will be made to that.

Nevertheless, it should be noted that ss3(4), 20(9) and 20(10) of the 1988 Act contain power for the Lord Chancellor to transfer to the Legal Aid Board any functions to do with criminal legal aid, and a transfer of some kind is being considered by the Board as we go to press.

Applying for criminal legal aid

A magistrates' court or Crown Court which is seized of a criminal case has power to grant legal aid to the defendant.[1] There are different rules for the House of Lords, Court of Appeal and Courts-Martial Appeal Court.[2]

In practice that means that most applications for legal aid are made to the magistrates' court, because all criminal cases start there. In addition, a magistrates' court has power to grant legal aid to cover proceedings in the Crown Court:

- where it commits a defendant for trial or sentence to the crown court;[3] or
- before it commits a defendant for trial where it is sitting as examining justices;[4] or
- where, in a serious fraud case, it has been given a notice of transfer under s4 of the Criminal Justice Act 1987;[5] or
- where notice of transfer has been given under s53 of the Criminal Justice Act 1991; or
- where a defendant is appealing to the Crown Court against the conviction or sentence of the magistrates' court.

In all those instances the Crown Court also has power to award legal aid once the case has reached that court.[6]

Any magistrates' court has power to grant legal aid where a suspect has been arrested but not brought before a particular court.[7]

The Crown Court also has power to grant legal aid for proceedings in the Court of Appeal for applications in that court for leave to appeal or for appeals in respect of orders or rulings made at preparatory hearings.[8]

Applications for criminal legal aid to the magistrates' court must be made on Form 1 and Form 5. Form 1 (see Part V) sets out the personal details of the applicant, the proceedings in respect of which s/he needs legal aid, any other outstanding criminal charges that the defendant might have, details of the solicitor that s/he wants as a representative and, lastly, and in most cases very importantly, the reasons that s/he wants legal aid. How to set out those reasons will be considered after we have looked at the basis of the court's discretion to grant legal aid. Form 1 must be signed

1   LAA s20(1).
2   LAA s20(2) and see below.
3   LAA s20(4)(a).
4   LAA s20(5).
5   LAA s20(4)(b).
6   LAA s20(1) and Criminal Regs reg 18(1).
7   LAA s20(8).
8   LAA s20(6).

by the applicant, unless s/he is under 16, in which case it must be signed by his or her parents or guardian. If the applicant cannot sign because of physical or mental disability, the solicitor should sign on the applicant's behalf and explain why in a covering letter.

An application can be made orally to the court instead of on Form 1.⁹ However, the court has the option of referring the application to the justices' clerk, in addition to granting or refusing it.

The normal way to make an application for legal aid is in good time in advance of the hearing under Criminal Regs reg 11(1)(b) as outlined above. It should always be remembered, however, that any court seised of the case has a general power to grant a legal aid order under Criminal Regs reg 10, whether or not an application has been made. Under the same provision an applicant who has previously been refused legal aid or whose legal aid order has been revoked may apply again. The grant and application may be made at the trial or any other hearing. In any event, the legal aid order must not be made before the applicant has submitted Form 5 and his or her means have been considered by the justices' clerk (or Form 5 has been dispensed with, see below).

Form 5 is concerned with the financial means of the applicant. The information on this form will enable the court to consider whether the defendant can afford to pay for representation privately and, therefore, whether s/he needs legal aid. It also provides the necessary information to enable the court to decide how much the defendant should be obliged to pay as a contribution. Its contents will be considered further in the next chapter in the context of the criminal legal aid means test.

There is limited power under Criminal Regs reg 23(4) to dispense with Form 5 where:

– the applicant is incapable of providing a statement of means because of physical or mental incapacity; or
– the applicant has previously submitted a statement of means in the same case and there has been no change.

Where the applicant is under 16 (not under 17 as is erroneously stated in Note for Guidance 17-05), the court may also require a completed Form 5 from an 'appropriate contributor' (see next chapter).

The same rules apply and the same forms are used in the Crown Court as in the magistrates' courts.¹⁰

It should be noted that whenever there is any doubt whether criminal

9   Criminal Regs reg 11(1)(b).
10   Criminal Regs reg 18.

legal aid should be granted, that doubt should be resolved in favour of the applicant.[11] That provision is most likely to be invoked in relation to the court's discretion to grant legal aid in the interests of justice, but is equally applicable in relation to whether or not the applicant can afford to pay for his or her defence.

Applying for legal aid in criminal appeals

A magistrates' court or Crown Court legal aid order includes giving advice and assistance on an appeal (see p247 below). However, to conduct an appeal requires a new legal aid order. On an appeal from the magistrates' court to the Crown Court, an application may be made either to the magistrates' court from which the appeal is made, or to the Crown Court to which the appeal is being made.[12]

For appeals to the Court of Appeal, the power to grant legal aid depends on whether the appeal is against an order or ruling at a preparatory hearing, or whether it is against conviction or sentence.

As already noted, the Crown Court has power to grant legal aid in respect of appeals, or applications for leave to appeal against orders or rulings at preparatory hearings.[13]

Where an appeal is contemplated to the Court of Appeal, that court has power to grant legal aid before notice of appeal is given or an application made for leave to appeal.[14] However, Criminal Regs reg 22(4) provides that the Court of Appeal shall not make a legal aid order until notice of appeal has been given. Therefore, work done before the giving of the notice of appeal must be done under the crown court legal aid order.

Application to the Court of Appeal can be made orally to the full court, a judge or the Registrar of Criminal Appeals, or it may be made in writing using forms which can be obtained from the Registrar. The applicant must provide evidence of means unless he or she is physically or mentally incapable of doing so, or has done so previously and there has been no change of circumstances.[15]

The same rules apply in respect of appeals to the Courts-Martial Appeal Court.

---

11   LAA s21(7).
12   LAA s20(2) and 20(4)(c).
13   LAA s20(6).
14   LAA s20(2).
15   Criminal Regs reg 22(5)(b).

Obligatory legal aid

Although, as we shall see, in most cases the court has discretion whether to grant criminal legal aid, there are some circumstances in which it must do so. They are not all contained in the LAA.

It should be noted that in all cases the defendant must show that he or she is eligible on financial grounds.[16]

Custodial sentences

In some circumstances a court is required to offer legal aid to a defendant before it imposes a custodial sentence. The requirement applies to any defendant who is under 21[17] and to a defendant who is 21 or over and who is receiving a custodial sentence for the first time.[18]

In respect of any such defendants, the court may impose a custodial sentence only if:

- the defendant is legally represented; or
- has been refused legal aid on grounds of means; or
- has declined to be represented after having been informed of the right to apply for legal aid and has refused or failed to apply.

The requirement applies where a suspended sentence of imprisonment is imposed and, in the case of a defendant who is 21 or over, it applies before a person who has been sentenced to a non-implemented suspended sentence may be imprisoned. In both instances the requirement is satisfied if the defendant is represented after conviction but before sentence.[19] That means that as far as these provisions are concerned, the defendant can be convicted without legal representation, and legal aid only needs to be granted for mitigation of sentence.

A sentence imposed in breach of s21 or s3 would be invalid and the magistrates would be acting in excess of their jurisdiction. A Crown Court hearing an appeal against such a sentence may impose only such sentence as the magistrates could have imposed on an unrepresented defendant, even though the appellant is represented at the appeal.[20]

---

16 LAA s21(5).
17 Criminal Justice Act 1982 s21(3).
18 Powers of Criminal Courts Act 1973 s21.
19 Powers of Criminal Courts Act 1973 s21(2), Criminal Justice Act 1982 s3.
20 R v Birmingham Justices ex parte Wyatt [1975] 3 All ER 897.

Committals in custody for sentence

Legal aid must also be granted, under s21(3)(d) of the LAA, for a defendant to be represented for the purposes of sentencing where he or she is committed in custody to the Crown Court for sentencing.

Murder

Under s21(3)(a) of the 1988 Act, legal aid must be granted to an accused to be represented on a trial for murder in the Crown Court. It should be noted, however, that legal aid is available as of right only for the Crown Court proceedings. As far as the magistrates' court proceedings before committal are concerned, the normal, discretionary rules apply (see below). On the other hand, the magistrates' court cannot leave the grant of legal aid to the Crown Court but must make the order on committal.[21]

Prosecution appeals to the House of Lords

Where the prosecution has appealed or applied for leave to appeal to the House of Lords, the accused must be granted legal aid to be represented.[22]

Bail applications

In addition, legal aid must be granted under LAA s21(3)(c) for a bail application where:

- a defendant is brought before the court having previously been remanded in custody; and
- is at risk of being remanded in custody again; and
- was not legally represented when the previous remand in custody was made; and
- is not, but wishes to be, legally represented on this occasion.

Two points should be made about this provision. First, it provides mandatory legal aid only for a bail application, not for the proceedings as a whole. Secondly, the requirement that there should have been no legal representation when the remand in custody was made would not be met where the applicant had been represented by a duty solicitor.

21   LAA s21(4).
22   LAA s21(3)(b).

Committals for trial without consideration of the evidence

Section 6(2) of the Magistrates' Courts Act 1980 provides a fast and convenient procedure for commiting defendants for trial to the crown court without consideration of the evidence. However, it can only be used if all the defendants in a case are legally represented, although the legal representatives do not need to be in court when the committal takes place. If defendants are not represented privately, a magistrates' court will have to grant legal aid if it wants to make use of s6(2).

Remands in absence of defendant

Section 128 of the Magistrates' Courts Act 1980 provides that courts may remand defendants awaiting trial in custody in their absence. However, the power can only be used where the defendant has a legal representative present in court. (Magistrates' Courts Act 1980 s128(1A)(d) and (1B).) Therefore if courts want to take advantage of this provision they will have to grant legal aid unless the defendant is privately represented.

Remands of young persons

A court may not declare a young person to be one who should be remanded in a remand centre or prison, without that person being legally represented in court unless:

- he (the provision only applies to males) has been refused legal aid on the grounds of means; or
- he has refused legal aid after being informed of his right to apply. (Children and Young Persons Act 1969 s23(4A)).

Discretionary legal aid

In the vast majority of cases the court has a discretion whether to grant legal aid. According to s21(2), the court 'may' grant legal aid 'where it appears . . . desirable to do so in the interests of justice'.

Section 22(2) sets out the factors which the court should take into account. Although prior to the 1988 Act none of these factors was set out in statute, they are, in fact, the 'Widgery criteria' which, despite their previous lack of statutory backing, had been applied by the courts since 1966 to determine whether a grant of legal aid was necessary in the interests of justice.

Section 22(2) does not pretend to set out an exclusive list but in practice usually is treated as such. The relevant factors include:

- whether the accused is likely to be deprived of liberty, or to suffer serious loss of livelihood or serious damage to reputation as a result of conviction; or
- whether the case 'may involve' a substantial question of law;
- whether the accused may be unable to understand the proceedings or state his or her case because of inadequate understanding of English, mental illness or other mental or physical disability;
- whether the case involves the tracing and interviewing of witnesses or expert cross-examination of prosecution witnesses;
- whether it is in the interests of someone other than the accused that the accused should be represented.

The Justices' Clerks Society/Legal Aid Board Guidelines

The Justices' Clerks Society has circulated guidelines to its members for use when they are considering legal aid applications. The Legal Aid Board also takes account of those guidelines when its area committees are considering appeals from the refusals of magistrates' courts to grant legal aid (see p223 below). They have been published in the *Law Society's Gazette*.[23]

In the introduction, the guidelines state first that they have been drawn up with adult offenders in mind and that different weight may need to be given to the criteria when applications are made by juveniles. Secondly, they note that the plea may be relevant but that a 'not guilty' plea will not by itself justify the grant of legal aid.

Offences triable on indictment only should always be granted legal aid, say the guidelines.

Some either-way offences should normally be granted legal aid. They are:

affray
assault occasioning actual bodily harm
burglary (all types)
criminal damage
drugs – possession with intent to supply/supplying
indecent assault
possession of offensive weapon
sexual offences involving children
theft of substantial amount from employer
unlawful sexual intercourse
violent disorder (Public Order Act 1986 s2)

23   (1992) 89/21 LS Gaz 31.

wounding

any case where the court declines jurisdiction.

Legal aid should also be granted in respect of the following offences where the s22 criteria are made out:

abstracting electricity
obtaining property by deception
possession of drugs
false accounting
forgery
going equipped to steal
gross indecency
handling stolen goods
making off without payment
reckless driving
theft of small amount from employer.

The following summary offences should normally be given legal aid:

assault on police officer (irrespective of plea)
indecent exposure where plea of 'not guilty'
breach of community service order.

If the s22 criteria are established, legal aid should also be given for:

common assault
criminal damage
driving while disqualified
indecent exposure – 'guilty' plea
interference with motor vehicle
obstructing police constable
false representations in relation to social security offences
taking motor vehicle without consent
threatening behaviour (Public Order Act 1986 s4)
breach of probation order, attendance centre order or supervision following sentence.

Unless the applicant can show exceptional circumstances, such as mental disability or language difficulty, legal aid should normally be refused for:

drinking under age
being drunk and disorderly
litter offences
possession of sharp pointed object (Criminal Justice Act 1988)
loitering or soliciting for the purposes of prostitution
evading railway fare

school attendance cases
television licence offences
threatening behaviour (Public Order Act 1986 s5)
urinating in the street.

Legal aid should normally be refused for all road traffic offences, although there may be some where legal aid is appropriate even with a 'guilty' plea because of the possibly serious consequences, and others where a technical legal defence might make the grant of legal aid appropriate.

The guidelines have no legal status and parts are clearly questionable. In any event, in exercising their discretion under ss21(2) and 22(2), magistrates' courts have shown serious inconsistencies and wide divergence of practice, which has received adverse comment on many occasions, most notably over the years from LAG (see eg 1978 *Bulletin* 6) and most recently from the Legal Aid Board in its 1989-90 Annual Report.[24] The completion of Form 1 may therefore be a task of skilled advocacy and, if possible, solicitors should complete the form themselves rather than leave it to their clients. The work involved may, of course, be paid for under the green form scheme (see chapters 2 and 11).

Completing Form 1

Form 1 (see Part IV) asks the applicant to set out the reasons legal aid should be granted. It is always useful to know the court's attitude to legal aid so that the reasons legal aid should be granted may be phrased in a way that is likely to find favour. Where a court takes a restrictive attitude to the grant of legal aid those reasons should be set out in full – and they may become of vital importance if later it is decided to apply for judicial review (see below).

What follows are suggestions of what might be relevant reasons to be put forward on Form 1. In putting them forward it should be remembered that the court probably has little information about the case or the applicant other than what appears on the charge sheet:

1. I am in real danger of a custodial sentence for the following reasons . . .

Is there anything about the offence, the offender or any victim which makes a prison sentence more likely? An allegation that the offence had been committed while on bail would be relevant but previous convictions, whether for offences similar to the present charges, would be less relevant following the coming into effect of the Criminal Justice Act 1991,

24   HMSO HC 489 (1990–91) and see (1992) 89/44 LS Gaz 23.

Allegations of violence or unrecovered losses are also worth putting forward, as are special factors such as breach of trust, eg, theft from an employer or sexual assault by a teacher on a pupil. Local knowledge might suggest that the offence is one which will be treated particularly seriously because of its prevalence.

2. I am subject to a suspended or partly suspended sentence; conditional discharge; probation order; supervision order; deferment of sentence; community service order; or care order.

It is a fact of life, for which court practice must take most of the blame, that criminal defendants are frequently uncertain about the sentences which have been imposed on previous occasions, especially where they were subjected to one of the many different non-custodial options. However, the applicant should try to be as accurate as possible and, if there is time, it is usually worthwhile for the solicitor to make enquiries to find out the exact position. If that cannot be ascertained, that should be explained on the form.

3. I am in real danger of losing my job because . . .

This is important where the applicant is in a job involving trust that may be lost as a result of a conviction for an offence involving dishonesty. Anyone handling cash, for instance, is at risk of losing their job if found guilty of any kind of theft or offence involving dishonesty. Someone who needs a driving licence for their job is at risk of losing that job if conviction is likely to lead to disqualification. Those in caring occupations, such as teachers or social workers, may lose their jobs if found guilty of sex offences.

In *R v Brigg Justices ex parte Lynch* (1983) *Times* 17 December, a magistrates' court refused legal aid to a serving soldier facing three separate summonses for indecent exposure. In granting judicial review of that decision the court said:

It is a matter of almost common knowledge that a serving soldier who is convicted of offences such as are here alleged is very likely indeed to find himself discharged from the army . . .

and

in exercising discretion [the magistrates] will have regard to . . . the Widgery criteria [now s22(2)]. Amongst the matters which they can take into account under [s22(2)] are threats to a person's livelihood . . . the identification of a person as a serving soldier, without more, should have led the justices to grant legal aid.

4. I am in real danger of suffering serious damage to my reputation because . . .

This may be relevant where the applicant who does not have anything to say in answer to question 1 has a strong case to put forward. The defendant with no previous convictions charged with a small theft from a shop is unlikely to go to prison. But the consequences of a conviction on such a person's reputation can be disastrous. The courts may be ready to accept that as a good reason for giving legal aid where the defendant is a person of public standing in the community. However, someone who is not in the public eye can suffer just as much damage to their reputation, and this is an argument which often needs to be put forcibly: some magistrates' courts, for instance, refuse legal aid to first-offence alleged shoplifters as a matter of policy. Others take the view that unemployed people have no reputation to lose.

Clearly, this reason is not one which can be relied on where the defendant has recent convictions for the same offence; but where the convictions are for dissimilar offences, or where they are 'spent' under the Rehabilitation of Offenders Act 1974, it would usually be worth arguing for legal aid to be granted under this head.

5. I have been advised by my solicitor that a substantial question of law is involved.

The question of law involved should be outlined on the form. This may be to do with the definition of the offence, general defences such as lack of intent, self-defence or mistake, or special defences arising in connection with the offence charged. This ground for granting legal aid is not confined to 'not guilty' pleas. The law of sentencing is complex, particularly following the Criminal Justice Act 1991, and may need to be dealt with as part of a plea in mitigation in a difficult case.

6. Witnesses have to be traced and interviewed on my behalf.

Under this head should be mentioned not just witnesses as to facts but also any expert witnesses required, such as doctors or forensic scientists, and whether there is a need to produce plans or photographs.

7. I shall be unable to follow the court proceedings because . . .

The form requires the applicant to set out why s/he would have difficulty following the proceedings. Again, it is worth setting out the reasons in some detail. Inexperience of the English courts, as well as a language problem, may be relevant. In R v Phillippe [1965] Crim LR 109, the Court of Criminal Appeal held that legal aid should have been granted to a French Canadian with no experience of the English courts who had been prejudiced by a refusal of legal aid.

8. The case involves expert cross-examination of a prosecution witness.

In arguing for legal aid under this head it will be normally be necessary to give an indication of the prosecution evidence which is challenged (or likely to be challenged).

9. The case is a very complex one, for example mistaken identity.

Under this head the form specifically states that the applicant may need the help of a solicitor to answer the question. Other relevant examples might be cases involving disputed confessions or scientific evidence.

10. Any other reasons.

The form does not contain a question to elicit facts which might bring into play s22(2)(e), which states that 'it is in the interests of someone other than the accused that the accused be represented'. That might be relevant where a victim would be distressed by being directly cross-examined by the accused. The place to put such a reason is box 10.

Other reasons might also go in there. It should be remembered that the list of factors set out in s22(2) is not exclusive. So, for instance, in R v Edgehill [1963] 1 All ER 181 at 185, Lord Parker CJ said in the Court of Criminal Appeal that

It may well be that, in cases where a recommendation for deportation is made, legal aid should be granted. The Court is not laying that down as an absolute rule, but it would seem to be only right . . . that a Commonwealth citizen, who may be liable to have a deportation order made, should have the assistance of legal advice, and the court thinks it clearly advisable that, in these cases, he should be granted legal aid.

Challenging refusals

If legal aid is refused, the clerk of the court must notify the applicant on Form 2, stating whether the refusal is because representation is not necessary in the interests of justice, or because of means or because of both. The form also states what the applicant's contribution would have been had legal aid been granted.[25]

A copy of Form 2 must also be sent to the applicant's solicitor, and if the case is one where there is a right to review by a legal aid area committee, both the applicant and his or her solicitor must also be sent a copy of the completed Form 1 which is required to accompany any application to the area committee.

Solicitors should make sure that they can contact their clients, or that their clients will contact them urgently if legal aid is refused, so that the following options may be considered in order to obtain legal aid.

Renewing the application

A legal aid application may be renewed orally or in writing at any time to a magistrates' court[26] or a Crown Court.[27] However, if solicitors intend to make an application for review to the area committee, they must not renew the application to the court before the application for review has been lodged with the area committee, otherwise the right to apply for a review will be lost (see below). When renewing an application, the notification of refusal from the court (Form 2) must be returned. If the renewal takes place after an unsuccessful application for review (see below), then the notification of refusal from the area committee must also be given to the court.

The renewed application may be dealt with immediately or referred for consideration.[28] The usual rules about providing a statement of means apply to renewed applications as they do to original applications.

Before renewing the application, it is advisable to find out from the court why it did not consider the case for legal aid to have been made out. Unless there are new reasons which make the solicitor very confident that legal aid will be granted – such as new charges, a remand in custody, or sometimes just the passage of time in custody – it is probably preferable to apply for a review to an area committee if that option is available:

---

25 Criminal Regs reg 12.
26 Criminal Regs reg 14.
27 Criminal Regs reg 18.
28 Criminal Regs regs 12(3) and (4).

especially so since a right of applying for review is lost if a second application is made to the magistrates' court.

In any event, there is much to be said for a practitioner orally renewing the application in front of the bench. Not only does that mean that any questions not covered in the application can be dealt with but some benches may find it more difficult to turn the renewed application down if faced with the applicant's representative.

The right to renew an application is not available to a defendant whose legal aid order has been revoked (*R v Liverpool City Magistrates ex parte Shacklady* (unreported, CO/0492/92 and CO/2011/92).

Applying for a review

In some cases it is possible to apply to the area legal aid committee for a review of a magistrates' court's decision refusing legal aid. A review may be applied for where:[29]

- the magistrates' court has refused legal aid after considering it for the first time; and
- the applicant is charged with an indictable or either way offence, or is brought before the magistrates' court to be dealt with in respect of a sentence imposed or order made in connection with such an offence; and
- the application was refused because legal aid was not considered necessary in the interests of justice; and
- the application to the magistrates' court had been made at least 21 days before any date fixed for trial or committal.

As already noted, the area committee will refuse to consider an application for review if, at the time that it is made, the magistrates' court has considered the application more than once. However, it does not affect the application for a review if the application to the magistrates' court is renewed after the submission of Form 3 but before the consideration of the application by the area committee.[30]

When the applicant has a right of review, he or she must be sent Form 3, the form for applying for a review by the magistrates' court, at the same time as Form 2, the notification of refusal.

The application for a review must be made by giving notice on Form 3 to the area committee within 14 days of the date of notification of the

29   Criminal Regs reg 15.
30   Note for Guidance 17-13(f).

refusal of legal aid.[31] There is power to extend the time under Criminal Regs reg 16(3).

The application must be accompanied by copies of the completed Form 1 returned by the court and Form 2, the notice of refusal.[32] It should be noted that Form 3 specifically invites the applicant to put forward any new or additional information in support of the application. A copy of the Form 3 must be sent to clerk of the magistrates' court to which the original application was made.[33]

The area committee applies the same criteria as the court. Nonetheless, the review procedure is a valuable option when dealing with the more eccentric courts.

It is not possible to apply for a review of Crown Court decisions on legal aid.

Electing trial in the Crown Court

If the applicant is charged with an either way offence and has the option of electing trial by jury in the Crown Court, that is one way, subject to means, of ensuring legal aid. As we have seen (above), after committal for trial the Crown Court has power to grant legal aid. Refusal on the interests of justice ground is virtually unknown in the Crown Court.

However, if it appears to the Crown Court judge that the accused should have had the matter dealt with in the magistrates' court, there is a risk of an order for costs against the accused. Therefore this option should be used only where it is not possible to apply for a review or legal aid has been refused after a review – and the accused seriously intends to plead 'not guilty'.

Applying to the Divisional Court for judicial review

An application for judicial review can be brought in the Divisional Court in respect of a refusal of legal aid by a magistrates' court. However, under the principles laid down in *Associated Provincial Picture Houses v Wednesbury Corporation* [1948] 1 KB 223, the Divisional Court will interfere with the magistrates' decision only where it is wrong in law, *ultra vires*, or a decision which no reasonable bench of magistrates could have reached. In the context of legal aid that means it is insufficient to show that the case falls within the criteria in s22(2). The magistrates may

31 Criminal Regs reg 16(1).
32 Criminal Regs reg 16(2).
33 Criminal Regs reg 16(1).

still, in their discretion, refuse legal aid. As Lord Widgery stated in *R v Highgate Justices ex parte Lewis* (1977) 142 JPN 178:

> The court would entirely lose control over the grant of legal aid if individual offences acquired, as it were, a label saying that they were or were not suitable for the grant . . . every case turns on its own circumstances.

That view was further confirmed in *R v Cambridge Crown Court ex parte Hagi* (1979) 144 JPN 145, where the Divisional Court refused to interfere with the magistrates' refusal of legal aid even though all three judges said that if the discretion had been theirs, they would have granted legal aid. Specifically the court rejected the argument that:

> in any case involving difficult facts or difficult points of law . . . it would be, and must be, mandatory on the court to grant a legal aid order because it would be in the interests of justice to make an order and contrary to those interests to refuse to do so.

In another case, *R v Havering Juvenile Court ex parte Buckley* 12 July 1983 (unreported) CD/554/83, where the justices had refused legal aid to a juvenile in circumstances which arguably satisfied four out of the five 'Widgery' criteria now replaced by s22(2), the court refused to intervene on the basis that:

> What this court has to do is to ask itself whether having regard to [s22(2)], a reasonable bench of justices properly directed, could have reached the conclusions reached by the magistrates in the present case.

On the other hand, that test was satisfied in the case of *R v Brigg Justices ex parte Lynch* (1983) *Times* 17 December, where the Divisional Court held that it was so obvious that a serving soldier would lose his livelihood if convicted of indecent exposure that legal aid should have been granted (see p220 above).

Although the above decisions were made before the 'Widgery' criteria were put into statutory form in s22(2), they are still authoritative.

Judicial review proceedings may be brought against decisions of the Crown Court as against those of a magistrates' court, except where the decision it is sought to challenge is in relation to a trial on indictment.[34] This means that judicial review proceedings can only be brought against

---

34   Supreme Court Act 1981 s29(3); *R v Chichester Crown Court ex parte Abodunrin* (1984) 79 Cr App R 293 DC; *R v Isleworth Crown Court ex parte Willington* (1992) *Times* 6 October.

the Crown Court over legal aid decisions in relation to committals for sentence, appearances to be dealt with, and appeals.

Lastly, it should be remembered that civil legal aid is available and should be applied for to bring proceedings for judicial review.

Appeals against conviction or sentence

The only way to challenge Crown Court decisions in relation to trials on indictment is by way of appeal against conviction or sentence. Some examples of that are given above.

In *R v McAlister* [1988] Crim LR 380, the Court of Appeal quashed the convictions of an accused in the main because he had been refused the means of proper representation on legal aid. The Court took the same course in *R v Chambers* [1989] Crim LR 367, because the trial judge, having allowed the accused's solicitors to withdraw, but not having revoked the legal aid order, refused to allow him to appoint new solicitors.

Where a magistrates' court refuses legal aid and the defendant is convicted, it might also be possible to appeal on the basis that the defendant had not been allowed proper representation.

Paying privately and/or using the green form scheme

In some circumstances it may be possible to provide advice, help and representation under the green form scheme or with the accused paying privately, perhaps until an indictable or either way case reaches the Crown Court.

It would not be possible, however, to make use of the limited ABWOR provisions of Scope Regs reg 7(1)(b), because they are not available where legal aid has been refused.

European Convention on Human Rights

An application to the European Court of Human Rights will not be dealt with in time to reverse a refusal of legal aid in criminal proceedings. However, refusal of legal aid may be in breach of art 6 of the European Convention which guarantees the right to a fair hearing on criminal charges and free legal assistance where required by the interests of justice.

In *Granger v UK* (ECHR Case No 2./1989/162/218) (1990) *Guardian* 10 May, the applicant, who had been denied legal aid by the Scottish courts to appeal against a conviction for perjury, was awarded £8,000 compensation.

Legal aid for prosecutions

Criminal legal aid is available for prosecutors only in very restricted circumstances. Section 21(1) provides specifically that legal aid

> shall not be available to the prosecution except in the case of an appeal to the Crown Court against conviction or sentence, for the purpose of enabling an individual who is not acting in an official capacity to resist the appeal.

In other words, private prosecutors who have been successful in the magistrates' court may be granted legal aid to resist any appeal in the Crown Court. The Crown Court has the normal discretion to award legal aid having regard to the interests of justice.

Successful prosecutors under s82 of the Environmental Protection Act 1990 would be eligible for legal aid to resist an appeal. It was held in *R v Inner London Crown Court ex parte Bentham* [1989] 1 WLR 408 that someone who was resisting an appeal by a defendant against an order made under ss94(2) and 99 of the Public Health Act 1936 (now replaced by s82 of the Environmental Protection Act 1990) was entitled to apply for legal aid under s28(5) of the Legal Aid Act 1974 (now replaced by the above exception in s21(1) of the 1988 Act).

Should the defendant appeal further, to the Court of Appeal, legal aid would not be available. However, in relation to an application for judicial review, whether it was made by the prosecutor or the defendant, the prosecutor would be entitled to apply for civil legal aid.

CHAPTER 13

Means test and contributions

Introduction

As already noted, an applicant may not be granted criminal legal aid unless it appears to the court that he or she is financially eligible[1] and has submitted a statement of means on Form 5.[2] The only circumstances in which the court may dispense with Form 5 are set out in Criminal Regs reg 23(4): where the applicant is physically or mentally unable to provide the form, or where the applicant has already done so and there has been no change in circumstances.

The rules about provision of financial information apply in all cases, including those where the court otherwise has no power to refuse an application for legal aid.

Where the applicant is under 16, the court may require a statement of means from 'an appropriate contributor' instead of or in addition to requiring a statement of means from the applicant.[3] 'Appropriate contributor' is defined in Criminal Regs reg 3(1) and means the applicant's father ('or anyone adjudged to be his father'), mother or guardian.

Form 5 requires the applicant to state his or her marital status and provide details of the financial means of his or her spouse, if they are living together, or co-habitee. If the spouse fails to provide information the court can make an estimate of his or her means.[4]

The court can ask for further information or evidence from either the applicant or an appropriate contributor,[5] and failure to provide the information means that the applicant's means will be deemed to be above the free limit (see below) and s/he will have to pay whatever the court decides by way of a contribution.[6]

---

1 LAA s21(5).
2 LAA s21(6) and Criminal Regs reg 23.
3 Criminal Regs reg 23(3).
4 Criminal Regs Sch 3 para 1(2).
5 Criminal Regs reg 24(1).
6 Criminal Regs reg 24(2).

The Criminal Regs should now also be read in the light of the Lord Chancellor's Circular MCD[92]1 to magistrates' courts. This said that applications for legal aid should not be granted if Form 5 (and Form 1) was not completed in full, or if there was insufficient information to enable the court to consider the application. In those circumstances the application would be returned with a request for further information. If that was not supplied, the application would be refused.

Originally, the circular also required that applicants in employment should submit pay slips covering a period of three months before the application, in the form of three monthly or 13 weekly payslips. That requirement was withdrawn on 8 June 1992. However, another part of the circular which instructed justices' clerks that they should require applicants in receipt of any social security benefit to provide written proof of receipt was stated to remain in force.

Under the LAA, the courts are given discretion to grant criminal legal aid, except in those cases where it is obligatory, and it is for the courts to decide whether the applicant is financially eligible.[7] To the extent that the Lord Chancellor has sought to interfere with the discretion of the courts, Circular MCD[92]1 would appear to be vulnerable to an application for judicial review.

The calculation

Anyone on income support, family credit or disability working allowance is automatically eligible for criminal legal aid free of contribution and it is not necessary for the court to carry out a calculation to determine eligibility and contributions (Criminal Regs reg 26(3)). In all other cases it must do so.

Though the expressions used are the same as in civil legal aid, the rules differ somewhat in detail. Eligibility and contributions are based on the applicant's disposable income and capital during the 'period of computation' calculated in accordance with Criminal Regs Sch 3. 'Period of computation' is defined in Criminal Regs reg 3(1) (as amended by Legal Aid in Criminal and Care Proceedings (General) (Amendment) Regulations 1993 reg 4(g)) as the period of three months following the application for legal aid.

The financial resources of the applicant's spouse, if living with him or her, are taken into account, unless the spouse has a contrary interest or 'in all the circumstances it would be inequitable' to take his or her resources

---

7   LAA s21(5).

into account.[8] 'Spouse' in this context includes anyone of the opposite sex with whom the applicant is living in the same household as husband and wife.[9]

Where the applicant is under 16, the means of 'an appropriate contributor' may also be taken into account[10] and that person may be ordered to pay any contribution.[11] As already noted, 'appropriate contributor' means the father, mother or guardian of the applicant.

No contribution is payable, and it is not necessary to carry out any calculation of disposable income or capital, where the applicant, or the applicant's spouse or the appropriate contributor is receiving income support or family credit.[12]

The court will disregard any reduction or conversion of resources made by the applicant with intent to reduce his or her disposable income or disposable capital.[13] As a result of an amendment introduced in 1990, it is immaterial whether the reduction or conversion was with the purpose of reducing liability to pay a contribution, and therefore *R v Legal Aid Assessment Officer, ex parte Saunders* (1989) *Guardian* 17 November is no longer applicable.

Disposable income

It is the projected income of the applicant (an expression which will be used to include an appropriate contributor) during the period of computation that is relevant.[14] This 'may', and normally will, be estimated on the basis of the applicant's income during the three months prior to the application for legal aid.[15] However, there will be circumstances where that would clearly be inappropriate – because, for instance, the applicant had been remanded in custody and was not earning an income. In that event that should be made clear on Form 5 in the box headed '5. Further information', and if necessary expanded upon in a letter or in an oral application to the court.

Where the applicant is self-employed the income to be received during the contribution period may be calculated on the basis of profits made during the last accounting period for which accounts were prepared.[16]

8   Criminal Regs Sch 3 para 1.
9   Criminal Regs Sch 3 para 2.
10 Criminal Regs reg 25(1).
11 LAA s23(2).
12 Criminal Regs reg 26(3).
13 Criminal Regs Sch 3 para 3.
14 Criminal Regs Sch 3 para 4(1).
15 Criminal Regs Sch 3 para 4(2).
16 Criminal Regs Sch 3 para 5.

Criminal Regs Sch 3 para 6 sets out a number of social security benefits which are ignored in the calculation of disposable income. The most important is housing benefit. The others are: attendance allowance, disability living allowance, constant attendance allowance and payments from the social fund.

The following deductions are made from the applicant's gross income, in order to ascertain disposable income:[17]

- income tax and national insurance contributions (para 7(a) and (b));
- travelling expenses to work (para 7(c));
- contributions to an occupational pension scheme, whether or not they are obligatory (para 7(d));
- child minding expenses (para 7(e));
- council tax (para 7A);
- rent or other housing expenses, including if an owner occupier an allowance for necessary repairs and maintenance, (para 8);
- maintenance payments to a spouse, former spouse, child or relative (para 11);
- payments under any court order, including civil courts, in any proceedings other than those for which legal aid is being applied (para 12).

There are also fixed allowances in respect of dependants of the same amounts as those for civil legal aid.[18] The present annual amounts, which came into force on 12 April 1993, are:

spouse £1,304;
dependant under 11 years £785;
dependant 11–15 years £1,155;
dependant 16–17 years £1,379;
dependant 18 years and over £1,815.

These allowances are automatically increased if and when income support is increased.

The assessing officer has a discretion to disregard any income if s/he considers it 'reasonable having regard to the nature of the income or to any other circumstances of the case'.[19]

Disposable Capital

The rules for calculating disposable capital are also similar to those applied for civil legal aid. Every resource of a capital nature owned by the

17   Criminal Regs Sch 3.
18   Criminal Regs Sch 3 para 10.
19   Criminal Regs Sch 3 para 14.

applicant is taken into account.[20] However, some assets are disregarded. They are:[21]

- the value of the applicant's main dwelling-house and its furniture and effects (paras 18(a) and 19);
- articles of personal clothing (para 18(b));
- tools and equipment of trade (para 18(c));
- savings from a mobility allowance to be used in connection with mobility (para 16(a));
- up to 12 months' arrears of attendance or mobility allowance, income support or family credit (para 16(b));
- payments out of the social fund (para 16(c)).

Furthermore, the value of any business assets wholly or partly owned by the applicant must also be disregarded, unless it is 'reasonable in the circumstances' to take them into account.[22]

The assessing officer also has discretion to disregard any capital which it is reasonable to disregard 'taking into account the nature of the capital or any other circumstances of the case'.[23]

When it comes to the assessment of any items of capital which do not consist of money, the assessing officer must estimate what the item would be worth on the open market, or in a restricted market if that is all that would be available, and deduct any expenses which would be incurred in a sale.[24] If such an estimate is not possible the assessing officer must provide a 'reasonable' valuation.[25]

Fixing and payment of contributions

The amount of contributions is set out in Criminal Regs Sch 4, which is usually revised annually. The applicant who has an average weekly disposable income of £45 or less and capital of £3,000 or less is entitled to free criminal legal aid. There are no upper eligibility limits for criminal legal aid, unlike for the civil version, and therefore potentially everybody is eligible (see, however, below on refusal on means). As with civil legal aid, contributions may be payable out of both income and capital.

An applicant with a weekly disposable income of more than £45 pays a weekly contribution of £1 for every £3 by which his or her weekly income

20   Criminal Regs Sch 3 para 15(1).
21   Criminal Regs Sch 3.
22   Criminal Regs Sch 3 para 17.
23   Criminal Regs Sch 3 para 20.
24   Criminal Regs Sch 3 para 15(2)(a).
25   Criminal Regs Sch 3 para 15(2)(b).

exceeds £44. That continues until the end of the case or the discharge of the legal aid order, whichever comes sooner.

The contribution out of capital is simply the whole amount by which the applicant's disposable capital exceeds £3,000.

If a contribution is payable the court will issue a contribution order. It may do so at the same time as the issue of the legal aid order, or at a later date. Copies are sent to the applicant and his or her solicitor. At that point the applicant may withdraw the application but will be liable to pay the costs of any work done to date.

Contributions payable out of income are payable weekly or, at the discretion of the court, fortnightly or monthly, during the period the legal aid order is in force. The first payment is due seven days from the making of the legal aid order or the making of the contribution order, whichever is the later.[26]

Contributions out of capital are payable immediately if the money is readily available, and if not, at such time as the court considers reasonable.[27] Where the contribution is payable immediately, the legal aid order cannot take effect until it has been paid.[28]

A restriction on higher courts making a contribution order where one has been made previously by a lower court has been removed in relation to legal aid orders applied for on or after 12 April 1993. (Criminal Regs reg 28 deleted by Legal Aid in Criminal and Care Proceedings (General) (Amendment) Regulations 1993 reg 5).

Refusals on ground of means

As already noted, there are no upper means limits for criminal legal aid. However, Criminal Regs reg 26(1) provides that legal aid shall not be granted unless the applicant's financial resources 'are such that he requires assistance in meeting the costs which he may incur for that purpose'.

The effect of this is that where the contribution exceeds the likely costs of the case, legal aid may be refused. However, it would be wrong for courts to refuse in every instance. The defendant who is paying the contribution out of income does not necessarily have the resources available to pay for representation. Solicitors instructed privately will want to be paid on account and may not be prepared to accept payment at the rate of so much per week over a period of six months. In any event, the courts have a much better machinery for assessing payments by

26   Criminal Regs reg 29(1).
27   Criminal Regs reg 29(2).
28   Criminal Regs reg 29(3).

instalments and collecting them. Therefore, in cases, and courts, where the contribution from income is likely to be such that legal aid might be refused under Criminal Regs reg 26(1), it is worth arguing why legal aid should be granted, either on the form under '5. Further information' or in a covering letter.

Where legal aid is refused because of the applicant's capital, a careful eye should be kept on any costs which are incurred privately. As and when a bill is submitted and those costs are paid, they will, of course, diminish the amount of disposable capital. Therefore, it should be permanently in the minds of solicitor and client to renew the application for legal aid, especially if the case proves more expensive than originally expected.

Appeals against means assessments

There is no right of appeal against means assessments or refusals of legal aid on grounds of means. However, the court can be asked to reconsider, and Criminal Regs reg 34 provides for a contribution order to be amended where there has been an error or a mistake.

In addition, it is possible to apply for judicial review in an appropriate case. Although, as previously noted, the remedy of judicial review is not available to challenge a judge's ruling in connection with a trial on indictment, it might be possible to apply for judicial review of a legal aid means assessment in connection with such a trial. In the House of Lords case of *Re Sampson* [1987] 1 WLR 194, Lord Bridge of Harwich stated, *obiter*, that:

> . . . as at present advised, I see no reason why a legal aid contribution order under section 7(1) of Act of 1982 [now s23 of the Act of 1988] should not be made subject to review on an appropriate ground, eg that the order was made in the face of unchallenged evidence that the defendant's disposable income and disposable capital did not exceed the prescribed limits. Such an order cannot affect the conduct of the trial and certainly cannot be regarded as an integral part of the trial process.

Variation and revocation of contribution orders

As already noted, the court has power to vary the contribution order if it has been made on the basis of a mistake. In addition, the order can be amended or revoked on a change of circumstances. The assisted person (which in this context includes an appropriate contributor) must inform

236 Pt III Criminal legal aid

the court of any change in financial circumstances.[29] The court must carry out a reassessment where the assisted person's circumstances have changed and his or her:

- disposable income may have increased by more than £750 pa or decreased by more than £300 pa; and/or
- disposable capital may have increased by more than £750.[30]

Where a reassessment results in a higher contribution being payable, the court may extend the period for payment beyond the end of the case.[31]

If the assisted person, or the assisted person's spouse, or the appropriate contributor begins to receive income support or family credit during the contribution period, the contributions come to an end as from the date when the benefits are first received.[32] However, the court must be informed.[33]

Failure to pay contributions

If the contributions are not paid the court 'may' (it is under no obligation to do so) take steps to revoke the legal aid order. Before doing so it must send a notice to the assisted person requiring him or her to comply with the order and to pay any sums due within seven days.[34] If that notice is not complied with the court must send a further notice inviting the assisted person to make representations to show why the order cannot be complied with.[35] Copies of both notices must be sent to the assisted person's solicitor.

The court may revoke the legal aid order (again it under no compulsion to do so) only if it is satisfied that the assisted person was able to pay the relevant contribution when it fell due and is currently able to pay the whole or part of it but has failed or refused to do so.[36]

It should be noted that Criminal Regs reg 36 refers only to failure to pay by the assisted person. Thus the sanction of revocation is not available to the court where the failure to pay is on the part of an appropriate contributor. However, the court may enforce payment of contributions

---

29 Criminal Regs reg 32.
30 Criminal Regs reg 33.
31 Criminal Regs reg 35(5) as amended by Legal Aid in Criminal and Care Proceedings (General) (Amendment) Regulations 1993 reg 8.
32 Criminal Regs reg 37(1).
33 Criminal Regs reg 37(3).
34 Criminal Regs reg 36(1)(a).
35 Criminal Regs reg 36(1)(b).
36 Criminal Regs reg 36(3).

against an appropriate contributor as against an assisted person who has failed to pay contributions when they were due. The relevant provisions are set out in Sch 3 to the 1988 Act. Enforcement may take place only after the order has been revoked or the proceedings have ended.[37] Then unpaid contributions may be collected in the same way as payments under an affiliation order. In particular, Sch 3 para 2(4) applies the following sections of the Magistrates' Courts Act 1980:

- s80, which empowers a court to have a person searched and take any money found;
- s93, which provides that enforcement shall be on complaint at least 15 days after the order for payment;
- s94, which provides no arrears can accrue while a person has been committed to custody for failure to pay;
- s95, which gives power to remit all or part of any arrears.

In addition, s92 of the Magistrates' Courts Act applies, although it is not specifically mentioned in Sch 3 to the 1988 Act. Therefore, magistrates' courts may issue a warrant to commit to prison for failure to pay a legal aid contribution.[38] However, imprisonment may only be imposed for default in payment where:[39]

- the defendant is present; and
- the court has inquired in the defendant's presence whether the non-payment was due to wilful default; and
- has decided that it is due to wilful default; and
- has decided that it is inappropriate to make an attachment of earnings order.

If a legal aid order is revoked the defendant cannot renew his application under Criminal Regs reg 14 (see p223) but may make a new application (Criminal Regs reg 10) to the court which is seised of the matter (see p212).[40]

On completion of proceedings

Irrespective of the result of a case, where the legal aid costs amount to less than the contributions which have been paid, the excess will be repaid to the assisted person and/or the appropriate contributor.[41] That does not

37   Sch 3 para 6.
38   Magistrates' Courts Act 1980 s92(1)(b).
39   Magistrates' Courts Act 1980 s93(6).
40   *R v Liverpool City Magistrates ex parte Shacklady* (unreported CO/0492/92 and CO/2011/92).
41   LAA s23(7).

require an order of the court, but at the end of the case the assisted person's advocate should always consider whether it is necessary to ask for an order in respect of legal aid contributions and/or costs.

Where the proceedings come to an end and the legal aid order is still in force, then, whatever the outcome, the court should be asked to remit any contributions which are still due to be paid after the conclusion of the proceedings, unless the assisted person is given a custodial sentence.[42] It is in the discretion of the court whether it will do so. A *Practice Note* from the Lord Chief Justice[43] simply, and not very helpfully, says that the decision 'will depend upon the circumstances of the case'.[44] The sort of circumstances which would be relevant would be the defendant's conduct during the proceedings, his or her financial circumstances and the sentence. If the assisted person is given a custodial sentence, the contributions come to an end automatically.[45]

If the assisted person was successful, ie, wholly or partly acquitted, the advocate should apply for an order that any legal aid contributions should be repaid and that any outstanding contributions be wholly remitted, and an order that the defence costs be paid from central funds or, in the right circumstances, be paid by the prosecutor. This means that the advocate should be able to give details of the contribution order and any payments, and any relevant expenses to the court. Any green form costs incurred before the grant of the legal aid order are treated as part of the costs incurred under the order.[46]

The Lord Chief Justice's *Practice Note* states that in normal circumstances a court should order full repayment and remission of contributions to a successful defendant or appellant.[47] Such an order should be made, says the *Practice Note*, 'unless there are circumstances which make such a course of action inappropriate'. The circumstances are not specified. They must include the same sort of reasons which would make an order for costs out of central funds inappropriate, but they must be considered in a wider context such as the defendant's financial position and public interest in defendants being legally represented (see *R v Spens* below).

An order for costs in favour of the defendant can be of advantage even if his or her legal aid contributions are fully repaid/remitted. It is particularly important where the client has paid privately for expert's reports under the 'topping-up' rule (see p252). However, in all cases, the

42 Criminal Regs reg 37(1)(b).
43 [1991] 2 All ER 924.
44 Ibid. para 11.2.
45 Criminal Regs reg 37(1)(c).
46 LAA s26.
47 [1991] 2 All ER 924 at para 11.1.

legal aid order does not cover any out of pocket expenses that the defendant has incurred in attending court. Such expenses may be recovered, however, as part of a costs order.[48] It should be noted, though, that only subsistence or travelling expenses can form part of a costs order; lost earnings can only be recovered as damages in a suit for malicious prosecution.

Payment of costs may be ordered to be made either out of central funds or by the prosecution personally. A defendant's costs order out of central funds under the Prosecution of Offences Act 1985 s16 is the more usual order if there is an acquittal, if a case is not proceeded with, or if a conviction is set aside or less severe sentence imposed on appeal. The Lord Chief Justice's *Practice Note* makes clear that an order for costs should normally be made in favour of the defendant in such circumstances, 'unless there are positive reasons for not doing so'.[49] Examples of such reasons are given:

- if the defendant has brought suspicion on him- or herself or has misled the prosecution into thinking that the case is stronger than it is;
- if there was ample evidence to support a conviction but the defendant was acquitted on a technicality without merit.

If the court makes a defendant's costs order but decides that the defendant shall not recover the full amount of costs incurred, it must assess what is fair and reasonable and make an order for that amount.[50] Otherwise the costs will be taxed by the court, unless the defendant agrees to a specified amount being stated in the order.[51]

In *R v Spens* (1992) *Independent* 18 March, the defendant, Lord Spens, applied for a 'not guilty' verdict to be entered, for a defendant's costs order of £400,000 in respect of pre-legal aid costs and for the remission of a legal aid contribution of £100,000. The trial had come to an end part of the way through when the prosecution decided to offer no evidence because it would have been oppressive and/or an abuse of process due to the deteriorating health of Lord Spens' co-defendant who was representing himself.

Mr Justice Henry refused to order that a 'not guilty' verdict be entered against Lord Spens, and also refused to make a defendant's costs order. The costs order, said the judge, would have been refused even if Lord Spens had been acquitted, because information which he had given to DTI inspectors before he was charged showed that he had brought the

---

48   Prosecution of Offences Act 1985 s16 and Costs in Criminal Cases (General) Regulations 1986 reg 23.
49   [1991] 2 All ER 924 at para 2.2.
50   Prosecution of Offences Act 1985 s16(7).
51   Prosecution of Offences Act 1985 s16(9).

prosecution on himself. However, the judge did order that the whole legal aid contribution should be remitted. The reasons were the strong public interest in a defendant being legally represented in a long trial, Lord Spens' financial position and his liabilities to his pre-legal aid lawyers. It should be added that this trial was exceptionally lengthy and complicated, and that a major factor which had led to it eventually being abortive was the fact that Lord Spens' co-defendant had represented himself. This undoubtedly influenced the judge.

An order for costs out of central funds under s16 of the 1985 Act only provides for payment of the defendant's expenses over and above the legal aid costs and contribution.[52] That is why it is necessary to combine the application for costs under s16 with an application for repayment/ remission of contributions.

Costs may also be ordered against prosecutors or their representatives under ss19 and 19A of the Prosecution of Offences Act 1985, but only where they have caused the costs to be incurred unnecessarily or improperly (see also next chapter).

Under s19, but not s19A of the 1985 Act, the amount the prosecution may be ordered to pay may include the defendant's legal aid costs but not the contribution.[53] If the prosecution is ordered to pay all the defendant's legal aid costs, any legal aid contributions will be repaid under s23(8) of the Legal Aid Act 1988. In that event, as in any other where repayment is due to the assisted person, repayment will come from the court which has collected the contributions, and that is usually the magistrates' court.[54]

52   Prosecution of Offences Act 1985 s21(4A)(a).
53   Prosecution of Offences Act 1985 21(4A)(b).
54   Criminal Regs reg 37(2).

CHAPTER 14

Grant and scope of orders

Introduction

When legal aid is granted, a copy of the order is sent to the assisted person and his or her solicitor (or counsel if only counsel is assigned). If the order was made by a legal aid area committee, a copy will also be sent to the court.[1]

The form of the order varies according to whether it is for proceedings in the magistrates' court, the Crown Court or the Court of Appeal, but in all cases it will contain details of the proceedings for which legal aid has been granted and the solicitor (or counsel) who has been assigned. It is important to check that information as soon as the order is received to ensure that the work to be done is within the scope of the order or whether it might be necessary to apply for an amendment.

As with civil legal aid, lawyers will be paid only for the work done which is within the scope of the order. However, unlike the normal position in civil legal aid, they may be paid under the order for work done before it was issued. Under Criminal Regs reg 44(7), representation or advice provided in magistrates' court proceedings before the order was issued 'shall be deemed' to be work done under the order provided three conditions are satisfied. They are that:

- the interests of justice required that the work be done urgently;
- the application for legal aid was made without undue delay;
- the work was done by the solicitor nominated on the legal aid order.

The Legal Aid Board has issued guidance on its interpretation of this regulation.[2] The first two criteria mentioned above are likely to be satisfied where there is a court hearing within at most 10 days of the date when initial instructions were taken and the application for legal aid is made no more than seven days after that date. Time starts to run from the

---

1 Criminal Regs reg 40.
2 (1991) 88/39 LS Gaz 15 and Note for Guidance 17-24.

day following initial instructions, and Saturdays, Sundays and bank holidays are counted. It is possible, says the guidance, that circumstances other than those mentioned may be accepted as constituting a matter of urgency and that applications made after more than seven days will not be considered to be unduly delayed.

In practice, the option of claiming under Criminal Regs reg 44(7) is a supplement to duty solicitor schemes and the green form scheme.

If the work involved falls under the police station duty solicitor scheme, it would be in the interests of the client for the work to be done under that scheme because, unlike criminal legal aid, it is not means-tested. If, before the grant of legal aid, the client is appearing in a magistrates' court which has a duty solicitor scheme (and it is much more likely to have one than not), then solicitors should consider whether, if legal aid is not granted on the day of appearance, they will be able to show that it was necessary in the interests of justice for them to represent the client on the appearance given the availability of the duty solicitor.

Under s26, work done under a green form may be claimed for as work done under a legal aid order by the same solicitor, and any green form contributions payable by the client are credited against a legal aid contribution. The rates payable to solicitors for criminal legal aid work are usually the same as for green form work. There is therefore little to choose between relying on s26 or relying on Criminal Regs reg 44(7), except that solicitors cannot be sure in advance that the Legal Aid Board will accept that the first two conditions of Criminal Regs reg 44(7) have been met. Therefore, in most cases the latter provision is likely to be of use when the green form cannot be used – for example, because the client is not eligible, the prescribed limit has been reached, or representation in court is involved.

Assignment of solicitors and counsel

Solicitors and counsel

In the magistrates' court, legal aid is normally granted for representation by a solicitor only, although it is always possible for the solicitor to instruct a barrister (who will be paid out of the costs allowed to the solicitor, see next chapter) and in some cases that may be specifically authorised (see below). In Crown Court proceedings where solicitors have rights of audience, a court may also grant legal aid limited to solicitors only. Representation by counsel only may be ordered in all cases by the Court of Appeal[3] and in cases of urgency by the Crown Court.[4] In all other

3   Criminal Regs reg 44(4).
4   Criminal Regs reg 44(5).

courts, and normally in the Crown Court, a legal aid order provides for representation by solicitors and counsel.[5]

Counsel may be authorised in magistrates' court proceedings only where the defendant is charged with an indictable offence and there are circumstances which make the case unusually grave or difficult so that representation by both solicitor and counsel would be desirable.[6] It is desirable for solicitors to obtain an order for counsel, even if they intend to do all the work themselves, because they will be entitled to claim enhanced payment as a result and will not in any event be subject to standard fees.

For the purposes of Criminal Regs reg 44(5), 'indictable' includes offences triable either way.[7] As far as the 'unusually grave or difficult' requirement is concerned:

- in committal proceedings for murder, even if the case is not difficult, legal aid should include representation by counsel;[8]
- if charges are straightforward and simple, their mere multiplicity does not mean that representation by counsel is desirable;[9]
- if there is no conceivable reason for opposing a paper committal under s6(2) of the Magistrates' Courts Act 1980, there is no reason for assigning counsel at that stage;[10]
- complex facts might make it desirable for counsel to advise whether good grounds might exist for opposing a s6(2) committal.[11]

Choice of representative

In all cases where a solicitor is nominated it is for that solicitor to choose counsel, if any.[12]

If the applicant does not nominate a solicitor, the court can assign one to act. Otherwise, the rule is that the court must assign any solicitor who is willing to act nominated by the applicant.[13] However, this is subject to two qualifications.

First, for proceedings in the Court of Appeal, the applicant's choice is not necessarily decisive. The court may assign any solicitor having regard 'as far as is practicable to the wishes of the legally assisted person, the

5   Criminal Regs reg 44(1).
6   Criminal Regs reg 44(3).
7   *R v Guildhall Justices ex parte Marshall* [1976] 1 All ER 767.
8   *R v Derby Justices ex parte Kooner and others* [1971] 1 QB 147.
9   *R v Guildford Justices ex parte Scott* [1975] Crim LR 286.
10   *R v Guildford Justices, supra.*
11   *R v Guildford Justices, supra.*
12   Criminal Regs reg 45(2).
13   Criminal Regs reg 45(1).

identity of the solicitor or counsel, if any, who represented him in any earlier proceedings and the nature of the appeal'.[14] While the effect of this is that, for reasons of cost, the court will tend to appoint existing solicitors, that is not always so. If the grounds of appeal, for instance, expressly or implicitly criticise the handling of the previous proceedings by solicitors or counsel, it would clearly be wrong for the existing solicitors to be appointed having regard to 'the nature of the appeal'.

Secondly, unless the interests of justice require otherwise, the court may assign the same solicitor (or counsel) to two or more assisted persons whose cases are to be heard together.[15] In practice, this means that where co-defendants apply for legal aid the court is likely to assign the solicitor named on the first application form received. The requirement about the interests of justice is usually interpreted by the courts to mean that it must be shown that there is a conflict of interest between the defendants. But it could also arise in other circumstances, for instance where a nominated firm acts for the same client in a number of different current cases, it could be in the interests of justice that all those cases should be dealt with together.

In the first instance it is the duty of the solicitor who has been assigned to consider whether he or she can act for co-defendants without a conflict of interest. In some foreign jurisdictions – for instance, most states in the United States of America – the answer would be considered obvious: that it is impossible to act for co-defendants without the risk of conflict. Not so here. In some cases it will be clear – for instance, where a 'cut-throat' defence is being run. In other cases it may be less obvious – for instance, where no defendant is making allegations against another but it seems to the solicitor, on the basis of the defendants' relative backgrounds, that s/he should ask whether one was under the influence of the other. Or where there is a conflict between solicitor and client.

If it appears that a conflict is likely or possible, an application should be made for a change of solicitor (see below). That application can be made not only by the solicitor nominated, but also by a solicitor who is asking to be nominated, who will, however, not be able to be paid out of the Legal Aid Fund for that work.

It should be noted that it is in the interests of solicitors themselves that they should not get involved in representing co-defendants who are running cut-throat defences. In that event, they will not be able to continue to act for any of them. In *Saminadhen v Khan*, Lord Donaldson of Lymington MR stated:[16]

---

14   Criminal Regs reg 46(2).
15   Criminal Regs reg 49.
16   [1992] 1 All ER 963 (note), CA.

I can conceive of no circumstances in which it would be proper for a solicitor who has acted for a defendant in criminal proceedings, the retainer having been terminated, to then act for a co-defendant where there is a cut-throat defence between the two defendants.

It should be noted that the court does not have a completely free hand in assigning a solicitor to co-defendants. Where the co-defendants have nominated solicitors and those solicitors are willing to act, the court must assign one of them; it cannot assign a solicitor who has been nominated by none of the co-defendants.[17]

Renewal of applications to the area committee and to the court

In some circumstances, where an application to amend a legal aid order to authorise counsel under Criminal Regs reg 44(3) or to assign a new solicitor is refused, it is possible to renew the same application to the legal aid area committee.[18] Those circumstances are:

- that the refusal was made by the justices' clerk or a Crown Court officer, rather than by the court itself or the area committee;
- in Crown Court proceedings, the original application had been made within 14 days or less from the committal for trial or the giving of notice of appeal;
- in magistrates' court proceedings, the original application had been made at least 13 days before any date fixed for trial or committal.[19]

Those restrictions do not apply to renewal of an application to the court. That can be done in any case.[20]

An application to the area committee is made by sending the legal aid order, the notice of refusal and any supporting papers or additional documents.

Assignment of Queen's Counsel and two counsel

Queen's Counsel, or two junior counsel, can only be assigned for proceedings in the Crown Court, the Court of Appeal or the House of Lords;[21] in other words they cannot be assigned for any proceedings in the

17   *Baker v Chichester Justices* [1984] Crim LR 240.
18   Criminal Regs reg 51(2).
19   Criminal Regs reg 51(6).
20   Criminal Regs reg 51(2).
21   Criminal Regs reg 48(2).

magistrates' court. In addition, before an order can be made for a Queen's Counsel or two counsel, the case must meet certain requirements:

- it must be on a charge of murder; or
- it is of exceptional difficulty, gravity or complexity and the interests of justice require that the accused should have two counsel.

A two-counsel order may be made in the following forms:[22]

- a QC with a junior counsel;
- a QC with a noting junior counsel;
- two junior counsel;
- a junior counsel with a noting junior counsel.

In deciding between the options the court must have regard to any choice of counsel made by the accused – for instance, s/he would like to be represented by a named junior counsel with another junior counsel to assist. The court is also required to consider whether a QC without a junior would be sufficient.[23]

An application can be made to the magistrates' court, a High Court judge or a circuit judge for crown court proceedings, or a judge or the Registrar for Court of Appeal proceedings. However, the magistrates' court has no discretion other than in cases of murder to order representation by a QC with a junior.[24]

A *Practice Note* [1989] 2 All ER 479, provides how applications for two counsel should be dealt with in the Crown Court:

- applications made during a pre-trial review or a trial should be dealt with by the judge at the hearing;
- applications in a case which is to be heard before a named High Court or circuit judge, should be referred to that judge;
- otherwise the application should be put before the resident or designated judge of the Crown Court, or, if that judge is absent, a judge nominated by the presiding judge of the circuit.

Scope

A legal aid order covers all the work that would normally be done by a solicitor, and if necessary counsel, to bring a case to a conclusion. However, there are some items of expenditure for which it might be wise to obtain authority in advance (see below) and some types of work which may need to be justified when a claim is made for payment (see next chapter).

22   Criminal Regs reg 48(3).
23   Criminal Regs reg 48(5).
24   Criminal Regs reg 48(4).

If a case in which a legal aid order has been made is transferred from a magistrates' court to a juvenile court or to another magistrates' court, the same legal aid order will continue to provide representation.[25] However, where a case is committed for trial to the Crown Court, the legal aid order needs to be extended by the magistrates' court to cover the Crown Court proceedings. If the magistrates' court refuses to extend the order, it will be necessary to make a new application to the Crown Court. The exception to this rule is where the magistrates' court has made an order under s20(5) LAA which covers proceedings both in that court and in the Crown Court – a so-called 'through order'.

The magistrates' court order needs to be extended to the Crown Court where cases are transferred by notice, as under s4 of the Criminal Justice Act 1987 or s53 of the Criminal Justice Act 1991. However, that does not mean that the magistrates' court legal aid order comes to an end as soon as the notice of transfer is served. The magistrates' court continues to be concerned with bail, witness orders and the grant of legal aid for the Crown Court, and until those matters have been dealt with the magistrates' court legal aid order remains in force. It follows that all work actually and reasonably done by the accused's solicitors can be claimed for under the magistrates' court's legal aid order.[26]

A legal aid order in the magistrates' court or in the Crown Court includes representation in any preliminary or incidental proceedings, and in particular bail applications, whether or not they are in the same court as the main proceedings.[27] This means that a legal aid order in the magistrates' court will cover a bail appeal to the Crown Court under the Criminal Justice Act 1982 s60. Solicitors have rights of audience under s60, and so the legal aid order provides only for representation by a solicitor unless counsel has been authorised. The magistrates' court has no power to issue a legal aid order solely for a s60 bail appeal. An application to a High Court judge in chambers is specifically excluded from a magistrates' court legal aid order.[28] However, civil legal aid is available to bring an application to a High Court judge in chambers and is granted in some circumstances (see p76 above).

As noted in the previous chapter, a legal aid order, whether in the magistrates' court or the Crown Court, includes advice and assistance in connection with an appeal against conviction and/or sentence.[29] It is the duty of solicitors and counsel to provide that advice and assistance in every

25   LAA s19(3).
26   Note for Guidance 17–47.
27   LAA s19(2).
28   LAA s19(4).
29   LAA s2(4).

case where the client is convicted or sentenced, and if they fail to do so, they may be at risk as to costs (see next chapter). A *Guide to Proceedings in the Court of Appeal, Criminal Division*, published in 1990 by the Criminal Appeal Office, sets out the procedure which should be followed, which requires that written advice should be given to the offender within 21 days of conviction or sentence. Appendix 1 to that *Guide* sets out instructions to counsel which solicitors should always include with their brief. Counsel should complete Appendix 1 immediately after the case has ended, and solicitors should provide the client with a copy. If counsel's advice is that there are no reasonable grounds of appeal, that is the end of the work done under the legal aid order. Otherwise counsel must advise further in writing within 14 days and a notice of application for leave to appeal or a notice of appeal lodged with the court.

In addition, as has already been noted on p225, a refusal of legal aid, or any other decision by a magistrates' court may be challenged in the Divisional Court, but only when it is considered wrong in law, *ultra vires* or totally unreasonable. Civil legal aid may be sought for this purpose. However, a Crown Court decision 'relating to a trial on indictment' is specifically excluded from judicial review (see pp226–227).

Advance authorisation of expenditure

Under Criminal Regs reg 54, it is possible for solicitors to apply to an area committee for advance authorisation of expenditure in a particular case. The effect of advance authority is that normally no questions will be raised about the propriety of the expenditure on assessment by the area office or taxation by the court.

Criminal Regs reg 54 sets out the expenses for which authority can be obtained in magistrates' court and crown court cases:

a) obtaining expert's reports;
b) employing someone other than an expert to provide a report or opinion;
c) obtaining transcripts of shorthand notes or tape recordings of any proceedings, including police interviews with suspects;
d) where solicitor and counsel is authorised, instructing a QC alone without a junior;
e) any act which is unusual in its nature or involves unusually large expenditure.

In each case the area committee should authorise expenditure if satisfied that it is necessary for the proper conduct of the case and reasonable in the circumstances.[30] Where the area committee authorises expenditure it must also, except where it authorises a QC, specify the maximum amount to be paid.[31] The amount will usually be in line with guideline rates issued by the Lord Chancellor's Department.

There is no appeal against an area committee's refusal but applications can be renewed at any time. In any event, if advance authority is refused, the expense may be allowed on assessment or taxation later, or the solicitor can obtain payment privately under the topping-up arrangements allowed by Criminal Regs reg 55.

Change of solicitor

The defendant may ask at any time for the legal aid order to be amended to assign new legal representatives.[32] Normally the best way to do this is for the defendant or the new solicitors to write to the court asking for the change of solicitors and explaining the reasons for it. It should be noted, however, that the new solicitors cannot be paid on legal aid for any work which is done before the transfer of the order. Criminal Regs reg 44(7) does not apply in these circumstances, and the green form scheme cannot be used where a legal aid order is in force in connection with the same proceedings.

That may be a problem, particularly where the client wants to change solicitors in order to appeal, since the legal aid order, as already noted, also covers giving advice and assistance on appeal. In those circumstances, if the trial court refuses to agree to a transfer, the new solicitors have the option of being paid privately or doing the work for free until a new order assigned to them may be obtained from the court to which an appeal is made.

If a new solicitor (or counsel) is assigned, the previous solicitor (or counsel) is required by Criminal Regs reg 50(4) to send him or her all the relevant papers and other items.

When an application is made to a court to change legal representatives because the existing representatives, or some of them, want to withdraw from the case, the court has the option of withdrawing the order if it thinks that because of the assisted person's conduct it should not be amended.[33]

---

30   Note for Guidance 17–17.
31   Criminal Regs reg 54(2).
32   Criminal Regs reg 50(1).
33   Criminal Regs reg 50(2) and *R v Dimech* [1991] Crim LR 846.

A refusal to amend a legal aid order, or a decision to withdraw it, may be challenged by renewing the application to an area committee in the same circumstances as renewing an application for counsel (see p245 above), or it may be renewed to the court. In addition, if the decision is wrong in law it may be challenged by judicial review if made by a magistrates' court or by an appeal against conviction and/or sentence if made by a Crown Court.[34]

34   R v McAlister [1988] Crim LR 380.

CHAPTER 15

Obtaining payment

Introduction

The rules about payment for criminal legal aid work are set out in the Legal Aid in Criminal and Care Proceedings (Costs) Regulations 1989 (the Criminal Costs Regs). Despite the full title, these regulations, as a result of the Children Act reforms, no longer have anything to do with care proceedings.

The outline of the system is quite simple. Claims for payment for magistrates' court work are made to the area offices of the Legal Aid Board, claims in respect of Crown Court and Court of Appeal work to the courts. In all cases claims must normally be made within three months. There are set standard fees, but these may be 'enhanced' in special circumstances.

The principles according to which legal aid costs are assessed or taxed by the Legal Aid Board, the Crown Court and the Court of Appeal (including the Courts-Martial Appeal Court) are all the same and are set out in the Criminal Costs Regs. Solicitors and barristers are paid for work 'reasonably' done and repaid disbursements 'reasonably incurred'.[1]

Where costs have been wasted as a result of acts or omissions by a defendant's legal representatives, they can be ordered to pay those costs under s19A of the Prosecution of Offences Act 1985 or under the court's inherent jurisdiction, but the latter only applies to solicitors. In addition, or as an alternative, the legal aid costs of legal representatives may be reduced or disallowed under the Criminal Costs Regs.

Time for claiming

All claims for costs must be made within three months of the end of the case.[2] It is possible to apply for an extension but it is advisable to have a

1 Criminal Costs Regs reg 6(2) and 7(1).
2 Criminal Costs Regs reg 5(1).

good reason for being late.[3] The Legal Aid Board has stated that the fact that a particular firm submits a large number of bills on time and only rarely is out of time, is not a good reason for delay in any particular case.[4]

Where the proceedings have not been concluded but an arrest warrant has been issued, the solicitor may make a claim for costs six weeks after the issue of the warrant and must do so within 19 weeks (Criminal Costs Regs reg 5(1A) inserted by Legal Aid in Criminal and Care Proceedings (Costs) (Amendment) Regulations 1993).

'Topping up'

In criminal legal aid, as in the civil scheme, solicitors and counsel are generally prohibited from accepting payment in a legally-aided case from any source other than the Legal Aid Fund.[5] However, there is a specific exception in the criminal legal aid scheme. Solicitors, and counsel, may accept private payment from another source – such as the assisted person or a friend or relative – to cover certain disbursements where authority to incur those disbursements has previously been refused by an area committee under Criminal Regs reg 54.

In such circumstances, 'topping up', as it is usually called, is allowed under Criminal Regs reg 55(b) in respect of the fees or expenses incurred in:

- preparing, obtaining or considering any report, opinion or further evidence, whether from an expert witness or otherwise; or
- obtaining transcripts of shorthand notes or tape recordings of any proceedings, including police interviews.

Solicitors should remember, however, that refusal of authority under Criminal Regs reg 54 does not preclude them from claiming disbursements on taxation, and such a claim should be made. If the claim is allowed on taxation, the topping-up payment should, of course, be returned.

Magistrates' court claims

Claims for work done in the magistrates' court are made to the area office of the Legal Aid Board. If the case is committed to the Crown Court, there is no need to wait for the proceedings to be finished there. With the claim form should be sent the documents required by the area offices which are listed on the form. The Legal Aid Board has made clear (Note for

3 See Note for Guidance 17-23.
4 Note for Guidance 17-38 and Legal Aid Board ref. CRIMLA 14.
5 Criminal Regs reg 55(a).

Guidance 17–36) that it will not meet claims unless they can be substantiated. The area office can call for the whole file if it so wishes. Standard fee provisions apply where the legal aid order was granted on or after 1 June 1993, unless the case is excepted from those provisions. The specifically excepted cases are those where counsel has been assigned under the legal aid order (Criminal Costs Regs Sch 2 Part III para 3(a), a new schedule inserted by Legal Aid in Criminal and Care Proceedings (Costs) (Amendment) Regulations 1983) or where enhanced rates apply (ibid para 3(b) and see below). In addition some cases are implicitly excepted through not being included in any of the categories listed in the Criminal Costs Regs Sch 2 Part III. They are extradition proceedings and 'old-style' (s6(1) Magistrates' Courts Act 1980) committals.

Calculation of standard fees

The standard fee payable in each case (see Note for Guidance 17–22) depends on two factors: the cost of the work actually done and the category into which the case falls.

The work is costed using the fees set out in Schedule 1 Part 1 of the Criminal Costs Regs. The rates for work done after 1 April 1992 (and not increased since) are:

	£ per hour
Preparation	43.25 (45.75)
Advocacy	53.00 (54.50)
Routine letters and telephone calls (£ per item)	3.35 (3.50)

The figures in brackets apply to fee-earners whose offices are within Legal Aid Area 1 (Greater London).

For the purposes of calculating which standard fee should apply only the so-called 'core costs' are included:

- all preparation, including listening to, or viewing, tape or video recordings of interviews or evidence;
- routine letters and telephone calls;
- advocacy, including bail and other applications made in either the magistrates' court or the Crown Court;
- work done by a fee-earner acting as the solicitor's agent;
- unassigned counsel's preparation, advocacy and waiting time, (Criminal Costs Regs Sch 2 Part III para 4).

It should be noted that time spent travelling and waiting, and disbursements, are excluded from the calculation of the standard fee (but, as we shall see, they are added later).

Where a solicitor acts for more than one defendant or in respect of more than one charge, one claim for payment covers everything.

Having worked out the cost of the work done, the solicitor consults a standard fees table to see in which band within its appropriate category the case falls. Costs up to the lower limit attract the lower standard fee; costs over the lower and up to the higher limit attract the higher standard fee. The categories are as follows (Criminal Costs Regs Sch 2 Part III para 2(2)).

Category 1

Guilty pleas, uncontested proceedings arising out of breach of a magistrates' court order, discontinued or withdrawn proceedings or proceedings which result in a bind over (other than committal proceedings), proceedings arising out of a deferment of sentence.

Category 2

Contested trials, cracked trials (including a bind-over on the date of the trial), contested proceedings arising out of a breach of a magistrates' court order, mixed pleas.

Category 3

Magistrates' Courts Act 1980 s6(2) committals (including those discontinued or withdrawn), committals withdrawn or discontinued before court has fixed the date for a s6(1) hearing, proceedings transferred under s4 of the Criminal Justice Act 1987 or s53 of the Criminal Justice Act 1991.

The standard fees for each category are set out in a table in the Criminal Costs Regs Sch 2 Part III para 8(1).

Type of proceedings	Lower standard fee	Lower limit	Higher standard fee	Higher limit
Category 1	£140	£261	£336	£451
London rate	£180	£335	£427	£565
Category 2	£247	£447	£566	£745
London rate	£317	£567	£711	£908
Category 3	£223	£395	£505	£689
London rate	£282	£479	£593	£733

The London rate applies to fee-earners whose office is within the Greater London area (legal aid area 1). Travelling and waiting time is paid at the rate of £24.25 per hour.

Where the cost of the work done, calculated as above and taking no account of travelling and waiting time, exceeds the higher limit, the solicitor will be paid for the work done on the basis of the fees set out in Sch 1 Part 1 of the Criminal Costs Regs and including travelling and waiting time (Criminal Costs Regs Sch 2 Part III para 8(3) and see p253).

To take a hypothetical example: the lower standard fee for the work done by solicitor outside London in connection with a s6(2) committal is £223. The solicitor who does work to a value of less than £223 will nonetheless be paid £223. The solicitor who does work to a value of more than £223 but less than £395 would also be paid £223. In each case the solicitor would also be paid in respect of travelling and waiting time and disbursements. But if the solicitor does work to a value of more than £395, say a value of £400, s/he will immediately become entitled to the higher standard fee of £505, but if the cost is more than this, s/he will not receive more by way of fees until costs reach the higher limit of £689. In other words, and leaving aside the fine tuning that will no doubt be applied in the assessment process, the solicitor who has done, say, £100-worth of work is paid the same as the solicitor who has done £394-worth, and the solicitor who has done £396-worth receives the same as the solicitor who has done £688-worth.

It will be difficult in many cases for solicitors to calculate, within the limits, whether it is financially worth their while to carry out additional work, but in some cases it will be possible. In some cases, when otherwise unenergetic solicitors are spurred to greater efforts by the incentive of reaching a higher limit, the result may be a higher standard of work. However, given the fact that Legal Aid Board assessment officers, with the twin benefits of hindsight and lack of practical experience, will penalise solicitors for doing too much rather than too little, it seems more likely that standard fees will lead to corner-cutting and a lowering of professional standards.

Some specific points should be noted, most of which are relevant whether fees are payable on the standard or assessed basis.

Working while travelling and waiting

The treatment of travelling and waiting time differs according to whether fees are to be paid on a standard basis or not and, if so, whether turning that time into preparation time will push the case into a higher fee band.

If fees are to be paid on an assessed basis, the position is simple. As can be seen from the above, travelling and waiting time is badly paid compared with preparation time. Therefore whenever possible, the former should be turned into the latter. Reading the file, for instance, or preparing a submission while travelling to court means that the time can be classified as preparation rather than travelling and the higher rate claimed. Taking instructions from and advising the client at court, or negotiating bail conditions with the prosecution, or discussing the case with them to obtain information or finding out how a guilty plea would be received, means that time can be classified as preparation or attendance rather than waiting and the higher rate claimed. Even more remunerative is to have a number of different cases at the same court so that not only can all waiting time be filled, but some of it can be filled with advocacy time which pays best of all, a question of good organisation of time.

However, where a standard fee is payable it will only be in the financial interests of practitioners to convert travelling and waiting time into preparation time where the effect of doing so is to reach a higher limit. Otherwise, since travelling and waiting time is added to the standard fee, but all preparation time is included in it, the effect would simply be to lose money that would otherwise be payable. However, such fine calculations and predictions, which, of course, should be made when the work is done, rather than at the time of claiming payment, might well be difficult to apply in practice.

Counsel's fees where not authorised

As noted above (see p242) in the magistrates' court legal aid normally covers representation by a solicitor only. However, the solicitor is free to instruct counsel to appear instead. When that happens the treatment of counsel's fees depends on whether or not the legal aid order was made before 1 June 1993.

If the order was made before that date, the area office will calculate the total fee for the case as though it had been done without counsel. It will then, on the basis of the documents submitted, assess counsel's fees. Counsel will be paid his or her fees direct and the balance of the original total will be paid to the solicitor (Criminal Costs Regs reg 7(3) and (4)).

Where the legal aid order was made on or after 1 June 1993, the Legal Aid Board will not assess counsel's fees. Instead the solicitor must agree the brief fee with counsel and state the amount in the claim for payment submitted to the Board.[6]

Formal committals and remands

Under the Magistrates' Courts Act 1980 s6(2), a defendant can be committed for trial to the Crown Court as long as s/he has a solicitor acting for him or her. There is no general requirement that the solicitor should be in court when the remand takes place. Therefore, to be paid for

6   Criminal Costs Reg regs 5(3)(f) and 7A, inserted by Legal Aid in Criminal and Care Proceedings (Costs) (Amendment) Regulations 1993.

attendance at a committal, a solicitor must be able to show that his or her attendance was necessary.[8] The circumstances which will justify attendance are:

- a submission of no case to answer was to be made; or
- there was a need to take oral evidence from witnesses; or
- there was to be an application for bail or to vary bail conditions; or
- there was to be an application to lift bail restrictions; or
- there was to be an application in relation to the trial venue; or
- the witness statements had been served less than 14 days before the date fixed for committal; or
- there was some other matter which reasonably required attendance at court (details must be given).

The factors which would justify attendance under the last-mentioned criterion would be, for instance, that the solicitor had some application to make, or that the court appearance was a convenient and an economical opportunity to obtain instructions from a client in custody some distance away.

Where clients appear at formal remand hearings, there is again no general need for solicitors to attend. Therefore, solicitors should similarly explain why they attended any formal remand hearings, or they will not be paid for doing so.[9]

Representation in a distant court

Only such work as has been done 'reasonably' will be paid for.[10] Further, any travelling expenses claimed as disbursements which are 'abnormally large by reason of the distance of the court or the assisted person's residence or both from the solicitors' place of business' may be reduced to what the area office considers a reasonable amount.[11]

Solicitors will have to show why it was reasonable for them personally to go to court rather than to instruct local agents. The factors which will be relevant are similar to those which are considered under the next head.

Attending clients remanded in custody

Where a client has been remanded in custody at a distance, the solicitor will normally be paid for going to see him or her to take instructions.

---

8 See Note for Guidance 17-25.
9 Note for Guidance 17-32 and CRIMLA (reference of Legal Aid Board Costs Appeals Committee) 7.
10 Criminal Costs Regs reg 6(2)(b).
11 Criminal Costs Regs reg 7(1)(a).

However, the area office will always consider whether it would have been more reasonable to instruct a local agent. The relevant factors include, for example: the nature and seriousness of the charge; whether the client is under a disability; the relationship, if any, between the solicitor and client; the practicality of taking instructions at court, and the likelihood of the client being given bail or being moved closer to the solicitor's office.[12]

Supervision

A fee-earner should normally be competent to deal with the cases allocated to him or her, and time spent on supervision cannot be claimed under the heading of practical instruction or practice management. Supervision may, however, also be part of the preparation of the case; but if claimed as such, an explanation of the circumstances which made it necessary and details of the supervisory participation must be provided.

Use of interpreter

Solicitors must justify interpreters' fees, taking into account all the circumstances, including the need to preserve confidentiality and the need for accurate understanding.

Medical or psychiatric reports in mitigation

Unless reports have been requested by the court, their cost will be allowed only in exceptional circumstances.

Listening to taped interviews

The Legal Aid Board has held that it is reasonable for solicitors to listen to taped police interviews where the client cannot confirm that the written summary is correct (Note for Guidance 17–59 and CRIMLA 35).

Transcription of taped interviews

Payment to an outside agency for transcribing tapes will be allowed if the area office is satisfied that it was necessary (and advance authority will normally be given in such circumstances by the area committee). However, if transcription is made in the solicitor's office, the area office will

---

12   Notes for Guidance 17-34, 17-45 and 17-55, CRIMLA 9, 21 and 31.

not normally accept it as fee-earner's work, and therefore will not pay for it. On the other hand, listening to the tapes and deciding whether they should be transcribed, and checking the accuracy of transcripts normally will be remunerated as fee-earner's work.[12]

The practical solution is to make sure, first, that adequate time is given to, and claimed for, listening to the tapes and comparing them with other evidence; and secondly, that if tapes are transcribed by a member of the solicitor's staff, that is done in his or her own time as part of a legitimate separate business, charged for privately, and that a receipt is provided to validate a claim for the payment as a disbursement (see Note for Guidance 10–06).

Factual enquiries

A claim for profit costs for time spent making factual enquiries may be disallowed if the area office thinks it would have been more reasonable to use an enquiry agent. It depends on all the circumstances of the case, including its nature, the nature and number of the enquiries to be undertaken, the travel involved and any unusual aspects of the case or the evidence. If a claim for profit costs is disallowed, the Board may allow a notional claim for the instruction of an enquiry agent as part of the profit costs.[13]

Witness expenses

In the first instance, witness expenses – including compensation for loss of time and out of pocket expenses – are payable out of central funds and not out of the Legal Aid Fund.[14] Therefore, witness expenses are only payable under a legal aid order if the court has directed that they shall not be paid out of central funds. In the absence of such a direction they will be disallowed by the area office. If there is a direction, witness expenses will be paid out of the Legal Aid Fund if the area office accepts that they were properly incurred under the Criminal Costs Regs reg 7.[15]

Separate representation

Two or more defendants in the same case represented by the same firm may be represented by different advocates in court. Where that is necessary in the interests of justice, the costs of separate advocates will be allowed.

12   Note for Guidance 17-43 and CRIMLA 19.
13   See Note for Guidance 17-49 and CRIMLA 25.
14   LAA s25(3) and Costs in Criminal Cases (General) Regulations 1986 regs 15 and 16.
15   See Note for Guidance 17-39 and CRIMLA 15.

However, if solicitors claim payment for separate representation on the basis of conflict of interest, the Board will consider whether it was reasonable for the firm to continue acting.[16]

See also the discussion about separate representation on p244.

Special features

Special features should be set out and would need to be in most of the circumstances referred to above and to support a claim for enhanced rates (see below). Practitioners should always explain why longer time than usual was spent on the case, and point out, for instance:

- why it was difficult to obtain instructions from the client or from witnesses;
- difficulties with the court, or the prosecution;
- the seriousness or complexity of the case or the volume of document- ation.

Counsel's fees where authorised

As already noted, when the legal aid order authorises representation by counsel, standard fees do not apply. In addition, solicitors may claim for attending court with counsel. The rate is £29.50 per hour.

Crown Court claims

Claims for payment for Crown Court work are made to the court in which the case has been heard. The court assesses or taxes the bills which are submitted and sends a cheque in payment to solicitors and counsel. The Crown Court has a system of paying standard preparation fees, and claims for payment in respect of them do not require a detailed bill. However, standard fees do not apply in all cases, and even where they do apply, solicitors always have the option to have a bill taxed in full. Claims are made on Forms 5144 (bill to be taxed) or 5144A (claim for standard fee) which are obtained from the court.

As noted earlier (see p247) a criminal legal aid order covers advice and assistance in connection with an appeal. In respect of a Crown Court legal aid order, the claim for payment for work done in connection with a possible appeal to the Court of Appeal is made in the Court of Appeal if a notice of appeal is given or application for leave to appeal is made as a

16   Note for Guidance 17-35 and CRIMLA 11 and see *R v Legal Aid Board (Area No 15) ex parte Malcolm Gregg & Co.* CO/1524/92, October 1992 *Legal Action* 23.

result of counsel's or the solicitor's advice. If no such notice is given or application made, then the costs of the advice and assistance should be included in the crown court bill.[17]

Standard preparation fees

The advantage of claiming a standard fee is that it is simpler and results in payment more quickly than submitting a bill for taxation. The disadvantage is that sometimes the payment is less than can be achieved on taxation.

In practice, it is a matter of choice in all cases for the solicitor whether to apply for a standard fee or not. The Criminal Costs Regs Sch 1 Pt II para 1(2), provides that standard fees shall apply only in trials of class 3 and 4 offences, which in everyday terms means everything except trials for homicide and the more serious sexual offences. In addition, they apply in appeals and committals for sentence. However, even in the more serious cases solicitors can elect to take standard fees.[18]

Further, standard fees are not compulsory even in cases that fall within para 1(2). A solicitor may submit a bill for taxation in any case.[19] If the taxed fees are more than the upper standard fee limit, the solicitor will be paid the amount determined on taxation. On the other hand, if they are less than the lower limit, then the lower standard fee will be paid. If they are between the lower and the upper limits, then the principal standard fee will be paid.[20] This is quite separate from any question of applying for enhanced fees (see below).

The claim is made on Form 5144A. Standard fees are set out in Criminal Costs Regs Sch 1 Pt II para 4(3), and are normally up-rated anually. The rates in respect of work done since 1 April 1992 (not increased for 1993) are as follows:

Preparation:

	Lower standard fee limit	Lower fee limit	Principal standard fee	Upper fee limit
	£	£	£	£
Jury trials	125.50 (135.00)	173.00 (180.00)	242.00 (254.00)	302.00 (316.00)
Guilty pleas	79.00 (85.00)	106.00 (110.00)	170.00 (180.00)	218.00 (228.00)
Appeals against conviction	49.50 (53.00)	66.00 (68.00)	148.50 (154.50)	225.00 (236.00)
Appeals against sentence	35.25 (38.00)	50.50 (52.50)	90.50 (95.00)	127.00 (131.00)
Committals for sentence	41.00 (43.50)	49.50 (51.50)	94.75 (100.00)	137.00 (141.00)

17 Criminal Costs Regs reg 3(3).
18 Criminal Costs Regs Sch 1 Pt II para 1(4).
19 Criminal Costs Regs Sch 1 Pt II para 3(1)(a).
20 Criminal Costs Regs Sch 1 Pt II para 3(2).

Lump sum standard fees apply only to preparation. Court work is claimed for at an hourly rate:

	£ per hour
Advocacy in bail applications	£25.25 (£27.75)
Attendance at court (including waiting where counsel assigned)	£20.75
Travelling	£18.00

Additional standard fees:

Preparation of brief for counsel to appear unattended £29.00 (£31.00);

Listening to tapes of police interviews £10.45 for every 10 minutes;

Acting for more than one accused: 20% added to preparation fee for each accused; 20% for each additional accused on bail application.

The figures in brackets apply where the fee-earner's office is in Legal Aid Area 1 (Greater London).

Where a solicitor is acting for an accused facing an indictment and is also involved in some other process in the same case, such as an appeal against conviction, then the greater of the appropriate standard preparation fees applies and is increased by 20 per cent for each additional process. The increases of 20 per cent also apply where an accused is facing, for instance, two or more indictments, appeals against conviction etc.[21]

There is also a system of standard brief and refresher fees for counsel.

Solicitors should always claim the principal standard preparation fee unless there is good reason not to do so. The only circumstances in which the lower standard fee is applicable is where little or no work has been done, for instance because instructions were withdrawn, the client failed to co-operate, the solicitors failed to do the work in time before the case was listed, or all the preparation had been done before committal and was therefore claimed for on Form Crim 5. If the assessing officer considers that the principal standard fee is excessive, the lower standard fee will be allowed instead.[22]

Bills for taxation in the Crown Court

As noted above, solicitors always have the option of having their bill taxed, rather than accepting the standard preparation fees. A bill for taxation is prepared on Form 5144. The same principles apply as in the assessment of magistrates' court fees (see above). It is important that the time taken in respect of each item of work is carefully and separately set

21 Criminal Costs Regs Sch 1 Pt II para 4(9).
22 Criminal Costs Regs Sch 1 Pt II para 2(1).

out. The grade of fee-earner should also be specified, and it should be remembered that it is not just qualifications that matter – experience and competence should also be taken into account.

The hourly rates which can be claimed on taxation are set out in Criminal Costs Regs Sch 1 Pt I para 1(1)(b). The rates payable from 1 April 1992 (not uprated in 1993) are:

Class of work	Grade of fee earner	Rate £ per hour
Preparation	Senior solicitor	51.50 (54.00)
	Solicitor, legal executive equivalent	43.50 (45.75)
	Articled clerk or equivalent	28.75 (33.00)
Advocacy	Senior solicitor	62.50
	Solicitor	54.50
Attendance at court where counsel assigned	Senior solicitor	41.25
	Solicitor, legal executive or equivalent	33.00
	Articled clerk or equivalent	20.00
Travelling and waiting	Senior solicitor, solicitor	24.25
	Legal executive etc	24.25
	Articled clerk etc	12.00

Routine letters out and telephone calls made or received per item £3.35 (£3.50)

The figures in brackets apply where the fee-earner's office is in Legal Aid Area 1 (Greater London).

It should be noted that non-routine letters and telephone calls should not be claimed for at the per item rate. Instead, whether written, made or received, the time spent should be claimed for at the hourly rate.

Court of Appeal claims

Work done under a Crown Court legal aid order after a notice of appeal or application for leave to appeal is paid for by the Court of Appeal. That includes advice and assistance given before the notice is given or application is made.[23] Work done under a Court of Appeal legal aid order is, of course, also paid for by the Court of Appeal.

The claim is made by submitting a bill for taxation to the Registrar of Criminal Appeals, on forms supplied by the court. There are no standard fees in the Court of Appeal. The rates which apply are those in Criminal Costs Regs Sch 1 Pt I para 1(1)(b), ie, the same as those which apply in a

23   Criminal Costs Regs reg 3(3)(a).

crown court taxation (see immediately above). Enhanced rates may also be claimed in respect of Court of Appeal work.

Enhanced rates

Under Criminal Costs Regs Sch 1 Pt I para 3, it is possible for legal representatives to claim for work done in magistrates' courts and the crown court at higher ('enhanced') rates than those set out in Criminal Costs Regs Sch 1 Pt I para 1(1)(b) (see above). In order to qualify for enhanced rates the representatives must show that, 'taking into account all the relevant circumstances of the case', the specified rates would not reasonably reflect:

(a) the exceptional competence and dispatch with which the work was done; or

(b) the exceptional circumstances of the case.[24]

A claim under Criminal Costs Regs Sch 1 Pt I para 3 must be justified in order to be successful, and Criminal Costs Regs reg 4(4)(b) specifically requires the solicitor to give 'full particulars in support of' a claim for enhanced payments.

In order to qualify for enhanced rates the work done or the demands placed by the case on the particular fee-earner must have been exceptional, unusual or out of the ordinary. The work done must show both exceptional competence and exceptional dispatch,[25] or the case must be exceptional compared with the general run of cases handled by the fee-earner. The question is not only whether the case was unusual but whether it increased the burden on the solicitor. Relevant factors could be the character of the defendant, the defendant's position in life, the effect the trial might have on the defendant, the number of defendants, the allegations made, the degree of public interest, difficulties in tracing or interviewing defence witnesses, and whether expert witnesses were needed.

The assessing or taxing authorities have a wide discretion but it is possible to give some indications:

- where a solicitor takes over a case from other solicitors which requires work at short notice for an imminent hearing, that will usually establish exceptional dispatch, but whether exceptional competence is involved depends on the circumstances;[26]

---

24   Criminal Costs Regs Sch 1 Pt I para 3.
25   Criminal Costs Regs Sch 1 Pt I para 3(a).
26   Note for Guidance 17-42, CRIMLA 18.

- if a solicitor is able to deal with a case without an interpreter because the solicitor speaks a foreign language, enhanced rates may be allowed;[27]
- murder cases often qualify;[28]
- the unusual length of a hearing is a factor which might help a case to qualify;[29] but
- representation of several defendants does not by itself entitle representatives to enhanced rates.

An enhanced rate might be payable for all the work done or for part only; usually it would not apply to travelling and waiting time or routine letters and telephone calls. Where enhanced rates apply, they replace the rates set out in Criminal Costs Regs Sch 1 Pt I para 1(b) and (c). Instead solicitors may claim, under the normal rates of taxation, the 'broad average direct costs' of doing the work.[30] The Law Society has suggested how such costs should be claimed in their publication *Expense of Time*, but taxing officers may prefer to take a broader view of what is appropriate for the relevant level of fee-earner at the time the work was done. The Legal Aid Board has said that it wil have regard to the enhanced rate likely to be allowed by the appropriate Crown Court for the relevant fee earner at the time. The resultant calculation will produce what the Legal Aid Board has called the 'A' figure.[31]

A percentage uplift should be added to the 'A' figure. This is meant to reflect the 'burden of the relevant circumstances', as it was put in *R v Backhouse*, or the exceptional circumstances of the case. The Legal Aid Board has suggested 35 per cent as a starting point for preparation, 40–60 per cent as normal for solicitor advocacy, and 20 per cent for attendances with counsel.[32]

Payments on account

The extent to which practitioners can apply for payments on account depends on whether or not the legal aid order was made before 26 April 1993.

For orders made before that date the position is governed by LAA s25(2) which provides that 'subject to regulations' fees and disbursements may be paid to a defendant's legal representatives. Since no regulations had been made, solicitors and counsel received payments on account from

27 Note for Guidance 17-29, CRIMLA 4.
28 Note for Guidance 17-44, CRIMLA 20.
29 Note for Guidance 17-48, CRIMLA 24.
30 *R v Backhouse*, Taxing Master's Decision March 1986.
31 Note for Guidance 17-37, CRIMLA 13 as amended.
32 Note for Guidance 17-37, CRIMLA 13.

Crown Courts in long-running cases and, more rarely in practice, from the Legal Aid Board.

Where the legal aid order is made on or after 26 April 1993 the position is governed by Criminal Costs Regs regs 4A to 4D, inserted by the Legal Aid in Criminal and Care Proceedings (Costs) (Amendment) Regulations 1993. Payments on account are only available in respect of Crown Court proceedings. Payment on account of disbursements will only be made where they exceed £100, prior authority has been given and they have actually been incurred. Solicitors and barristers have the right to be paid 40% of their outstanding fees on account where:

- three months have elapsed since the bill was lodged for taxation;
- in the case of solicitors the total claim for costs is £4,000 (exclusive of VAT) or more;
- in the case of barristers the basic fee is £4,000 (exclusive of VAT) or more.

Wasted and disallowed costs

As mentioned in the introduction to this chapter, in some circumstances the courts can order that legal representatives should pay all or some of the costs of a case, or that they should not be paid for some or all of the legally-aided work that they have done.

If such an order results in a saving of money on the part of the Legal Aid Fund so that the costs are less than any contribution paid by the assisted person, then a repayment of contribution will be made under Criminal Regs reg 39.

Wasted costs orders under the Prosecution of Offences Act 1985

Under s19A of the Prosecution of Offences Act 1985, a court may disallow the costs of legal representatives or order them to pay part of the costs if those costs have been 'wasted'. The power may be exercised by a magistrates' court, Crown Court, or the Court of Appeal. An order can be made under s19A to disallow legal aid costs. Costs which have been incurred as a result of improper, unreasonable or negligent acts or omissions on the part of a legal representative are 'wasted costs' which the court considers that the parties to the trial should not reasonably be asked to pay.

Section 19A was incorporated into the Prosecution of Offences Act 1985 by s111 of the Courts and Legal Services Act 1990, which is in the same terms as s4 of that Act which applies to costs in civil cases. Further, s4 simply puts into statutory form the rules which, with one exception, existed since the introduction of RSC Ord 62 r11 in 1986 and which were explained by the Court of Appeal in *Sinclair-Jones v Kay* [1988] 2 All ER 611 and *Gupta v Comer* (1990) *Independent* 8 November. Therefore, in any consideration of s19A of the Prosecution of Offences Act 1985, it would be appropriate to look at those earlier cases and the discussion above at p162.

The Costs in Criminal Cases (General) Regulations 1986 Pt IIA (the General Criminal Costs Regs) and the Lord Chief Justice's *Practice Note* [1991] 2 All ER 924, set out the procedure which a court should follow before it makes an order against a legal representative under s19A. Under the General Criminal Costs Regs reg 3B, the court must:

- specify the amount of the wasted costs; and
- allow the legal representative and any party to make representations; and
- take into account any other orders for costs (and take the wasted costs order into account when making any other orders for costs); and
- notify any interested parties (including the Legal Aid Board and central funds determining authorities) of the order and the amount.

The *Practice Note* also specifies that the court should normally give reasons for its decision (para 8.2), and that the hearing should normally be in chambers with a shorthand note being taken, but that the decision and the reasons may be announced in open court (para 8.3). Although the court should not delegate its decision, it might ask court officials to calculate the amount involved and postpone the making of the decision until the end of the case for that, or any other, reason (para 8.3). In particular, it might be necessary to postpone the decision in order to avoid a conflict of interest between legal representatives and their client (para 8.4).

A s19A wasted costs order could be an alternative to making observations about the disallowance of legal aid costs (see below). The *Practice Note* states (para 8.5) that the court should use s19A rather than making observations unless 'the extent and amount of the costs wasted is not entirely clear.'

Section 19A of the Prosecution of Offences Act 1985 (and s4 of the Courts and Legal Services Act 1990) goes further in one respect than the pre-existing provisions as far as civil costs and criminal costs are concerned. For the first time barristers may be made liable for wasted costs. At the same time, no doubt only as a coincidence, the Court of Appeal has made clear that judges must act carefully before they impose an order under s19A. Thus the Court of Appeal allowed the appeal in the only case to have reached it so far, *Re Wasted Costs Order (No 1 of 1991)* (1992) 142 NLJ 636, and quashed a wasted costs order against a barrister. The Court held that before an order could be made, the General Criminal Costs Regs and the Lord Chief Justice's *Practice Note* had to be strictly complied with, and it laid down further guidelines before a court could take the 'Draconian' measure of making an order:

a) a judge or court intending to make a wasted costs order must carefully and concisely formulate the complaint and grounds on which the order is sought; and

b) where necessary a transcript of the relevant parts of the proceedings should be available; and

c) a transcript must be made of any wasted costs order; and

d) the defendant should be present if his or her interests might be affected;

e) there may also be cases where prosecution counsel should be present;

f) the judge or court should follow what the Court of Appeal called a three-stage test or approach:
   i) has there been an improper, an unreasonable or a negligent act or omission by a legal representative?
   ii) if so, as a result have any costs been incurred by a party?
   iii) if so, should the court disallow or order the representative to meet the whole or any part of the relevant amount and, if so, what specific sum is involved?

g) it is inappropriate for the court or the judge to propose any deals or settlement or to enter into any discursive conversations.

Strictly speaking, the guidelines were *obiter*, but they will no doubt be binding. For a time it seemed, following *Re Wasted Costs Order (No 1)*, that any practitioner challenging a wasted costs order should, if possible, ensure that the appeal was heard in the Civil rather than the Criminal Division of the Court of Appeal. *Re Wasted Costs Order (No 1)* was in the Criminal Division, and the judges there held, with regret, that they had no power under the General Criminal Costs Regs reg 3C(6) or the court's inherent jurisdiction to order that the successful appellant's costs should be paid out of central funds, and as a result he had to bear his own costs of the appeal.

The Civil Division, on the other hand, in the earlier case of *Holden & Co v Crown Prosecution Service (No 2) and others* [1992] 2 All ER 642, ordered that costs could be ordered out of central funds under Supreme Court Act 1981 s51 when solicitors had successfully appealed against an order to pay 'wasted' costs which had been imposed under the court's long-standing inherent jurisdiction (see below). That decision was reversed by the House of Lords in *Steele, Ford & Newton and others v CPS* (1993) *Independent* 10 June, and so practitioners are equally disadavantaged whichever division of the Court of Appeal they use.

Solicitors may be able claim against the Solicitors Indemnity Fund in respect of any order made. If possible, they should try to inform the SIF before a hearing, although failure to do so would not be fatal to a claim. The SIF might also finance an appeal (see below).

Wasted costs orders under the court's inherent jurisdiction

The Crown Court and the Supreme Court have always had an inherent jurisdiction over solicitors based on their position as officers of the court. No similar jurisdiction existed over barristers until s19A of the Prosecution of Offences Act 1985. The inherent jurisdiction over solicitors still exists but, like the same jurisdiction in civil cases, it has no practical effect since the implementation of s19A.

In order for solicitors to be liable under the inherent jurisdiction, they must be shown to have acted in grave dereliction of duty.[33] The test under s19A is much lower, mere negligence will suffice.[34] Therefore, there would appear to be no point in anyone now relying on the inherent jurisdiction in order to obtain an order against solicitors.

Disallowing legal aid costs

In addition to the powers to order legal representatives to pay wasted costs, there are specific powers for legal aid costs to be disallowed. Under Criminal Costs Regs Sch 1 Pt I para 2, the area office, Crown Court taxing officer, or Registrar of Criminal Appeals may reduce fees below the basic rates where it seems reasonable to do so 'having regard to the competence and dispatch with which the work was done'. Further, under Criminal Costs Regs Sch 1 Pt II para 1(3), in the Crown Court cases where standard fees are payable, if the trial judge is dissatisfied with the solicitors' conduct of the case, s/he may direct that the fees should be taxed.

In addition, the Lord Chief Justice's *Practice Note* [1991] 2 All ER 924 provides (para 10.1) that any trial, or appeal, judge may make observations for the benefit of the taxing authorities if s/he thinks that costs have been wasted by work unreasonably done, by conducting the case unreasonably or without reasonable competence or expedition. If so,

---

33   *Myers v Elman* [1940] AC 282.
34   *Sinclair-Jones v Kay* [1988] 2 All ER 611.

the judge should specify as precisely as possible the items which should be investigated, and the observations must be entered on the court record.

Before taking any such steps, the judge should inform the legal representatives of what s/he proposes to do and hear any representations in chambers, although any decision or observations may be made in open court (para 10.4). In addition, the taxing officer must also allow solicitors or counsel to make representations (para 10.6). As already noted, the Lord Chief Justice also states that, if possible, the wasted costs procedures of s19A should be followed rather than those of the Criminal Costs Regs where it is possible to ascertain the amount of the wasted costs (para 8.5).

Appeals

Appeals may be made against determinations of costs by area offices, crown court taxing officers and the Registrar of Criminal Appeals. The procedures are set out in the Criminal Costs Regs regs 12–17.

It is also possible to appeal against orders to pay or disallow costs under s 19A. The procedure is set out in the General Criminal Costs Regs reg 3C.

Part IV

Franchising

CHAPTER 16

Franchising

Over the next few years it seems that those solicitors' firms – and law centres – who undertake a heavy volume of legal aid work will want to apply for a franchise from the Legal Aid Board. In fact, if some of the more threatening noises emanating from the Lord Chancellor's Department turn out to have substance, practitioners may have no choice if they want to be able to undertake work on legal aid (see, eg, April 1993 *Legal Action* 4).

As this book goes to press, the proposals from the Legal Aid Board have gone through a number of drafts and, although not yet fully determined, the version set out in the document *Franchising Specification – Draft for Consultation* published in April 1993, may be taken as nearly representing their final form. The refererences that follow are to this document.

Advantages of holding a franchise

Franchised organisations will be given a number of advantages over other legal aid providers (paras 2.1–2.13). First, full franchisees will be able to exercise some of the powers of a legal aid area office in relation to the green form scheme, ABWOR and emergency certificates. Second, they will receive special payments on account. Third, they will be able to make slightly wider use of the green form scheme.

Devolved powers

Devolved powers will only be exercisable within the categories of work for which a franchise is held (para 2.10). Only full franchisees will have devolved powers – others only receive the enhanced payments.

Franchisees with devolved powers will receive a franchise manual which will include guidance on how they should exercise them and will

273

also be able to obtain guidance from their area office (para 2.1). Franchisees who consistently fail to follow the guidelines may find that their devolved powers are suspended or withdrawn. Continued breach could lead to loss of the franchise (para 2.8).

Green form scheme

Franchisees will be able to take all the decisions of an area office in respect of green forms within the category, or categories, of work for which they hold a franchise. Most importantly, that means that they can exceed the financial limit without authority (see below).

However, their bills will continue to be scrutinised by the area office, especially where they have authorised an extension.

ABWOR

Franchisees will be able to grant their own ABWOR applications without financial limit and give their own authorities for disbursements. However, if they have commenced ABWOR outside the guidelines, they will not be paid.

Emergency legal aid

Franchisees may grant their own emergency certificates, but must apply for a full certificate within seven days of doing so. If the grant of emergency legal aid was outside the guidelines, the solicitor's costs will be disallowed and the Board will not pay the usual £250 on account (see immediately below).

Financial incentives

At the time of writing the financial incentives for practitioners to become franchisees were still under discussion between the Legal Aid Board and the Law Society, but the Board had proposed that franchisees should be paid (para 2.9):

a) £250 on exercising the devolved power to grant an emergency certificate;

b) £150 on exercising the devolved power to grant ABWOR;

c) for two or three hours work, as appropriate, on exercising the devolved power to exceed the green form financial limit;

d) the lower standard fee on grant of a criminal legal aid order;

e) 75% of costs incurred nine months after the grant of a civil legal aid certificate and thereafter at nine-month intervals. This would apply to certificates issued up to three months before the franchise contract was signed.

The payments would only be available in the categories in which franchises are held.

Franchisees without devolved powers would receive payments (a), (b) or (c) when emergency legal aid, ABWOR or an extension of the green form was authorised by the area office.

Wider use of the green form scheme

Franchisees will be able to claim for telephone advice and for the outward journey on a home visit to give green form help (para 2.13).

Categories of work

Franchises will be available in one or more of the following categories (para 5.1):

Matrimonial/family
Personal injury
Crime
Welfare benefits
Housing
Consumer/general contract
Debt
Immigration/nationality
Employment

Who can apply?

Any solicitor's firm can apply for a franchise and so can any law centre or independent advice agency employing a solicitor with a current practising certificate and complying with the requirements for independent advice laid down by the Law Society, Federation of Independent Advice Centres, Law Centres Federation or the National Association of Citizens Advice Bureaux (para 1.5).

In order to qualify, an applicant must show that it is capable of providing advice, assistance and representation at the magistrates' court, county court, or tribunal as appropriate to the category of work being applied for. If representation cannot be provided by the applicant's own staff, the applicant should be able to refer clients to an appropriate source of representation (para 1.6).

The Legal Aid Board has stated that size is not a criterion: sole practitioners and small agencies will be considered for a franchise. However, it seems likely that smaller organisations will find it more difficult to meet some of the Board's requirements.

How to apply

On present plans, it will be possible to apply for a franchise at any time after 1 October 1993, though area offices are happy to discuss applications before that date. There is no date by which applications must be received and no limit on the number of franchises that will be granted either by category of work or geographical area.

There is no need, therefore, to rush to make an application. In fact, a premature application could be prejudicial because failed applicants may have to wait before their further applications are processed.

The Board will issue a self-assessment audit checklist so that prospective applicants can see whether they are ready. The completed checklist should be sent with the application form to the area office covering the geographic location of the office which is applying.

On receipt of the application the area manager will appoint a liaison manager who will check the application for completeness and accuracy, check the status of the applicant and its employees with the appropriate professional bodies, and undertake a preliminary audit of the applicant to see if the applicant meets the mandatory requirements (para 4.1).

Preliminary audit and mandatory requirements

In order to be considered for a franchise, applicants must meet a number of general management requirements. They must appoint a named representative, the 'franchise representative', who will act as a focal point for the Legal Aid Board liaison manager (para 4.2).

In addition they must have at least one member of staff suitably qualified to recognise the need for welfare benefits advice and responsible for ensuring that all caseworkers in the franchised categories are able to recognise the need for welfare benefits advice and refer clients to appropriate sources of advice (paras 4.6–4.9).

Other requirements are to do with non-discrimination and equal opportunities; management structures, including an office manual; a services plan; a named supervisor for each franchised category of work; systems of file management and file review; financial and personnel management, including appraisal and training; client care and complaints; and legal reference materials (paras 4.16–4.59). They are likely to be identical with the Law Society's practice management standards (see *Legal Aid Focus* 8).

If the preliminary audit (paras 5.20–5.24) shows that the applicant meets the mandatory requirements, the application will move into the pre-contract monitoring period.

Pre-contract monitoring and the transaction criteria

During the pre-contract monitoring period the Board's staff will continue to carry out audits to ensure that the mandatory requirements are being met. In addition auditors will seek to measure the competence of the work carried out by the applicant. This will be done by the application of 'transaction criteria' to a random selection of files in order to seek objective evidence of:

a) the information obtained from a client;
b) the advice given on the basis of the information;
c) the steps taken following that advice (paras 5.41–5.52).

Transaction criteria have been developed for green form work, emergency certificates and ABWOR (Sherr, Moorhead, Paterson, *Transaction Criteria*, HMSO 1992). Transaction criteria covering personal injury litigation, crime (including police station duty solicitor work) and matrimonial litigation are being finalised as this book went to press. The aim is to publish a single set of criteria covering the advice and assistance stages and litigation stages of personal injury and matrimonial work and, in respect of crime, a single set of criteria covering advice and assistance, duty solicitor work in the police station and preparation and presentation of cases in the magistrates' courts.

During the pre-contract monitoring period the area office will also be monitoring the applicant's work in the areas for which the application has been made. The area office will be checking:

– *applications for green form extensions* to see if any have been refused or not fully granted. If so, the liaison manager will want to discuss supervision of the devolved powers;
– *emergency legal aid applications*. Again, if any are refused, the liaison manager will want to discuss the supervision of devolved powers;
– *applications for civil legal aid*. A consistent rejection rate of more than

5%, without a reasonable explanation, could lead to the grant of a franchise being delayed;
- *claims for costs in criminal cases.* If more than 5% of claims are reduced from a non-standard fee, then the grant of a franchise will be postponed until the Board is satisfied that claims are being properly submitted;
- *average cost of cases.* The Board will take into account whether an applicant's costs are higher than average before deciding whether to grant a franchise;
- *bills rejected for technical deficiency.* If more than 5% of bills are rejected for technical deficiency the grant of a franchise will be delayed until the rejection rate is reduced below that figure (paras 5.53–5.66).

The decision

At the end of the audit process the liaison manager will prepare a franchise report recommending or refusing a franchise. This will be submitted to the area manager, who must make the decision and notify the applicant within 14 days of the end of the audit. A copy of the franchise report must accompany the notification to the applicant. The area manager must decide and notify the applicant within 14 days of the end of the audit (para 5.66).

Post-contract monitoring

The franchise contract is initially likely to be for five years. After it has been awarded the Legal Aid Board will continue to monitor the performance of the franchisee and carry out periodic audits using the criteria outlined above. If there is cause for concern, a higher level of monitoring might be instituted or specific audits carried out. If the franchisee does not deal adequately with the Board's concerns, the franchise might be suspended or terminated (paras 5.81–5.87).

Appeals and reviews of refusal, suspension or termination of franchise

Practitioners will be able to appeal to the relevant area manager against a liaison manager's decision not to accept their application (para 5.25).

They will also be able to challenge refusal of a franchise or suspension or termination by the area manager. The present proposal (paras 5.71–5.80) is that the area manager's decision should be reviewed by a panel consisting of another area manager, a representative from a nearby local law society and a representative from the advice services alliance.

The panel would be able to confirm the original decision or refer it back to the original area manager for reconsideration. Whether there should be a further right of review is under consideration at the time of writing.

Part V

Precedents and forms

Contents

Specimen letter on statutory charge and emergency legal aid

Ref . . . .

Dear . . . .

(Case heading)

Your legal aid forms have now been sent to the Legal Aid Board. The Board will take about (four) weeks to deal with the forms. I will contact you as soon as I hear from them.

When we met I explained what would happen about your legal costs if you won your case and what would happen if you lost. You will remember that I described to you how the legal aid statutory charge worked and I handed you a copy of the leaflet 'The Legal Aid Statutory Charge — What it means to you'. However, I also write to all my legal aid clients to set out the position about costs.

If you win

If you win your case and [obtain compensation/recover the property you are claiming/successfully resist all or part of the claim being made against you], legal aid works like a loan. The Legal Aid Board can deduct the cost of your case out of your winnings or out of what you have successfully retained. That is known as the statutory charge.

How much will be deducted depends on how much your opponent pays towards your legal costs. In most cases there is a shortfall of about 10% of the total legal aid costs, but you must understand that it could be more in any particular case. [*Add in matrimonial cases involving property*: The workings of the statutory charge mean that in most disputes over matrimonial property the parties end up paying the full legal aid costs. However, the statutory charge does not attach to maintenance orders or to property below a value of £2,500. If the statutory charge applies to a dwelling house, it is normally possible to postpone payment. In that case the charge will work like a mortgage on which interest will be charged but which you will not have to pay until you sell the house.]

If you lose

All litigation involves a measure of uncertainty. If you lose your case the Legal Aid Board will not ask you for any more money. But the court might order you to pay something to cover your opponent's costs. [*Omit rest of this paragraph in mortgage possession actions*; see p155.] How much you would have to pay would usually depend on your financial

Specimen letter on statutory charge and emergency legal aid page 2

situation. Most likely it would be the same or less than you have had to pay as a contribution towards your legal aid — unless your financial situation had improved in between the time you applied for legal aid and the case was decided.

I will advise you again about legal costs and the statutory charge when necessary but it is important that you should understand the possible costs of legal action before you become involved. Therefore keep this letter and if you have any questions please contact me.

Finally, I would remind you that it is your duty to inform the Legal Aid Board if your financial circumstances improve while you have legal aid. It is in your own interests to inform the Board if your financial circumstances worsen. I therefore suggest that you let me know of any change either way so I can inform the Board on your behalf.

Yours sincerely

Specimen paragraphs where client has applied for emergency legal aid

You have applied for emergency legal aid. As soon as we hear that it has been granted we can start work for you. However you will remember that I advised you about the fact that your emergency certificate could be revoked:

- if you fail to co-operate with the Legal Aid Board and the Department of Social Security in assessing your means; or
- if, once an assessment has been carried out, it shows that you are not entitled to legal aid.

If your certificate is revoked you can be required by the Legal Aid Board and by this firm to pay the full cost of the work that has been done on your behalf.

GF 1: Green Form

Green Form

GF 1

Notes for the solicitor

LEGAL AID BOARD LEGAL AID ACT 1988

1. Where you give advice and assistance in connection with **divorce or judicial separation proceedings** and the work will include preparing a petition, you can ask for your claim for costs and disbursements to be assessed up to the higher amount referred to in Regulation 4(1)(b) Legal Advice and Assistance Regulations 1989.
2. You can only give advice and assistance about making a **will** in the circumstances set out in The Legal Advice and Assistance (Scope) Regulations 1989. In such circumstances, your client must fill in Form GF 4.
3. Do not use this form for advice to suspects at police stations.
4. Supplementary Claims (see note on Key card): please give the date you sent the first claim for payment: __/__/__

Client's details *Please use block capitals*

Surname Mr/~~Mrs~~/~~Miss~~/~~Ms~~: **ELLIOTT**   Male/~~Female~~

First names: **PETER**

Permanent address: **73 MONK STREET, LEEDS LS95 2XY**

Capital details *(give these details even if the client gets income support, family credit or disability working allowance)* [A]

How many dependants (partner, children or other relatives of his/her household) does the client have? **1**

Give the total savings and other capital which the client has (and if relevant his or her partner)

Client: £	**300**
Partner (if living with the client as man and wife): £	**—**
Total: £	**300**

Income details [B]

Does the client get Income Support, Family Credit or Disability Working Allowance?

[✓] Yes: ignore the rest of this section   [ ] No: Please give the total weekly income of

The client: £ _____

The client's partner (if living with the client as man and wife): £ _____

Total: £ _____

Calculate the total allowable deductions: Income tax: £ _____ [C]

National Insurance contributions: £ _____ [D]

Partner (if living with the client as man and wife): £ _____

Attendance allowance, disability living allowance, constant attendance allowance and any payment made out of the Social Fund: £ _____ [E] [F]

Dependent children and other dependants:

	Age	*Number*	
	Under 11		£
	11 to 13		£
	16 to 17		£
	18 and over		£	[G]

Less total deductions: £ _____

Total weekly disposable income: £ _____

Client's declaration

I confirm that:
> I am over the compulsory school-leaving age (or, if not, the solicitor is advising me under Regulation 14(2A) Legal Advice & Assistance Regulations 1989);
> I have/have not *(delete whichever one is not correct)* previously received help from a solicitor on this matter under the Green Form; and
> I understand that I might have to pay my solicitor's costs out of any property or money which is recovered or preserved for me.

As far as I am aware, the information on this page is correct. I understand that if I give false information I could be prosecuted.

Signed: **P. Elliott**   Date: **1/10/92**

GF 1 page 2

CLAIM FOR PAYMENT TO ACCOMPANY FORM GF2

Name of Client: . . . .

Has a Legal Aid Order been made?   Yes/No
If so, give date: . . . .

PLEASE ATTACH ANY AUTHORITIES GIVEN BY THE AREA OFFICE

TICK THE APPROPRIATE LETTER TO INDICATE THE NATURE OF THE PROBLEM

A   Divorce or judicial separation (Petitioner)
M   Divorce or judicial separation (Respondent)
B   Other family matters (specify in the summary)
C   Crime
D   Landlord/tenant/housing
E   H.P. and debt
F   Employment

G   Accident/injuries
H   Welfare benefits/tribunals
J   Immigration/nationality
K   Consumer problems
N   Child Support Agency - child maintenance
L   Other matters (specify in the summary)

Has any money or property been recovered?
If so, give details:

NO

No. of letters written	3
No. of telephone calls made	2
received	4
Time otherwise spent: specify in summary	1 hr 15 min

Summary of work done:

Preliminary instructions, taking statement from client and spouse, inspecting premises, making application for legal aid

Has a legal aid certificate or order been granted? Yes/No
If not, is one being applied for?   Yes/No

Certificate or Order No. if appropriate: _____

PARTICULARS OF COSTS

	£			£
1. Profit costs	87.70	Details of disbursements:-		
2. Disbursements (including Counsel's fees)	—	Counsel's fees (if any):		
3. Add VAT as appropriate	13.30	Other disbursements (listed):		
TOTAL CLAIM	101.00			

Have you previously made a claim for legal advice and assistance for your client in respect of divorce or judicial separation proceedings or matters connected therewith?   YES/NO   If Yes, how much was allowed?   £ . . . .

Signed . D. White . . . . Solicitor   Date 10-10-92 Solicitor's ref DW . . . .

Firm name (in full) . BLACK, WHITE & Co . . . .

Address . . . . . . 30 COLD HARBOUR LANE, LEEDS LS94 1EQ . . . . .

NOTICE OF ASSESSMENT

Date . . . .

The Area Director has assessed your costs in this matter as set out below. In view of the fact that the sum assessed is less than that claimed, you may appeal in writing to the Area Committee in support of your claim as originally submitted or on any item in it, if you wish. These representations must be received within 21 days of receipt of this notice. I have deleted this matter from the consolidated claim form GF2 with which it was sent and I should be obliged if you would do the same. If you accept the assessment, please include this matter on your next consolidated claim form as assessed below AND RE-SUBMIT THIS FORM WITH IT.

Authorised Signatory Legal Aid Area No:
£

1. Profit costs

2. Disbursements (including Counsel's fees)

3. Add VAT as appropriate

TOTAL CLAIM

NOTE:- You are advised to keep a copy of this page because if in the same matter your client obtains a L.A. Certificate or Order, you may on taxation of your costs and disbursements be required to produce to the Taxing Officer a copy of this form indicating work done and quantum of payment. You may also require a copy of this page if after submitting your claim for payment you apply to the Area Office for a financial extension to enable you to give further advice and assistance to your Client.

GF 3: Application for extension of green form financial limit

GF 3

To be submitted in duplicate

LEGAL AID BOARD
LEGAL AID ACT 1988

APPLICATION FOR EXTENSION OF GREEN FORM FINANCIAL LIMIT

PLEASE USE BLOCK CAPITALS

Surname: CASSON   Forenames BRIDGET   ~~Male~~/Female

Address: 32 AUSTIN HOUSE, ORCHARD ESTATE BLACKBURN, LANCS

Date of Green Form 25.6.92   Area No. 7

(a) NATURE OF MATTER:-

If matrimonial and you are acting for Petitioner has petition been drafted? N/A   YES/NO (Delete as appropriate)

(b) COSTS and DISBURSEMENTS
Already incurred*
costs £ 91:50
disbursements £ — : —
total £ 91:50

(c) To be incurred but not yet incurred*
*include estimate if exact figure not known.
costs £ 100: 00
disbursements £ 125: 00

(d) NEW FINANCIAL LIMIT REQUESTED   £ 316:50

(e) VALUE OR ESTIMATED VALUE OF CLIENTS CLAIM OR CLAIM AGAINST (if this can be assessed in monetary terms) £2,000

(f) GROUNDS FOR EXTENSION:-

(i) Please give details of work already done:-

Proof taken and advice given on issue of proceedings

(ii) Please give details of work to be done:-

Obtaining and considering report from environmental health consultant on cockroach infestation
Detail special features (if any) overleaf

(g) DATE AND REFERENCE OF ANY PREVIOUS EXTENSION GRANTED OR REFUSED None
(Please attach any extensions granted)
(h) REFERENCE NUMBER OF ANY LEGAL AID APPLICATION None
OR CERTIFICATE

IMPORTANT
When you submit your claim for payment you MUST forward all authorities granted.

GRANTED TO £   REFUSED

SIGNED EBrown   Solr's Ref: EB
Date: 3.9.92   Tel. No (088 std) 926 5168

BROWN & PARTNERS
DX 329876 BLACKBURN

Please set out in the box above your firm's full name and address or DX number

Authorised Signatory
Legal Aid Area No.
Date

OAKLEY PRESS April 1989

CLA 1: Application for Legal Aid
(non-matrimonial proceedings)

PAGE 1

Application for Legal Aid CLA 1

Non Matrimonial Proceedings

Application number: _____   LEGAL AID BOARD   LEGAL AID ACT 1988

This form should be used for all non matrimonial cases. Applications relating to proceedings under the Children Act 1989 (as well as adoption and wardship) should be submitted on forms CLA 5 and CLA 5A. Form CLA 2A should be used for matrimonial proceedings and Children Act applications dealt with in family proceedings.

When complete, this form should be sent to the Legal Aid Area Office with the following form(s):
> CLA 4A (CLA 4B if the applicant is in receipt of income support)
> L 17 completed by the applicant's employer
> L 17 completed by the applicant's partner's employer (unless the partner is opposing the applicant in these proceedings)
> CLA 4C if the applicant is resident outside the United Kingdom

---

Applicant's details

Surname: Mr/Mrs/Miss/Ms   CROSS

Forename(s):   JEAN

Date of birth: 23 / 8 / 48   Occupation: MESSENGER

Permanent address: 14 TALBOT HOUSE, ROSE ESTATE,
ANYTOWN, CORNSHIRE

Correspondence address:
(if different from above)

Name of next friend or guardian ad litem if appropriate: (i.e. a person applying on behalf of the applicant)

Solicitor's details

Solicitor to be nominated: ROBERT BLUE

Legal Aid account no: W 356

Address of firm: 25 CHURCH STREET,
ANYTOWN, CORNSHIRE

Dx no: 329876 CORNSHIRE   Fax no: 022-926 8321

Tel no: 022-926 5968   Ref no: RB-00601

Crystal Mark
Clarity
approved by
Plain English Campaign

CLA 1 page 2

PAGE 2
General Questions

Please complete this page in all cases
The Area Office will not be able to enter into correspondence about this application.
The merits of the case must therefore be clear from the information provided. If there is insufficient information,
Legal Aid may be refused.

Green Form Advice

1 Did the applicant sign a Green Form and receive advice about the case for which he/she is now applying
for Legal Aid? ☑ Yes ☐ No

2 If you ticked yes, please give the date of the claim for payment (i.e. the date given on form GF2) if
submitted: NOT YET SUBMITTED

Previous Legal Aid

3 Has the applicant ever had or applied for Civil Legal Aid?
☐ Yes ☑ No ☐ Don't Know

4 If you ticked yes, please tell us the reference number(s) of the Legal Aid certificate(s) / applications if you
can: _____

5 If you do not know the reference number(s) please tell us when Legal Aid was applied for:

6 If the applicant's surname at that time was different from his/her present one, please give the old one:

7 If the applicant's address at that time was different to his/her present one, please give the old one:

Other Persons

8 Does any other person stand to gain anything if these proceedings are successful?
☐ Yes ☑ No ☐ Don't Know

9 If anyone does stand to gain anything, will they be involved in the court proceedings?
☐ Yes ☐ No ☐ Don't Know

10 If you ticked yes to boxes 8 and 9, please provide details:

Help from other sources

11 Is any other person or body (*e.g. Motoring Organisation, Insurer, Trade Union*) willing to help out with any or
all of the legal costs? ☐ Yes ☑ No ☐ Don't Know

12 If you ticked yes, please give details:

If you ticked don't know, you should make sure whether or not the applicant qualifies for help from another
source before proceeding with this application.

Please go on to page three

CLA 1 page 3

PAGE 3

The Opponent

Please complete this page in all cases

1 Opponent's full name: CORNSHIRE COUNTY COUNCIL

2 Opponent's occupation: LOCAL AUTHORITY/HOUSING AUTHORITY

3 Is the opponent insured against the applicant's claim (if appropriate)?:

☑ Yes   ☐ No   ☐ Don't Know

4 If you can not answer the previous two items please tell us why you believe the opponent has the means to pay the claim (if appropriate). For example, the opponent may have more than one property or other valuable items that could be sold to pay the claim.

_____

_____

_____

_____

5 Has the opponent been granted Legal Aid for these proceedings?

☐ Yes   ☑ No   ☐ Don't Know

6 If you ticked yes, please provide the Legal Aid reference number if known:

Costs and merits

To be completed by or on behalf of nominated Solicitor only:

1 Based on your existing knowledge of the case, which of the following best describes the prospects of a successful outcome? Please tick as appropriate:

☑ A Very good (80%+)   ☐ B Good (60-80%)   ☐ C Average (50-60%)

☐ D Below average   ☐ E Impossible to say. Limited certificate sought at this stage.

2 If you are estimating the chances of success as below average , please say why you believe legal aid should be granted: _____

_____

3 If you have not ticked box E above, please estimate your likely final costs, including disbursements. Your estimate will need to take account of your view of likely settlement.

☐ Less than £1,500   ☑ £1,500 – £2,500   ☐ Over £2,500

4 If you have ticked box E above, please say what work needs to be done under a limited certificate and at what cost:

I need to carry out the following work: _____

_____

_____

_____ at an estimated cost of: £ _____

Please go on to the rest of this form

CLA 1 page 4

Personal Injury Actions

Please complete this page if the applicant sustained or caused personal injury in any kind of accident (including medical negligence). If this page does not apply, please go on to page five.

1 Please tick whether the applicant is the:

☐ Plaintiff   ☐ Defendant   ☐ Other Party

2 Have the proceedings commenced?

☐ Yes   ☐ No   ☐ Don't Know

If you ticked yes, please make sure you enclose copies of all appropriate court documents.

3 Please describe clearly what injuries were sustained by the applicant:

N/A

4 Please provide the date when the personal injuries were sustained: _____ / _____ / _____

5 If the injury was caused by a pavement trip or other tripping incident, please give the exact height of the trip in inches or centimetres:

[ ] inches   [ ] cms

6 Please provide the value of the claim being made by/against the applicant: £ _____

7 Please now write a statement of case on page seven, making clear why the opponent named on page three was at fault or stating why the applicant has a defence to the action. It may help to bear in mind the following points:

- ► Please describe events in the order that they occurred. Photographs and medical reports if available are helpful.
- ► If there were witnesses, say whether they agree with what the applicant says and send statements if available.
- ► If the accident happened at work, try to show whether the employers may have operated an unsafe system/unsafe machinery or did not provide competent fellow employees.
- ► Draw a diagram or picture of the scene of the accident if it helps explain what happened. If you have a photograph, please enclose it.
- ► If the level of damages is in dispute, state the extent of the disagreement and say what evidence there is to support the applicant's view.
- ► If the police were involved, please provide details of any prosecutions and the police report if available.

Please go on to page seven and write a statement of case.

CLA 1 page 5

Breach of Contract/Faulty Goods and Services Actions

Please complete this page if the applicant is making a claim or defending an action for breach of contract or faulty goods and services. If this page does not apply, please go on to page six.

1   Please tick whether the applicant is the:

☑ Plaintiff   ☐ Defendant   ☐ Other Party

2   Have the proceedings commenced?

☐ Yes   ☐ No   ☐ Don't know

If you ticked yes, please make sure you enclose copies of all appropriate court documents.

3   Please describe briefly an outline of the agreement entered into (if appropriate):

TENANCY AGREEMENT
(copy enclosed)

4   Otherwise, please say what goods or services are alleged to be faulty:

SEE STATEMENT

5   Please provide the date of the agreement (if appropriate) and a copy of the agreement: 10 / 6 / 88

6   Please provide the date when the goods or services were purchased (if appropriate):   ___ / ___ / ___

7   Please provide the value of the claim being made by/against the applicant: £ _____

8   Please now write a statement of case on page seven, making clear why the opponent named on page three was at fault or stating why the applicant has a defence to the action. It may help to bear in mind the following points:

➤   Please describe events in the order that they occurred.
➤   If possible, state what specific area of law is being relied on.
➤   If a written contract is available, please enclose a copy.
➤   Photographic evidence can often help us, e.g. in building disputes.
➤   If an expert's report is available, please enclose a copy.

Please go on to page seven and write a statement of case

CLA 1 page 6

PAGE 6

All Other Non Matrimonial Actions

If the applicant's case was not covered by pages four and five, please complete this page.

1 Please tick whether the applicant is the:

☑ Plaintiff ☐ Defendant ☐ Other party

2 Have proceedings commenced

☐ Yes ☑ No ☐ Don't Know

If you ticked yes, please make sure you enclose copies of all court documents.

3 Please provide the value of the claim being made by/against the applicant (if appropriate):

£ _____

Please tick the box that is relevant to the applicant's case and read the guidance on what the statement on page seven should include:

4 **Landlord and Tenant**

Housing Disrepair ☑

Please give details of defects and their causes. Please also provide details of complaints to the landlord and how the applicant has been affected.

Possession ☐

Please provide a copy of the Lease or agreement and say why the applicant has a defence or needs representation.

5 **Property Dispute**

Jointly owned property ☐

Please give details of the basis on which the applicant seeks/opposes a sale, together with the value of the property and the amount of the mortgage.

Claim to an interest
in property ☐

Please give details of ownership, why the interest is claimed or denied and the value of the property together with the amount of the mortgage.

6 **Assault/Trespass** ☐

Please give details of recent incidents and say if an injunction is required.

7 **Probate and Inheritance** ☐

Please give details of the size of the estate, details of other beneficiaries, the grounds for the claim (e.g. dependency) and provide a copy of the Will.

8 **Other** ☐

Please specify proceedings:

_____

_____

_____

_____

Please give full details of why the applicant has a valid claim/defence and provide all relevant documentation.

Please now provide a statement of the Applicant's case on page seven having regard to the guidance given above.

CLA 1 page 7

PAGE 7

Statement of Case

Statement
Please type or write clearly.

The applicant rents a two-bedroomed flat from the proposed defendants. She lives there with her three children aged 14, 12 and 8. Under the tenancy agreement (copy enclosed) the landlord is obliged to maintain the roof, windows and brickwork in good condition.

For the last two years water has poured through a hole in the roof whenever it rains and it is also seeping through the window frames and the walls. As a result, the living room and one of the bedrooms have been unusable since October 1990 and her three piece suite, two beds and the carpets in the living room and bedroom have been damaged beyond repair. Complaint was first made to the proposed defendants housing officers in November 1990 and on many occasions since then. However, no steps have been taken to carry out any repairs.

Last week water started pouring through the ceiling of the second bedroom and the applicant and her children have had to move out and sleep on a friend's floor.

If more space is required, please attach a separate sheet to the inside of this form.

Please now turn to the back page.

CLA 1 page 8

PAGE 8

Declaration to be signed by applicant

I declare that I have received the leaflet "The Legal Aid Statutory Charge - What it means to you" which has been explained to me by my solicitor and given to me to keep.

I have been given a copy of the leaflet "What Happens Next?"

I understand that:

➤ even if I win I may have to pay all or some of my legal aid costs.

➤ if my means change my contribution may be re-assessed.

➤ my legal aid certificate could be cancelled and I might have to pay the costs in full if I do not deal promptly with Legal Aid Board requests.

➤ if I make a false statement I may be fined £1000 or imprisoned or both as well as losing my legal aid.

I declare that to the best of my knowledge, the information given by me is true.

Signed *J. Cross* **Date** 26 / 8 / 92

Statement by or on behalf of nominated solicitor

I certify that:

➤ the statutory charge has been explained to the applicant and he/she has been given the leaflet "The Legal Aid Statutory Charge - What it means to you."

➤ the applicant has been given the leaflet "What Happens Next?"

➤ the applicant has been advised about his/her obligations including changes of means and address.

➤ the information requested on page 3 of this form relating to the costs and merits of this case has been provided and that the information is as accurate as possible.

➤ The nominated solicitor holds a current practising certificate and has given an undertaking not to act or delegate the conduct of this matter under a Legal Aid certificate whilst uncertificated.

Signed by or on behalf of nominated solicitor: *R. Blue* **Date** 26 / 8 / 92

To the solicitor: *Please complete the following. It will help us process the application more quickly:*

1 Please tick what proceedings this application relates to:

☐ Personal injury   ☐ Breach of contract

☐ Property dispute   ☐ Assault and trespass

☑ Landlord and tenant   ☐ Probate/inheritance

☐ Other

If other, please specify: _____

2 Please tick this box if the applicant's opponent is his/her spouse or cohabitee   ☐

3 Please tick the boxes confirming that: ☑ page 3 has been completed in full

                                             ☑ there is a statement of case on page seven

CLA 3: Application for emergency legal aid certificate

CLA 3

LEGAL AID BOARD
LEGAL AID ACT 1988

APPLICATION FOR
EMERGENCY LEGAL AID CERTIFICATE

IMPORTANT: This application cannot be considered unless either a substantive application has already been submitted or accompanies this application.

OFFICIAL USE
ONLY

*delete as appropriate

Please use block capitals and answer all questions

Surname   CROSS   (Mr/Mrs/Miss*)   Forenames   JEAN

Home Address   14 TALBOT HOUSE,
ROSE ESTATE,
ANYTOWN, CORNSHIRE

Correspondence Address
(If different from above)

I apply for an emergency   TAKE PROCEEDINGS AGAINST CORNSHIRE COUNTY COUNCIL FOR BREACH
Legal Aid Certificate to: OF COVENANT, NEGLIGENCE AND BREACH OF STATUTORY DUTY

Have the proceedings already begun?   YES/NO*   Do the proceedings relate to an Appeal?   YES/NO*

I require legal aid as a matter   WATER PENETRATION HAS MADE MY HOME
of urgency because: UNINHABITABLE AND I AM SLEEPING ON
A FRIEND'S FLOOR WITH MY 3 CHILDREN.

NB. If you have difficulty in completing this form you may be eligible for advice and assistance from a solicitor under the Green Form Scheme.

DECLARATION TO BE SIGNED BY APPLICANT
1. I enclose or have already submitted an application form for a legal aid certificate to replace any emergency legal aid certificate issued to me.
2. I understand that if an emergency legal aid certificate is issued it will entitle me to receive temporary legal aid for a limited period and may authorise only those steps necessary to deal with the emergency that has arisen.
3. I understand that if, after an emergency legal aid certificate has been issued, I am offered a legal aid certificate to replace it, the offer will set out the financial terms upon which I can obtain such a certificate and I shall have an opportunity of making up my mind whether to accept it.
4. I understand that any emergency legal aid certificate issued to me may be revoked or discharged if:-
    (a) I fail to provide sufficient information or documents or attend for interview (if required) so that my means can be assessed and my contribution (if any) towards the cost of the case determined.
    (b) I am not financially eligible for legal aid.
    (c) I fail to accept an offer of a legal aid certificate to replace the emergency legal aid certificate.
    I understand that if I do not obtain a legal aid certificate replacing any emergency legal aid certificate issued to me, I shall become liable:-
    (a) To pay the Legal Aid Board the expense to which the legal aid fund has been put as a consequence of the work done by my solicitor and/or counsel, and
    (b) To pay such solicitor and/or counsel the difference between the amount they receive from the legal aid fund and the costs and fees to which they would have been entitled if I had not been legally aided.
IMPORTANT: IF THE PROCEEDINGS COME TO AN END YOU MUST STILL PROVIDE SUFFICIENT INFORMATION SO THAT YOUR MEANS MAY BE ASSESSED AND YOUR CONTRIBUTION TOWARDS THE COST OF THE CASE DETERMINED.

Signed   J. Cross

Date   26.9.92

OAKLEY PRESS PLC.   April 1989

CLA 2A: Application for Legal Aid
(matrimonial proceedings)

PAGE 1

Application for Legal Aid CLA 2A

Matrimonial Proceedings
(including Magistrates' Courts)

Application number: _____ LEGAL AID BOARD LEGAL AID ACT 1988

IMPORTANT: READ CAREFULLY BEFORE COMPLETION
➤ If instructed your solicitor should complete this form on your behalf.
➤ Do not use this form for freestanding applications under the Children Act 1989 which are not being dealt with in family proceedings. Children Act forms CLA 5 and CLA 5A should be used for care, supervision and emergency protection proceedings as well as for all other Children Act applications which are not to be dealt with in the proceedings listed at Section 2 of this form. Form CLA 5 must also be used for wardship and adoption.
➤ If you have any difficulty filling in this form, your solicitor will be able to help you.
➤ This form must be submitted with financial application form CLA 4A, CLA 4B or CLA 4C.
➤ Many people think that legal aid is free. This is not necessarily so. You may have to make a contribution toward the costs of your case and some or all of any money or property recovered or preserved in the proceedings may be used to pay your solicitor's fees. It is therefore most important that you read the leaflet attached to this form. It explains what happens when you apply for legal aid and what you have to pay towards it. You should detach the leaflet from this form and keep it. Please read it carefully, it is for your use and will help you to understand what is involved if legal aid is granted to you. It will tell you about the way legal aid works.

Section One

Surname: ~~Mr/Mrs/Miss/Ms~~ HILL

Forename(s): OLIVIA

Date of birth: 16 / 8 / 45

Permanent address: 15 ASHBRIDGE ROAD, EASTVILLE, GRIMSHIRE

Correspondence address: /
(if different from above)

Telephone no: 076-654 0923

Name of next friend or guardian ad litem if appropriate: (i.e. a person applying on behalf of the applicant)

Solicitor to be nominated: CLARE GREEN

Legal Aid account no: W356

Address of firm: GREENS
100 HIGH STREET, EASTVILLE, GRIMSHIRE

Dx no: 329876 GRIMSHIRE Fax no: 076-926 8321

Tel no: 076-926 5968 Ref no: CB-00901

Have you previously applied for legal aid in:

	Yes	No
this matter?	☐ Yes	☑ No
any other matter?	☑ Yes	☐ No

If the answer is YES, please quote references. 01 01 89 53468 M

These may be found on any correspondence you may have had with the area office.

CLA 2A page 2

PAGE 2

Section One continued

If you do not know the reference, when did you apply for legal aid?

_____/_____

If your address at that time was different from your present one, please give the details of the old one.

_____/_____

_____

If your surname at that time was different from your present one, please give the old one.

_____/_____

Have you ever been advised/assisted under the Green Form scheme in connection with the present proceedings?

☑ Yes   ☐ No

If yes, please ask the solicitor involved to give the date of his/her claim for payment on form GF2.

_____NOT YET SUBMITTED_____

(* Delete as appropriate)

Section Two

I am the: ☑ petitioner/applicant*   ☐ respondent   ☐ other party

I apply for legal aid to:

    a bring a suit for nullity of marriage   ☐

    b defend a suit for nullity of marriage   ☐

In connection with proceedings for:

    ☐ divorce   ☐ judicial separation

    c prosecute a petition since I cannot proceed without legal aid because of physical or mental incapacity   ☐

    d continue to prosecute a petition directed to be heard in open court   ☐

    e continue to prosecute a petition to which an answer has been filed   ☐

    f defend a petition   ☐

    g defend a petition and to cross-pray   ☐

    h defend/intervene* as "other party"   ☐

    i be heard in residence/contact* proceedings   ☐

    j be heard on financial provision or property adjustment   ☑

    k take/defend* proceedings for an injunction/specific issue order/ prohibited steps order*   ☐

    l take/defend* proceedings under the Domestic Violence and Matrimonial Proceedings Act 1976   ☐

    m take/defend* proceedings under the Married Woman's Property Act 1882   ☐

    n take/defend* proceedings under the Matrimonial Homes Act 1983   ☐

    o take/defend* proceedings under the Domestic Proceedings and Magistrates' Courts Act 1978   ☐

    p take/defend* proceedings under the Children Act 1989 in connection with *l* to *o*. (Please specify order(s) sought/opposed in statement).   ☐

    q any other matter, namely: ☐

Have the proceedings already begun?   ☑ Yes   ☐ No

CLA 2A page 3

PAGE 3

Section Three

Full name of applicant: OLIVIA HILL

Brief details about proceedings:

TO APPLY IN DIVORCE PROCEEDINGS FOR
FINANCIAL PROVISION AND/OR PROPERTY
ADJUSTMENT

Full name of opponent: CHARLES HILL

Full address of opponent: 29 CHICHESTER DRIVE,
EASTVILLE, GRIMSHIRE

Is your opponent your spouse? ☑ Yes ☐ No

Full name and of address of opponent's solicitors (if known)

NONE

Has your opponent been granted Legal Aid in these proceedings? ☐ Yes ☑ No ☐ Don't Know

If yes, please quote the legal aid reference number (if known)

Information for the Solicitor

1 The Provisions relating to the Legal Aid Board's Statutory Charge are to be found in Part XI of the Civil Legal Aid (General) Regulations 1989.

2 You should ensure that the leaflet attached is given to the applicant and that its contents are explained and understood. It is important that the effect of the statutory charge is understood by the applicant as this particular matter gives rise to more misunderstandings and complaints than any other aspect of legal aid. You will find the leaflet "What Happens Next?" particularly helpful.

3 To ensure that the application is dealt with as quickly as possible by the area office it is important that the facts of the case are set out concisely and accurately. Copies of the pleadings, relevant documents and reports and opinions of counsel, if any, should be supplied with the application. It will help if details can be given (if appropriate) of the evidence and law on which the applicant will rely in support of the case. *If proper details are given there is no need to send voluminous correspondence to the area office.* It is for the solicitor to sift and summarise the material.

4 You are under a duty *forthwith* to inform the area office of any property or money recovered or preserved for the applicant in the proceedings. You should not wait until you submit your report on case and claim for costs to give this information. If you do not inform the office forthwith, and the legal aid fund incurs a loss, payment of your profit costs may be deferred.

5 If money is recovered by you for the applicant as a result of the proceedings then unless it is exempt or partly so from the statutory charge it must be paid to the area office and should not be retained on client account, even on deposit. In case of doubt please contact the area office.

6 If you are prepared to give an undertaking to the area office that your costs will not exceed a specified amount, then the release of the balance of the monies to the assisted person may be authorised. The area office can supply a form of undertaking on request. When estimating your costs you should have in mind that although the work authorised under the certificate may be completed, further work might be needed for which an amendment might be granted. Payment of costs in excess of the amount specified in your undertaking will not be authorised in respect of work carried out under the same certificate.

7 You must not pay any money or transfer any property recovered or preserved in the proceedings either to your client or on your client's instructions without prior authority of the area office. If you do so the area office has the power to defer payment of your profit costs.

8 You must not advise your client to stop making payment of his/her legal aid contributions even in circumstances where your client has recovered or preserved property and been awarded costs.

I certify that I have explained to the applicant how the statutory charge may affect the outcome of this case, and this has been confirmed by letter to the applicant. I have also advised the applicant that he/she has a duty to disclose a change of address or financial means and that, if there is any increase in financial means during the currency of any legal aid certificate that may be issued, this may affect the amount of any contribution to be paid towards the costs of the case. I have also explained to the applicant the effect of a legal aid or emergency certificate being revoked/discharged.

I certify the nominated solicitor holds a current practising certificate and will not act or delegate the conduct of this matter whilst uncertificated.

Signed by or on behalf of
nominated solicitor: Black

Date 1 / 9 / 92

CLA 2A page 4

PAGE 4

Section Four: Your Marriage

Date of Marriage: **14-3-73**

Date last lived together: **16-8-89**

Did you leave your opponent?   ☐ Yes   ☐ No

Are you still married to your opponent?   ☑ Yes   ☐ No

Occupation of opponent: **DENTIST**

Opponent's income: £ **50,000+** _____ Opponent's capital: £ **30,000 (estimate)**
     (Estimate)   *(Estimate) (not including matrimonial home)*

If there are children of the marriage or any former marriage who are children of the family, please complete the details below:

Date of Birth	Name	With whom are they living?
17-7-73	TAMSIN	ME
5-8-80	SEBASTIAN	ME

If there have been previous proceedings in respect of your marriage to your opponent or the children mentioned above, please complete the details below:

Date	Court	Result of proceedings

Section Five: Details of the Matrimonial Home

Address of the property where you live or last lived with your opponent

**15 ASHBRIDGE ROAD,
EASTVILLE, GRIMSHIRE**

Is the property owned by: ☐ You   ☐ Your opponent   ☑ Jointly

Is the property rented?   ☐ Yes   ☐ No

If the property is owned, what is its current value?   £ **150,000 (estimate)**

What amount, if any, is owing on the mortgage?   £ **40,000 (estimate)**

Are you making a claim over the property or its value?   ☑ Yes   ☐ No

Are you making any other monetary claims, e.g. Maintenance?   ☑ Yes   ☐ No

CLA 2A page 5

Section Six: Statement of Case

Give full details of the facts of the case, what claims are being made in the proceedings or, if defending, the nature of the defence. (*Continue overleaf if necessary*).

I have obtained a degree nisi of divorce on the basis of my husband's unreasonable behaviour as set out in the enclosed petition.

I now want to apply for maintenance for myself and the children and a property adjustment order.

I have worked throughout the marriage as a computer analyst and until recently my earnings have always been about the same as my husband's. He is a gambler who regularly lost money and so over the years I have borne the main burden of paying the outgoings on the house and housekeeping expenses.

For the last year I have suffered from Repetitive Strain Injury and have been unable to work.

Since my husband left the matrimonial home, he has made no payments whatsoever, either to me or in respect of the children.

I am advised by my solicitors that I qualify for income support and I am applying for that.

Both I and my solicitors have made repeated requests to my husband to discuss the amount

(contd)

CLA 2A page 6

PAGE 6

Section Six continued

of maintenance he should pay and what arrangements
should be made about the house and other capital,
but he has ignored all approaches

Signed: O. Hill
(Applicant)   Date 1 / 9 / 92

Have any steps or proposals been made to settle the case?   ☑ Yes   ☐ No

If yes, please give details, including previous legal aid or Green Form work done.

see Correspondence

The following documents are submitted in support of this application for legal aid:

petition, decree nisi, medical report,
letters to my husband

Declaration and authority to be signed by the applicant

Please read the following declaration carefully before you sign below. If you deliberately make a false statement on this form you may be fined or imprisoned, or both.

I DECLARE that I have read the attached leaflet which has been given to me to keep. I understand that I may have to pay all or part of the costs of the proceedings at the end of the case even if I am successful in the proceedings. I also understand that in certain circumstances my financial means may be re-assessed, resulting in a contribution or higher contribution being paid by me towards the costs. I also understand that in certain circumstances a legal aid certificate granted to me can be cancelled and the Legal Aid Board may claim from me the amount which is owed to my solicitor and counsel for costs.

I DECLARE that the information given by me is correct to the best of my knowledge.

Signed: O. Hill   Date 1 / 9 / 92

CLA 2A page 7

Note for the applicant

Please read this note carefully and ask your solicitor to explain any part which you do not clearly understand.

This note should be detached from the application form and retained by you.

What Happens To Your Application

Your signed application will be sent by your solicitor to the Area Office.

Your income and savings will have to be considered by the Department of Social Security (DSS). The DSS will report to the Area Office.

The Area Office will consider your application and will decide whether:

> ➤ you have a reasonable chance of success; and
> ➤ it is reasonable for legal aid to be granted

You may have to give more information to the DSS or the Area Office. You must send the information as soon as possible.

If Your Case Is Urgent

Your solicitor can ask for emergency legal aid. This can be granted at once by the Area Office. Emergency legal aid lasts only until a decision has been taken on your full application. When you apply for emergency legal aid you must agree:

> ➤ to co-operate with the DSS in their enquiry into your financial position, and
> ➤ also to pay any contribution that is decided; and
> ➤ to pay the full costs of your case if it is found that you do not qualify for legal aid
> or if you refuse legal aid when it is offered to you.

If Your Application Is Refused

You will get a notice explaining why the application has been refused. There is a right of appeal against a refusal of legal aid for legal reasons. There is no appeal if the DSS says you are above the financial limit. You will be told if you can appeal and how to do it.

If Your Application Is Granted

If you have to pay a contribution, or there is some limitation on the work your solicitor can do for you, you will get an offer of legal aid. You will have 28 days to accept. If you do accept you will have to sign the form and send it to the Legal Aid Accounts Department with your payment. A legal aid certificate will then be issued.

If you do not have to pay a contribution and your application is granted in full you will get a legal aid certificate straight away.

What Will You Have To Pay?

When a legal aid certificate is issued you will have to pay your contribution (if any). If your income and savings change while you have legal aid the DSS will reconsider your contribution. You may be asked then for an extra contribution. If at the end of your case your contribution is more than the actual costs of your case, then the difference will be returned to you. As well as your contribution you may have to pay from any money or property you get with the help of legal aid (see *If You Win* below).

If You Win

Your solicitor will have told you that if you get money or property with the help of legal aid, some (or all) of it may be used to pay your solicitor's and barrister's bills. This is the Statutory Charge.

Where you get money your solicitor must usually pay to the Area Office straight away enough to cover the statutory charge.

Where you get a house, if the statutory charge applies, the Area Office will put a charge on it to secure what you owe. You will not have to pay the charge until you sell BUT when you pay it off you must pay INTEREST on the amount of the charge.

Sometimes where you get money to buy a house, the Area Office may agree to put a charge on that house rather than you paying it you straight away. You will not have to pay the charge until you sell BUT when you pay it off you must pay INTEREST on the amount of the charge.

Your solicitor will also have told you that what you have to pay will depend on what your opponent pays towards your costs and whether your case comes within any of the exceptions or exemptions to the statutory charge.

If You Lose

If you lose you will still have to pay your contribution. The Legal Aid Fund will be responsible for the rest of your solicitor's and barrister's bills.

The court may order you to pay some or all of your opponent's bills. You will only have to pay what the court thinks is reasonable.

CLA 2A page 8

PAGE 8

Remember

➤ You must pay your contribution (if any) and any extra contribution if your income or savings go up.

➤ You must tell your solicitor and the Area Office of any change of address.

➤ You must tell the Legal Aid Accounts Department of any change in your financial position.

➤ You must give your solicitor instructions and deal with any requests from your solicitor or the Area Office promptly.

➤ You must not ask your solicitor to act in a way that causes unnecessary expense to the legal aid fund. If you do your solicitor will have to tell the Area Office straight away which may result in withdrawal of your legal aid certificate.

➤ Keep your legal aid certificate carefully. You will need to use the number if you want to make any enquiries. You are not on legal aid until either an emergency certificate or a full legal aid certificate is issued to you.

CLA 5: Application for Legal Aid
(Children Act proceedings)

PAGE 1

Application
for Legal Aid CLA 5

Children Act Proceedings

Application number: _____   LEGAL AID BOARD LEGAL AID ACT 1988

This form should be used for proceedings under the Children Act 1989 unless the client qualifies for non-means, non-merits tested legal aid, i.e. where he/she is a child, parent or person with parental responsibility who is a party to proceedings under Section 25 (use of secure accommodation – child only), 31 (care and supervision orders), 43 (child assessment orders), 44 (emergency protection orders) or 45 (extension/discharge protection orders) Children Act 1989. In such cases, form CLA 5A "Legal Aid for Special Children Act Proceedings" must be completed by the solicitor. Form CLA 5 should also be used for wardship and adoption proceedings but not where a Children Act order is being applied for/opposed in other family or matrimonial proceedings (in which case form CLA 2A must be used).

Where the client involved in the Children Act proceedings under the sections specified above is someone other than a child, parent or person with parental responsibility, he/she will not be subject to the legal aid merits test but will have to satisfy the means test. Please use this form, completing only the section below, page 2 and the back of the form.

Note that only one form needs to be completed for each applicant for legal aid even if more than one child (and therefore more than one set of proceedings) is involved. If you act for more than one child, you must submit an application form for each child who is applying for legal aid.

If you intend to commence proceedings in a court other than the Magistrates' Court, you must support this in your statement but you should note that certificates issued in respect of public law proceedings will permit transfer in accordance with the Children (Allocation of Proceedings) Order 1991.

When complete, this form should be sent to the Legal Aid Area Office with the following form(s):

> CLA 4A (CLA 4B if the applicant is in receipt of income support)
> L 17 completed by the applicant's employer (wage slips are acceptable with an emergency application)
> L 17 completed by the applicant's partner's employer (unless the partner is opposing the applicant in these proceedings) (wage slips are acceptable with an emergency application)
> CLA 4C if the applicant is resident outside the United Kingdom
> If the matter is urgent, form CLA3 – emergency application – should also be submitted.

Applicants for whom the legal aid means test, but not the merits test, applies – proceedings under Section 31, 43, 44 or 45 Children Act 1989.

A ☑ Tick this box if your client is a party/applying to be joined in proceedings under Section 31 (care and supervision), 43 (child assessment orders), 44 (emergency protection orders), or 45 (extension/discharge of emergency protection orders) Children Act 1989 but is not a child, parent or person with parental responsibility.

Please indicate the proceedings by ticking below:

1 ☑ An application for a care order under Section 31
2 ☐ An application for a supervision order under Section 31
3 ☐ An application for a child assessment order under Section 43
4 ☐ An application for an emergency protection order under Section 44
5 ☐ An application for extension/discharge of an emergency protection order under section 45

B If it is known at this stage that the client requires representation in related proceedings, give exact details of any order to be applied for. A Section 8 order made on the court's own motion will be covered in any event. If the position is not yet known an amendment may be applied for at a later date.

My client also requires representation in the following related matter:

_____

because   _____

(if necessary, please continue on a separate sheet)

Please complete page two and the back page only

CLA 5 page 2

PAGE 2

Applicant's and Solicitor's Details

Applicant's details

Surname: ~~Mr/Mrs/Miss/Ms~~ MORTON

Forename(s): BEATRICE ROSE

Date of birth: 12 / 4 / 40   Occupation: SHOP ASSISTANT

Permanent address: 32 LANDSEER AVENUE
CROYLEY, SURREY

Correspondence address:
(if different from above)

Telephone no: 081 - 935 2854

Name of next friend or guardian ad litem if appropriate:

Solicitor's details

Solicitor to be nominated: CLARE BROWN

Legal Aid account no: W356

Address of firm: 25 CHURCH STREET
LONDON SW2

Dx no: 329876 LONDON SOUTH   Fax no: 081-926 8321

Tel no: 081-926 5968   Ref no: CB-00461

Green Form Advice

1 Please tick box if the applicant has signed a Green Form in respect of advice about this case: ☑

2 If you ticked the box, please give the date of the claim for payment (the date of form GF2) if already claimed or write 'not applicable'

NOT YET SUBMITTED

Previous Legal Aid

3 Please tick box if the applicant has had civil legal aid before ☐

4 If you ticked the box, please give the legal aid reference number(s) _____

5 If you do not know the reference number(s), please give the date of the application(s) ____ / ____ / ____

6 If the applicant's surname was different at that time, please give the old one: _____

7 If the applicant's address was different at that time, please give the old one: _____

Please go on to page three *(But turn to the back page if the client is entitled to means tested only legal aid under Section 15(3E) Legal Aid Act 1988)*

CLA 5 page 3

Details of Proceedings

There is no need to complete this page if the client qualifies for means tested only Legal Aid under Section 15(3E) Legal Aid Act 1988.

I am: ☐ the applicant ☐ the respondent ☐ applying to be joined

I apply for legal aid to (you may tick more than one box, e.g. if you wish to apply for/oppose more than one type of order or if you wish to take and defend proceedings)

(* delete whichever does not apply)

1 ☐ Make/defend* an application for a contact order (see also 13 and 14 below)

2 ☐ Make/defend* an application for a prohibited steps order

3 ☐ Make/defend* an application for a residence order

4 ☐ Make/defend* an application for a specific issue order

5 ☐ Make/defend* an application for a parental responsibility order

6 ☐ Make/defend* an application for periodical payments for a child/children

7 ☐ Make/defend* an application for secured periodical payments for a child/children

8 ☐ Make/defend* an application for a lump sum order/settlement* for a child/children

9 ☐ Make/defend* an application for transfer of property for a child/children

10 ☐ Make/defend* a variation or discharge of periodical payments/secured periodical payments order* for a child/children

11 ☐ Discharge a care order

12 ☐ Vary or discharge a supervision order

13 ☐ Make an application for contact with a child subject to a care order

14 ☐ Vary or discharge a contact order

15 ☐ Defend an application for an education supervision order

16 ☐ Other – give details, including Children Act Section number (unless for wardship or adoption proceedings)

Please go on to page four *(But turn to the back page if the client is entitled to means tested only legal aid under Section 15(3E) Legal Aid Act 1988)*

CLA 5 page 4

PAGE 4

Statement of Case

There is no need to complete this page if the client qualifies for means tested only legal aid under Section 15(3E) Legal Aid Act 1988.

Information about myself

I am:

☐ the child　　　　　　　　　　☐ the child's mother or father

☐ a Guardian of the child　　　　☐ a person with parental responsibility

None of the above. I am: _____

Complete only if leave is required:
Leave to make this application to the court:

☐ will be sought　　　　　　　　☐ has been given

Information about the child/children

Full name: _____
(Forenames first)
Date of birth: _____ / _____ / _____　　　☐ Male　　☐ Female

Living with: _____

Usually living with: _____
(if different)

Full name: _____
(Forenames first)
Date of birth: _____ / _____ / _____　　　☐ Male　　☐ Female

Living with: _____

Usually living with: _____
(if different)

Full name: _____
(Forenames first)
Date of birth: _____ / _____ / _____　　　☐ Male　　☐ Female

Living with: _____

Usually living with: _____
(if different)

Full name: _____
(Forenames first)
Date of birth: _____ / _____ / _____　　　☐ Male　　☐ Female

Living with: _____

Usually living with: _____
(if different)

If necessary continue on a separate sheet in the same format.

Please go on to page five　*(But turn to the back page if the client is entitled to means tested only legal aid under Section 15(3E) Legal Aid Act 1988)*

CLA 5 page 5

Statement of Case

There is no need to complete this page if the client qualifies for means tested only legal aid under Section 15(3E) Legal Aid Act 1988.

If you are a respondent in the proceedings please forward a copy of the court application(s).

Whether you are an applicant or respondent you must in any event provide the following information, either in the copy application or in this statement:

> ➤ the child/children's family history
> ➤ any previous proceedings relating to the child
> ➤ details of the applicant/the (proposed) respondent(s)
> ➤ if you are the applicant, the reason(s) why you wish to start proceedings in a court other than a magistrates' court.
> ➤ if you are the applicant or are cross-applying:
>   – why you believe any order is necessary
>   – why you believe the court will intervene and make an order in the particular circumstances, given the non-intervention principle in Section 1(5) Children Act 1989
> ➤ why you believe the application will be opposed/you wish to oppose the application or why you need representation.

Please go on to the back page

CLA 5 page 6

Declaration to be signed by applicant

I have been given a copy of the leaflet 'What Happens Next?'.

I understand that:

> ➤ if my means change my contribution may be re-assessed.

> ➤ my legal aid certificate could be cancelled and I might have to pay the costs in full if I do not deal promptly with Legal Aid Board requests.

> ➤ if I make a false statement I may be fined £1000 or imprisoned or both as well as losing my legal aid.

> ➤ even if I win I may have to pay all or some of my legal aid costs, but only if I recover or preserve property or money (other than maintenance) and I do not recover my costs from another party.

I DECLARE that, to the best of my knowledge, the information given by me is true.

Signed: _____   **Date** 3 / 9 / 92

This declaration need not be signed by children or next friends/guardians ad litem.

Statement by nominated solicitor

I certify that:

> ➤ I have given the applicant/guardian the leaflet 'What Happens Next?'

> ➤ I have advised the applicant/guardian about his/her obligations including changes of means and address.

> ➤ the nominated solicitor holds a current practising certificate and will not act or delegate the conduct of this matter whilst uncertificated.

Signed: _____   **Date** 3 / 9 / 92

By or on behalf of the nominated solicitor

**CLA 5A: Legal Aid for special
Children Act Proceedings**

Legal Aid for
Special Children
Act Proceedings CLA 5A

(non-means, non-merits tested)

Application number: _____ LEGAL AID BOARD LEGAL AID ACT 1988

The Solicitor must use this form to certify to the Legal Aid Board that a client qualifies for non-means and non-merits tested legal aid for representation in proceedings under Section 25 (use of secure accommodation – child only), 31 (care and supervision orders), 43 (child assessment orders), 44 (emergency protection orders) or 45 (extension/discharge of emergency protection orders) Children Act 1989.

If correctly certified, and lodged with the area director within three working days of receipt of instructions to act, the solicitor will be covered under the Legal Aid Act 1988 for his/her costs immediately he/she signs the form.

The completed form must be sent to the solicitor's legal aid area office where it will be immediately checked and a legal aid certificate issued if the certification is correct, or, if not, the solicitor notified that he/she is not covered for costs.

If it is known at this stage that the client requires representation in related proceedings, give exact details of any order to be applied for. A Section 8 order made on the court's own motion will be covered in any event. If the position is not yet known, an amendment may be applied for at a later date.

Applicant's details

Surname: Mr/Mrs/Miss/Ms MORTON

Forename(s): ELIZABETH JULIE

Date of birth: 23 / 8 / 68

Permanent address: 49 MORRIS HOUSE, COWLEY ESTATE,
LONDON N25

Correspondence address: _____
(if different from above)

Guardian ad litem: _____
(if applicant is a child and a guardian has been appointed)

Solicitor's details

Solicitor to be nominated: JAMES CANE

Legal Aid account no: B.926

Address of firm: 13 HIGH STREET, LONDON N25

Dx no: 428936 LONDON NORTH   Fax no: 071-329 8864

Tel no: 071-329 8694   Ref no: JC

Please complete the back page

Oakley Press PLC, McB, September 1991.

CLA 5A page 2

Solicitor's Certification

Tick appropriate boxes

I was instructed by the above-named on: ___2_/_9_/_92___

and my client is: ﹐

        a ☐ a child   b ☑ a parent   c ☐ a person with parental responsibility

who is entitled to non-means, non-merits tested civil legal aid under Section 15 (3B) or (3C) Legal Aid Act 1988.

The proceedings in which I have been instructed to act are:

      1 ☐ An application for authority to use secure accommodation under Section 25
           – child only

      2 ☑ An application for a care order under Section 31

      3 ☐ An application for a supervision order under Section 31

      4 ☐ An application for a child assessment order under Section 43

      5 ☐ An application for an emergency protection order under Section 44

      6 ☐ An application for extension/discharge of an emergency protection order
           under Section 45

My client also requires representation in the following related matter

        because: _____

_____

_____

_____

NB. Completing details of related proceedings does not necessarily mean that the proceedings will be covered by the Certificate. The solicitor will be on risk as to costs until confirmation of cover is received from the area office.

I confirm:

    ➤ That I hold a valid practising certificate and will not act in this matter whilst
      uncertificated.

    ➤ That the client, or Guardian ad litem where applicable, has been informed that the
      certificate may be discharged if the case is required to be conducted unreasonably.

    ➤ That the client or Guardian ad litem has been informed that the area office must
      be informed of any change of address (including correspondence address).

Solicitor's signature: _____﹐_____ **Date** _2_/_9_/_92_

Notice of issue of certificate

Legal Aid Board

LEGAL AID ACT 1988

NOTICE OF ISSUE OF CERTIFICATE

IN THE ANYTOWN

[COUNTY COURT ~~Division~~]

Between JEAN CROSS [Plaintiff][~~Petitioner~~]

and

THE CORNSHIRE COUNTY COUNCIL [Defendant][~~Respondent~~]

TAKE notice that [~~an Emergency~~][a Legal Aid] Certificate No. 010192
01930F
dated the 8 SEPTEMBER 1992 has been issued in Area No. 1
to the plaintiff

in connection with the following proceedings:-

to take proceedings in a County Court against the Cornshire
County Council for damages and for an order for specific
performance of breach of covenant to repair and/or
for breach of statutory duty.

TAKE further notice that, in consequence thereof, the

in these proceedings is and has been from that date an assisted

person and that all monies payable to him/her shall be paid to

his/her solicitor or, if he/she is no longer represented by a

solicitor, to the Legal Aid Board.

Dated this 10 day of SEPTEMBER 1992

(Signed). Black, Blue & Co. . . . .
of 25 CHURCH STREET, ANYTOWN, CORNSHIRE
Solicitor for the Defendant

To the Defendant

Notice of amendment, discharge or revocation of certificate

Legal Aid Board

LEGAL AID ACT 1988

NOTICE OF AMENDMENT,
DISCHARGE OR REVOCATION OF CERTIFICATE

IN THE *ANYTOWN*

[*COUNTY* COURT   ~~Division~~]

Between   *JEAN CROSS*   [Plaintiff][~~Petitioner~~]

                    and

THE CORNSHIRE COUNTY COUNCIL   [Defendant][~~Respondent~~]

TAKE notice that [a Legal Aid] [~~an Emergency~~] Certificate
[~~dated the   day of   199 has been issued to the above~~
~~named *   in respect of the proceedings hitherto covered by~~
~~an Emergency Certificate~~] [dated the *8th* day of *SEPTEMBER* 199*2*,
issued to the above named *PLAINTIFF*] has on the *4th* day of
OCTOBER   199*2*, been [amended] [~~discharged~~] [~~revoked~~].

[The amendment provides:

                    that the certificate shall [~~not~~] extend
to the following proceedings:-

TO TAKE PROCEEDINGS IN THE HIGH COURT   ]

Dated this *10TH* day of *OCTOBER* 199*2*

(Signed). *Black, Blur & Co*.....................................
of *25 CHURCH STREET, ANYTOWN, CORNSHIRE*
Solicitor for the ~~Defendant~~ *Plaintiff*
To ~~the~~ *Defendant*

* Insert Plaintiff, Petitioner, Defendant, Respondent etc, as the
case may require.

Applicant's bill of costs

```
                                    V.A.T. Registration no: _____
IN THE HIGH COURT OF JUSTICE        CASE NO: CO/329/92
QUEEN'S BENCH DIVISION


B E T W E E N :
                                                        Applicant

                            and

                                                        Respondents
```

Applicant's Bill of Costs payable by the Respondents to be taxed if not agreed pursuant to order dated 1st May 1992 and for Legal Aid taxation in accordance with Regulation 107 of the Civil Legal Aid (General) Regulations 1989 pursuant to Order dated 1st May 1992.

Civil certificate no: 01/01/91/62591/Z dated 7th January 1992 replacing emergency certificate dated 11th December 1991.

Taxed Off		Date and Item	Value Added Tax	Legal Aid		Value Added Tax	Inter Partes	
Legal Aid	Inter Partes			Disbursements	Profit Costs		Disbursements	Profit Costs
		Legal Aid granted to apply for Leave and if granted to apply in the Divisional Court for judicial review of a decision made by the Respondents to deny the Applicant and her child accommodation and to seek possession of temporary accommodation the matter proceeded upon the question of tenancy in respect of the applicant's temporary accommodation the Respondents were advised that the tenancy was secure, however they refused to revise their decision, following which counsel was instructed to advise generally and duly did so, the advice given was unfavourable and the applicant was informed of same and was requested to submit further information, a statement was obtained, following which counsel advised further and thereafter settled the requisite documentation, correspondence followed between the parties whereupon agreement was reached whereby the application be withdrawn in consid-							

-1-

Applicant's bill of costs page 2

Taxed Off		Date and Item	Legal Aid			Inter Partes		
Legal Aid	Inter Partes		Value Added Tax	Disbursements	Profit Costs	Value Added Tax	Disbursements	Profit Costs
		eration of the Respondents making a further offer of accommodation, upon hearing a consent order was made in the terms sought; conducted by a solicitor.						
		1991/92 Time charged at £55.00 per hour Telephone calls at £5.50 each Letters written at £5.50 each Counsel Ms Lesley Luton throughout						
		1992 4th February preparing instructions to counsel to advise 1xA4						
		6th February Counsel's advice 7xA4 paid fee to counsel on advice					19 69	112 50
		12th March Preparing instructions to counsel to further advise 1xA4						
		16th March Further advice 4xA4 Paid fee to counsel on advice					13 13	75 00
		31st March Preparing instructions to counsel to settle 2xA4						
		6th April Preparing form 86A 8xA4 Paid fee to counsel to settle (moiety)					16 41	93 75
		6th April Preparing Affidavit in support 5xA4+1Ex Paid fee to counsel to settle (moiety)					16 41	93 75
		16th April Counsel's draft Defence and counterclaim 4xA4 paid fee to counsel to settle					23 63	135 00
		30th April Preparing brief to counsel 1xA4						
		1st May Draft consent order prepared and draft letter to Council Paid fee to counsel on draft consent order and letter					7 00	40 00
		1st May 1(a)(i) Attending Court with						

-2-

Applicant's bill of costs page 3

Taxed Off — Legal Aid	Taxed Off — Inter Partes	Date and Item	Legal Aid — Value Added Tax	Legal Aid — Disbursements	Legal Aid — Profit Costs	Inter Partes — Value Added Tax	Inter Partes — Disbursements	Inter Partes — Profit Costs
		counsel upon inter alia the Respondents having agreed to withdraw decision of 20.2.92 refusing to revise a decision of 21.11.91; by consent order made application for judicial review be withdrawn, costs of applicant be taxed by a taxing master if not agreed and paid by Respondents. Legal Aid taxation.						
		engaged on hearing 10 mins £9.17						
		(ii) care and conduct at 40% £3.67						
		(b) engaged travelling 45 mins £41.25						
		£54.09						54 09
		Paid fee to counsel on hearing				26 25	150 00	
		4. Preparation						
		PART A – WORK DONE						
		(i) Client						
		Attending upon and corresponding with the applicant, obtaining detailed lengthy periodic instructions views and comment upon all aspects of the matter, informing of the Respondent's views and comment throughout as required, informing of counsel's advices and requesting further information and documentation pursuant to same, informing of the Respondents' proposal, receiving views upon same and subsequent agreement, informing of hearing and terms made thereon, informing and advising in detail throughout as required.						
		3 personal attendances engaged 1 hour 35 mins £87.08						
		7 untimed telephone calls £38.50						
		5 letters written £27.50						
		£153.08						
		iii) Experts						
		Dr Bolton						
		Corresponding with him requesting medical details as to the applicant's medical condition in respect of depression and insomnia, receiving relevant details						
		1 letter written £5.50						
		(vii) Other Parties The Respondents and solicitors						
		Attending upon and corresponding with them as to the filing of						

-3-

Applicant's bill of costs page 4

Taxed Off		Date and Item	Value Added Tax	Legal Aid		Value Added Tax	Inter Partes		Profit Costs
Legal Aid	Inter Partes			Disburse- ments	Profit Costs		Disburse- ments		

Pleadings; informing of the
applicant's views and comment
upon all aspects as required,
receiving their views and
comment, conducting correspondence culminating in agreement,
informing and advising upon the
matter generally throughout as
required.
3 untimed telephone calls £16.50
6 letters written   £33.00
                           £49.50

(vii) Homeless Persons Unit
Attending upon and corresponding
with them as to the applicant's
circumstances, receiving their
views and comment, informing in
detail as required
1 personal attendance engaged
15 mins   £13.75
2 untimed telephone calls £11.00
1 letter written   £5.50
                           £30.25

(vii) Counsel and Clerk
Attending upon them as to advices
and to arrange representation
furnishing all additional
information as required and
necessary throughout
6 untimed telephone calls £33.00

(ix) Documents
Considering documents facts and
evidence including counsel's
draft form 86A (8 pages),
Affidavit (5 pages and 1Ex),
defence and counterclaim (4
pages), counsel's advices (7
pages and 4 pages), draft
consent order and letter and
all other relevant documentation,
collating documents facts and
evidence to prepare 86a form,
Affidavit to prepare and
preparing instructions and brief
to counsel (1 page, 1 page, 2
pages and 1 page), Applicant's
statement (7 pages), reviewing
files from time to time and the
relevant law involved, preparing
for hearing, general detailed
consideration as necessary.
engaged 3 hours 50   £210.83

(xiii) Notices
preparing notice of acting,
notices of issue of full and
emergency legal Aid and report
on case to the Legal Aid Board

-4-

Applicant's bill of costs page 5

Taxed Off		Date and Item	Value Added Tax	Legal Aid		Value Added Tax	Inter Partes	
Legal Aid	Inter Partes			Disbursements	Profit Costs		Disbursements	Profit Costs
		engaged 30 mins £27.50						
		TOTAL PART A – £509.66 B. care and conduct at 50% £254.83						
		TOTAL	79 50				684	99
		5(a)(i) Taxation of costs Preparation hours mins taxation hours mins (ii) care and conduct at % (iii) travelling and waiting _i_ hours _10_ mins paid travel	10 00				50	00

Applicant's bill of costs page 6

Taxed Off		Date and Item	Value Added Tax	Legal Aid		Value Added Tax	Inter Partes	
Legal Aid	Inter Partes			Disbursements	Profit Costs		Disbursements	Profit Costs
		Summary						
		Page 1						
		Page 2						
		Page 3						
		Page 4						
		Page 5						
		Less taxed off						
		V.A.T.						
		Counsel's fees						
		V.A.T.						
		Disbursements						
		V.A.T.						
		Taxing fee						
		TOTAL						

Legal Aid Summary

Profit Costs	£
V.A.T.	£
Counsel's fees	£
V.A.T.	£
Disbursements	£
V.A.T.	£
Costs of taxation allowed inter partes	£
V.A.T.	£
Costs of taxation allowed against the Legal Fund	£
V.A.T.	£
TOTAL	£

Application for legal aid in criminal proceedings (Form 1)

INNER LONDON MAGISTRATES' COURTS

Application for Legal Aid in Criminal Proceedings
Magistrates or Crown Court

Form 1.

Regs. 11 and 18

I apply for Legal Aid — *Cross out whichever does not apply*

For the purpose of proceedings before   the Highbury Corner   ~~Crown~~/Magistrates/~~Juvenile Court~~ *

1. Personal Details: (Please use BLOCK letters and BLACK ink)

1. Surname   ABEL   5. Date of birth   16-6-73

2. Forenames   DAVID THOMAS

3. Permanent address   32 MARRIOTT WAY LONDON N1 9DT

4. Present address (if different from above)

2. Case Details:

1. Describe briefly what it is you are accused of doing, e.g., "stealing £50 from my employer", "kicking a door causing £50 damage."

   TAKING AND DRIVING AWAY MOTOR CARS WITHOUT THE OWNERS' CONSENT

2. The following other person(s) is/are charged in this case.

   RICHARD EVANS

3. Give reasons why you and the other persons charged in this case, if any, should not be represented by the same solicitor.

   HE IS BLAMING ME FOR TAKING CARS WHICH I SAY WERE TAKEN BY HIM

3. Court Proceedings: *(Complete section 1 or 2 whichever applies)*

Cross out whichever does not apply

1. I am due to appear before . . . . . .   the HIGHBURY CORNER   Magistrates/~~Juvenile Court~~ *

   On THURSDAY 8 OCTOBER   1992 at 10   a.m./~~p.m.~~ *

   or

2. I appeared before . . . . . .   the   Magistrates/Juvenile Court *

   On   19   at   a.m./p.m. *

   and   ☐   I was Committed for trial to the Crown Court

   (tick whichever applies)   ☐   I was convicted and committed for sentence to the Crown Court

   ☐   I was convicted and/or sentenced and I wish to appeal against   conviction and/or sentence *

1.

Form 1 page 2

4. Outstanding Matters:

1. If there are any other outstanding criminal charges or cases against you give details including the court where you are due to appear (only those cases that are not yet concluded)

None

5. Your Financial Position   *(Tick the box which applies)*

1. ☐ I attach a statement of my means in these proceedings (details of your income and expenditure)

2. ☐ I have already given a statement of my means to the [   ] Magistrates Court and there has been no change in my financial position *(A new statement is required if there has been any change)*

3. ☐ I am under 16 and attach a statement of my parents' means. If you are unable to provide a statement of their means give their name and address

6. Legal Representation:

Note: 1. If you do not give the name of a solicitor the court will select a solicitor for you.
2. You must tell the solicitor that you have named him, unless he has helped you complete this form.
3. If you have been charged together with another person or persons, the court may assign a solicitor other than the solicitor of your choice.

1. The Solicitor I wish to act for me is
JAMES SMITH

2. Give the firms name and address (if known)
SMITH, SMYTH & CO
25 LOWER STREET
LONDON N1 9KB

7. Signature:

I understand that the court may order me to make a contribution to the costs of legal aid, or to pay the whole costs if it considers that I can afford to do so and if I am under 16, may make a similar order with respect to my parents.

Signed *James Smyth*   Dated: 2-9-92

8. Reasons for wanting legal aid

● To avoid the possibility of your application being delayed or legal aid being refused because the court does not have enough information about the case, you must complete the rest of this form.

● When deciding whether to grant you legal aid, the court will need to know the reasons why it is in the interests of justice for you to be represented.

● If you need help completing the form, and especially if you have previous convictions, you should see a solicitor. He may be able to advise you free of charge or at a reduced fee.

2.   *Please complete pages 3 and 4*

Form 1 page 3

Reasons for wanting Legal Aid	Note: If you plead NOT GUILTY neither the information in this form nor in your statement of means will be made available to the members of the court trying your case unless you are convicted or you otherwise consent. If you are aquitted, only the financial information you have given in your statement of means will be given to the court. Tick any boxes which apply and give brief details or reasons in the space provided.	
1. I am in real danger of a custodial sentence for the following reasons (You should consider seeing a solicitor before answering this question)	☑ I have 12 previous convictions for similar offenses	For court use only
2. I am subject to a: suspended or partly suspended prison sentence ☑ conditional discharge...... ☐ probation order.......... ☐ supervision order........ ☐ deferment of sentence..... ☐ community service order... ☐ care order.............. ☐ Give details as far as you are able including the nature of offence and when the order was made	I was sentenced to 6 months imprisoned suspended for 2 years by this court for similar offenses about 1 year ago	
3. I am in real danger of losing my job because: ☐		
4. I am in real danger of suffering serious damage to my reputation because: ☐		
5. I have been advised by a solicitor that a substantial question of law is involved ☐ (You will need the help of a solicitor to answer this question)		
6. Witnesses have to be traced and interviewed on my behalf ☑ (State circumstances)	The police say they stopped me in a car, but I was standing outside my house and witnesses can confirm that.	

3.

324   Pt V   *Precedents and forms*

Form 1 page 4

Reasons (Cont.)   *Tick any boxes which apply and give brief details or reasons in the space provided.*

7. I shall be unable to follow the court proceedings because: a) My understanding of English is inadequate ☐ b) I suffer from a disability ☐ *(give full details)*	☐	For court use only
8. The case involves expert cross examination of a prosecution witness ☐ *(give brief details)*		
9. The case is a very complex one, for example, mistaken identity *(You may need the help of a solicitor to answer this question)* ☐		
10. Any other reasons: ☐ *(give full particulars)*		

Reasons for Refusal   For court use only

This section must be completed by the Justices' Clerk if the application is refused because:

(a) It does not appear desireable in the interests of justice, and

(b) The applicant is entitled to apply for legal aid to the area committee.

State briefly the reasons for that decision.

Signed...Justices' Clerk

Date...

4.   Form LA1 M.P.89

Solicitor's claim for standard fees in criminal proceedings (Crown Court) (5144A)

The Crown Court at	**Case No.**	Court copy	
1. R-v- or Appeal of	**Standard Fees**		
Messrs	**Solicitors**		
Address	*Notes for guidance may be obtained from the court*		Date received

		Fee Claimed	For official use Fee allowed
Date of legal aid order			
Date of case disposal			

2 STANDARD FEE FOR PREPARATION *tick where appropriate*

Jury trial ☐	Appeal against conviction ☐	**Principal standard fee** ☑	254 00
Prepared for trial no jury sworn ☑	Appeal against sentence ☐	**Lower standard fee** ☐	
Guilty plea ☐	Committal for sentence/breach ☐		

Additional defendants (state number)

3 ADDITIONAL CASES (state number)

Additional indictments
Additional defendants

Additional appeals
Additional appellants

Additional committals for sentence/breaches
Additional defendants

4 ADDITIONAL FEES *tick where appropriate*
Prepared for counsel to appear alone ☐
Listened to tape of police interview ☐

5 STANDARD FEE FOR BAIL APPLICATIONS CONDUCTED BY SOLICITOR (please give details)   Date

Additional defendants (state number)

6 ADVOCACY BY SOLICITOR (No standard fee provided) (please give details)

	Hrs	Mins		Hrs	Mins
Waiting time					

7 STANDARD HOURLY FEES FOR ATTENDANCE AT COURT AND WAITING TIME WHERE COUNSEL ASSIGNED (please give details)

	Hrs	Mins	Date		
Attending Court when application withdrawn 10am – 11.40pm	1	40	6·4·92		
Attending Court when client pleads not guilty x2. Prosecution offer no evidence. Verdicts NG entered 9.30am – 2.50pm	4	20	4·6·92	} 121 50	

8 TRAVELLING TIME (please specify with reference to sections 2, 5, 6 and 7)

	Hrs	Mins	Date		
Sect 2 Travelling to Counsel's chambers & return (lon) & includes 30 minutes waiting	1	30*	1·5·92		
Sect 7 Travelling to Court & return	1	00	6·4·92	} 66 00	
Sect 7 " " "	1	10	4·6·92		

9 SOLICITORS DISBURSEMENTS LIABLE TO VAT (please specify journeys with reference to section 8)

			Date	Miles	Rate	Miles	Rate
Sect 8 Travelling to chambers & return			1·5·92	2	50		
Sect 8 Travelling to court & return			6·4·92	–	–		
Sect 8 " " "			4·6·92	2	70		
Sect 8 " " " Laxia ram			3·6·92	12	00		

*sub-totals

5144A Solicitors claim for standard fees in Legal Aid in Criminal and Care Proceedings (Costs) Regulations 1989

Printed in the UK for HMSO 12 91 D 8252578 C1000 30625

Solicitor's claim for standard fees (5144A) page 2

Standard Fees

● Boxes 2 *only* is to be completed by the solicitor

The Crown Court at Inner London

R-v-or Appeal of

Determining Officer:

Date:

To:

Leagl Aid cost in the above case have been determined and a payable order is enclosed. Details of the determination are shown in the summary below. The rate codes 1, 2, 3 are as follows:

1 = basic rate, all work;
2 = more than basic rate, all or part work;
3 = less than basic, all or part work.

1.	Form No.	3092689 ▸1
● 2.	Solicitor's L.A. code	▸2
3.	Record type	
4.	Court location code	
5.	London weighting	A▸ 3 ▸4 ▸5
6.	Case number	▸6
7.	Date of conclusion of case	▸7
8.	Date of receipt of claim	▸8
9.	Date of determination	▸9
10.	Date of payment	
11.	Tape recording	
12.	Counsel alone	▸10
13.	Class & Offence code	
14.	Type of case	11 12 13
15.	Duration code	
16.	Length of case	Q▸ 14 15 16
17.	Scheme year	
18.	No. of defendants	
19.	No. of cases	17 18 19
20.	Amount claimed	20

Summary of Fees allowed		Fee Earner	Time/Items	Rate Code	Amount allowed	
STANDARD FEE FOR PREPARATION AND PERCENTAGE UPLIFTS	Principal Standard fee	SPF	—	—		21
	Lower Standard fee	SLF				22
STANDARD FEE FOR BAIL APPLICATIONS		SBA	—	—		23
ADVOCACY BY SOLICITOR		ADV	A			24
			B			25
				—	—	26
STANDARD FEE FOR ATTENDANCE & WAITING		SAW		—		27
SATNDARD FEE FOR TRAVELLING		STF		—		28
TRAVELLING		TRA	A			29
			B			30
			C			31
WAITING		WAI	A			32
			B			33
			C			34
HOW ORIGINALLY CLAIMED			0 0	—		35
SOLICITORS DISBURSEMENTS LIABLE TO VAT		17 20		DIS		36
VAT No.		458 70	TOTAL FOR VAT PURPOSES			37
OTHER DISBURSEMENTS (inclusive of VAT where appropriate) Please specify, e.g. expert fees, medical reports, agency work and include receipted vouchers and accounts.		8C 27	VAT			38
						39
		TOTAL	538 97			40
Solicitor's signature		LESS ANY PAYMENT ON ACCOUNT				41
Ref: Tel. No.		TOTAL CLAIMED AND ALLOWED	538 97			42

5144A Solicitor's claim for standard fees in Legal Aid in Criminal and Care Proceedings (Costs) Regulations 1989

Addresses

Legal Aid Accounts Department, Legal Aid Board, 12 Roger Street, London WC1N 2JL. Telephone 071-405 4333.

Specialisation Unit, The Law Society, Ipsley Court, Berrington Close, Redditch, Worcs. B98 8TD. Telephone 071-242 1222.

Directories Co-ordinator, The Law Society, Ipsley Court, (*as above.*)

Index